HOCKEY CANADA

HOCKEY CANADA

THIRTY YEARS OF GOING FOR GOLD
AT THE WORLD JUNIORS

EDITED BY GARE JOYCE

PENGUIN
an imprint of Penguin Canada

Published by the Penguin Group
Penguin Group (Canada), 90 Eglinton Avenue East, Suite 700, Toronto, Ontario, Canada, M4P 2Y3

Penguin Group (USA) Inc., 375 Hudson Street, New York, New York 10014, U.S.A.
Penguin Books Ltd, 80 Strand, London WC2R 0RL, England
Penguin Ireland, 25 St Stephen's Green, Dublin 2, Ireland (a division of Penguin Books Ltd)
Penguin Group (Australia), 707 Collins Street, Melbourne, Victoria 3008, Australia
(a division of Pearson Australia Group Pty Ltd)
Penguin Books India Pvt Ltd, 11 Community Centre, Panchsheel Park, New Delhi – 110 017, India
Penguin Group (NZ), 67 Apollo Drive, Rosedale, Auckland 0632, New Zealand
(a division of Pearson New Zealand Ltd)
Penguin Books (South Africa) (Pty) Ltd, 24 Sturdee Avenue, Rosebank, Johannesburg 2196, South Africa

Penguin Books Ltd, Registered Offices: 80 Strand, London WC2R 0RL, England

First published in Viking hardcover by Penguin Canada, 2011
Published in this edition, 2012

1 2 3 4 5 6 7 8 9 10

Copyright © Canadian Hockey Association, 2011

The credits on page 248 constitute an extension of this copyright page.

Manufactured in Canada.

ISBN: 978-0-14-318181-1

Library and Archives Canada Cataloguing in Publication data available upon request to the publisher.

Visit the Penguin Canada website at **www.penguin.ca**

Special and corporate bulk purchase rates available; please see
www.penguin.ca/corporatesales or call 1-800-810-3104, ext. 2477.

ALWAYS LEARNING   PEARSON

CONTENTS

INTRODUCTION

MURRAY COSTELLO,
FORMER PRESIDENT,
HOCKEY CANADA

Getting the Program of Excellence off the ground wasn't easy. We had to sell the program before we built it.

In the late 1970s and early '80s, the Canadian Amateur Hockey Association sent the defending Memorial Cup champions to the International Ice Hockey Federation's world under-20 tournament over the holiday season. You might think that would have given Canada a fairly representative team in the tournament. It didn't play out that way, however.

Major junior teams are built to win one season, and often they'll load up on older players to make that run. The following season, though, many if not most of their top players have graduated and the best have gone on to the pros—an experienced team one season is often a rebuilding one the next. You have a 16-year-old skating in place of a 19-year-old elite player, a very tough place to put a young man in.

The Memorial Cup champions sometimes picked up a few top players from other teams in their league, but that still wasn't enough to be competitive. I think this point was driven home when the Cornwall Royals went to Füssen in 1981. They were a great team when they won the Cup, but they struggled the next year. They had Dale Hawerchuk, who would be a Hall of Famer, but he was only 17 at the time. What we had in place wasn't fairly representing the Canadian game, and it wasn't fair to the players either. I remember Canada losing to West Germany 7–6, and we just said that it's no longer acceptable.

In the spring of 1981, we went to the Canadian major junior hockey leagues with a proposal for a national junior program. The first part of our plan was to bring together the best tournament-eligible players at a training camp during the summer. The second part of our plan was going to require the major junior teams to loan us their best players for the duration of the world junior tournament. We also proposed instituting a feeder system: an under-17 program. As we laid it out, major junior leagues would send their best young players to play regional teams in a tournament that would give the CAHA an opportunity to identify talent for world junior tournaments down the line. It would also give young players an opportunity to test themselves against the best in their class and a chance to get acquainted with our program.

In other words, we went to the leagues with a proposal that three decades later remains the foundation of the Program of Excellence.

If you were to look at our best moments—the gold medals, the great games and players—over the course of those years, you might think that it was an easy sell. It wasn't, and we knew it wouldn't be.

The initial resistance was understandable, really. Major junior teams were going to be reluctant to give up their best players if they were contending for playoff spots, especially over the holidays when teams would draw some of their biggest crowds of the season. And then there was the risk of injury. We had to use all our powers of persuasion to make our case. Over several meetings, we were able to convince the WHL, OHL, and QMJHL that the tournament would benefit their teams and players. Pretty quickly they came to understand that club teams raised their profiles and focused attention on junior hockey when their top players represented Canada internationally. At the start some teams and players were reluctant, but it has been a long time since a team or a player looked at an invitation to the world junior camp as anything less than the chance of a lifetime.

The three major junior leagues each have a seat on the Program of Excellence's policy committee, and Hockey Canada has a fourth vote. In a short time, those on the committee developed a solid working partnership.

We had a vision of what we could do and how we wanted to do it, and key to that was attention to detail at every level and in every aspect of the program. For instance, we wanted coaches to dedicate 100 percent of their attention to getting the team ready. Often, coaches at all levels of hockey have to handle logistics—whether it's travel, accommodations, or meals. From the start we had to have staff to clear the table for the coaches who came in. There would be no worries about schedules, buses, travel—we'd look after all of that. We also wanted the coaches to have the last word on the selection of the team with no input or veto from the CAHA on the final roster. In the management of any team or program, you don't want to give a coach a chance to pin a loss on a decision that wasn't his or her own.

The attention to detail had to carry over to the players, of course. We had to reinforce the idea to players that we were doing everything we could to give them the best chance to win. We also had to get them to understand it's a different game that's played internationally on Olympic ice. They were going to see different calls. They had to understand that pick plays called for interference penalties in the WJC were just part of the international game, or that good clean checks by our standards would get penalties in Europe. We wanted the players to know all this going in, and be able to adapt instead of finding out the hard way.

One of the worst images of Canada in international hockey came back in the Summit Series in 1972, when J.P. Parisé skated up to a referee in Moscow and threatened him with his stick, swinging it like he was going to take the ref's head off. I joke with J.P. every time I see him that for 30 years we've been able to use his stunt as an example of what not to do. Part of understanding that it's a different game is accepting that there are going to be frustrations and that you just have to check your emotions and move on. That attitude and emotional control are keys to winning internationally. To be frank, when we were starting up the program I wasn't sure that we would be able to get that message across. But in '82, the first year for the Program of Excellence, we had two big defencemen, Gord Kluzak and Gary Nylund, who were as tough and mean as anybody in major junior hockey. When I saw that they couldn't be goaded into retaliation penalties, I knew that players—the best players—are fast learners and capable of adapting.

I'm not going to say that it was only our planning that has put the Program of Excellence where it is today. We've evolved and grown over the years, but still the core values have stayed in place. And we've been lucky.

Because of the players we've had the pleasure of working with, the program has enjoyed good fortune. Those players always looked to measure themselves against the most talented players in the country. We've been lucky because the best coaches in junior hockey have come to view the Program of Excellence as an opportunity for their development, too. And we've been fortunate to be able to maintain a great working partnership with the major junior leagues.

On the ice, we were lucky to have immediate success, coming away with gold in Minnesota in 1982. That gave the program instant credibility and momentum. We were able to get off to a flying start. There's no overestimating how important that gold medal was 30 years ago.

We were also lucky that the world juniors became a huge television event. In the first years, CBC would broadcast only one tournament game—and the network was obliged to do that only if Canada was contending for a gold medal. Later, we found a great partner in The Sports Network and Réseau des sports—basically, the Program of Excellence, TSN, and RDS grew together.

And I consider myself lucky to have had a chance to work with some of the best and brightest people in the sport. Going back to those first years, that list would include Dennis McDonald, our technical director; Dave Draper, our scout in the launch years; and Dave King, who was coaching at the University of Saskatchewan when he helmed the 1982 team.

When we went to the major junior leagues with our plan in '82, we were aiming to improve our performance at the under-20 tournament. We also thought that the Program of Excellence would help our organization send better-prepared players to international hockey events, including the Olympics. I think we've been successful on that count, given that so many of the players on two Olympic championship teams had ties with the program.

We never imagined that the world junior tournament would grow like it has and become so significant in the sport. That's just a happy by-product of the success. The Program of Excellence was tough to get off the ground, but once we were able to do that, over the years it took flight thanks to the top-notch players, coaches, and officials I've had the honour of working with behind the scenes.

1982

ROCHESTER
THE OFF-KEY ANTHEM

DAVE MORRISON

The Program of Excellence's team-building strategies paid immediate dividends in Minnesota.

I was in a unique position. I experienced the world juniors before the Program of Excellence, and then again with the program in place.

I played my junior hockey for the Peterborough Petes and we went to the 1980 tournament in Finland as the Memorial Cup champions. I say "we" but the fact is I didn't play. I was just 17 and the team picked up a few top players in the OHL. We took the top line from the Ottawa 67's, Shawn Simpson, Jim Fox, and Yvan Joly, and we brought in Dino Ciccarelli from London, among others. The younger guys on the Petes went on the trip and practised with the team but didn't dress for games. We went for the experience and it wasn't pretty. We lost our first two games to the Finns and the Soviets and ended up in fifth place. It wasn't that we didn't have the personnel. We had a lot of talent. And it wasn't that we didn't have the coaching. Mike Keenan was our coach and he was one of the best coaches at any level of the game. Mike did everything he could to prepare the team for the tournament but we weren't positioned to win. We had a lot of things working against us. Too much, as it turned out. Just when the team started to come together, the tournament was over.

It was a completely different experience two years later. A lot of what you see in the Program of Excellence today was there in '82, including the summer camp and

Coach Dave King delivered what would be an enduring message to Canadian players: disciplined play is the key to victory.

the tryout camp in December. When we had gone to the 1980 tournament, it was like we had a standing start, but in '82 we weren't starting at square one. Our coach, Dave King, let us know just what to expect in the tournament. He let us know that staying out of the penalty box was key—if we just played our usual game, we'd get penalty calls going against us and the European teams' power plays could hurt us.

We weren't the most talented team that ever represented Canada in the world juniors but we were a good fit to our roles. I don't think that would have been possible if we didn't have the opportunity to play together in the summer and get to know each other. Having to play your way onto the team in December raised the stakes—you couldn't possibly take a shift off or you could lose your chance to play for your country. The competitiveness of our selection camp carried over to the tournament.

That year the WJC was being played in Manitoba and Minnesota. The Soviet Union had been the dominant team in the tournament's history—I remember in 1980 Vladimir Krutov had two or three goals against us and it seemed like there was nothing you could do to stop him. It was a different story in '82, though. We beat

Troy Murray, here flying through the air, and his teammates played in a packed arena in Winnipeg, but a near-empty rink in Minnesota.

the Soviets 7–0 in Winnipeg in front of a crowd that was just going crazy. It was an amazing atmosphere. I can't say the same about the scene when we went to Rochester, Minnesota, for our game against Czechoslovakia, the last game in the round robin. We were playing in this little arena that sat about 3,000 and probably wasn't half-filled. In Winnipeg, on home ice, it felt like we were involved in something historic. It really wasn't like that in Rochester.

In that final game we needed only a tie against Czechoslovakia to win the gold. Before the game the coaches somehow got hold of a gold medal and brought it into the dressing room and everyone in the room touched it. I don't know that we could have been any more motivated than we were before that, but it got our attention.

We were down 2–1 to the Czechoslovaks after two periods, and the score could have been a lot worse. Our goaltender Mike Moffat kept us in the game for 40 minutes. We poured it on in the third—we had 19 shots in the last 20 minutes. Marc Habscheid and Mike Moller scored to give us the lead but then the Czechoslovaks came back to tie it up. I just remember how tense the last few minutes were—we were just hanging on. It was a tough time, but we had come together and understood our roles well enough that we could handle it.

Mike Moller (left) and his teammates stayed out of the penalty box but didn't totally sacrifice physical play en route to the gold medal.

People who have followed the world junior program over the years might not know the name of a single player on that team, or might never have seen a video of the action from that game, but a lot of them know what happened afterwards. The hosts didn't have the Canadian national anthem—or it wouldn't play, we never really heard the definitive story on that. So we stood on the blue line and sang "O Canada." It was really just a spontaneous thing but it's the first thing people think about when they think about that '82 team, our signature moment. And 30 years later it's become one of the great stories in the history of the Program of Excellence. At the time, though, we had no idea that it would have so much staying power. In fact, it wasn't until my hockey career was over that it really hit home.

I finished my career playing a few seasons in Europe, and over that time the world junior tournament really took off. When I retired and our family was spending our first holiday at home, my wife and I bumped into our daughter's teacher at the supermarket and we asked her what she was planning to do at Christmas. She said that her family did the same thing every year—about 30 of them gathered for a party and to watch the world junior tournament. My wife and I just looked at each other—we couldn't believe the tournament had taken on a life of its own.

Dave Morrison (third from the left) didn't realize the impact of his team's victory until after his retirement years later.

1983

LENINGRAD
THE TOUGHEST ROAD GAME

MIKE SANDS

Canadian junior players about to go on to NHL stardom struggled in the pivotal game against the Soviets in Leningrad. Here, Dave Andreychuk is run into the boards by defenceman Ilya Byakin as Mario Lemieux looks on.

There are tough road games, and then there are *tough* road games.

A tough game on the road might be your third game in three nights and you're up against one of the league's best teams. Those types of road games are tough. I had seen enough of them as a goalie with Sudbury in the Ontario Hockey League.

Being in another country and playing a game you're not used to—that makes your life tougher. If you ask anyone involved in the Program of Excellence who ever played or coached in a tournament held in Europe, they'll tell you that it's a challenge.

To be a Canadian team playing in Russia? That's *tough*. And it was even tougher back in the days of the former Soviet Union. If you were a bunch of teenagers—well, let's say that, no matter how good and experienced you were in major junior, you had never been in a situation quite like it.

We went to Leningrad as the defending world junior champions, taking a really talented team there, a lot more talented than we actually realized at the time. We didn't know that Mario Lemieux was someday going to be in the conversation when people talked about the most talented players ever. We didn't know that Steve Yzerman would be the captain of three Stanley Cup winners. That Dave Andreychuk, our leading scorer, would end up with 640 goals in his NHL career.

The Canadian juniors had no answers for the Soviets' speed and skill. Here, Vladimir Turikov slips by Mike Eagles.

That Gary Leeman was going to have a 50-goal NHL season down the line. Or that James Patrick, who was back from the '82 gold-medal winners, would play in the NHL until he was 42. No, we didn't lack for talent. We had enough that a future Hockey Hall of Famer, Doug Gilmour, was one of the last cuts.

We were just teenagers—a few amazingly talented; the rest very good juniors. But teenagers.

We were just old enough to remember Team Canada going to play in Moscow in 1972—we would have been in elementary school at the time. We all had heard about the teams from the Soviet Union when we were growing up—we had seen the USSR's best beat our best NHL players. We knew enough about hockey to understand that these guys could really *play*.

The Soviets were good. And they were at home.

I think it's different now. I think kids are more worldly than we were. Most of us had never been to Europe. None of us had been to Eastern Europe. And what we knew about the Soviet Union we learned from the movies: spies lurking around the corners, soldiers in the streets, people living in fear of the gulag. Were we scared when we took on the Soviets in Leningrad in '83? On the ice, I'd say no. Were we comfortable? Not even close.

We'd won our first three games at the tournament, beating West Germany, the United States, and Finland pretty comfortably, and went into our round-robin game against the Soviets looking at it as the contest that would decide the gold medal.

Even before we hit the ice, we knew it was going to be a different game completely. In our first three tournament games, the arena was practically empty and almost silent. When I was standing in the crease in those games, I could hear guys talking on the bench. But for our game against the Soviets, we could hear the crowd while we were sitting in the dressing room.

Then there were the head games. We got the call to go out and we got our game face on—but when we were just about to step on the ice, the officials sent us back to the dressing room. It seems like a small thing but it wouldn't happen anywhere else. It wasn't a big thing; it was just *another* thing. We had been through the long stare-down with customs officers, dirty looks from soldiers, sneers from people working around the arena, and other stuff. We were warned that the food was bad but we couldn't have imagined just how bad it was—I thought they might have been trying to poison us. All that wouldn't rattle you if you were a professional, but we were teenagers. For sure, it unsettled us.

Dave King returned to the head coaching post for a shot at a second gold. The Canadians stayed with their game plan from the year before, and it came up just a bit short.

So did the whistling.

As soon as we stepped on the ice, the whistling started—the European equivalent of booing. And whenever we touched the puck, the whistling got even louder. It was just ear-splitting. We'd gone from playing in a silent rink to one where you couldn't hear yourself think.

It was a whistle that really threw us off. We thought it was a referee's whistle. We were sure it was. Maybe it was just the ringing in our ears.

We were on a power play in the first period. The Soviets had scored a couple of goals against us on consecutive shifts at about the 10-minute mark and I was doing my best to keep us in the game. The power play was going to be our chance to get back in it. A goal at that point would have given us a huge boost. James Patrick, who was playing the point on our power play, had the puck at the Soviet blue line when he heard a whistle and figured it was an offside call. He came to a dead stop and so did everyone else. It was a whistle from the crowd—at least that's the story we were told. Before anyone could react and get back in the play, a Soviet player picked up the loose puck, skated the length of the ice, and beat me. It was a backbreaker. I guess it's like boxing—you have to defend yourself at all times, even after the bell.

Dave King was our returning coach and, even though we had guys who would score hundreds of goals in the NHL, he had really set us up to be a defensive team. Mike Eagles probably had a bigger role than a lot of the better known players on

Sylvain Turgeon celebrates after putting the puck by goaltender John Vanbiesbrouck in Canada's 4–2 victory over the United States. The win left Canada undefeated after the first two games in Leningrad.

our team. We didn't play a run-and-gun style of game, but instead were going to win our games with a few goals and tight checking. Mounting a comeback from that 3–0 hole would be tough anytime. In Leningrad, in 1983, we didn't get close to pulling it off. I'll shoulder my share of the blame. I wasn't good enough. I gave up six goals in 40 minutes and I was pulled in favour of Mike Vernon.

The final score was 7–3.

We were rattled. The next game, we tied Czechoslovakia 7–7, and then lost to Sweden 5–2. We were still thinking about the Soviet game. It was like the whistles were still ringing in our ears.

Canada ended up with the bronze medal. It could have been a silver pretty easily with a better effort against the Czechs or the Swedes.

I played for Canada's national team for a stretch a few years later. I've worked as a scout in the NHL for more than a decade. When I've seen a Canadian team perform well and win in Europe, I know all about the challenges those players and coaches have overcome. The Program of Excellence does a great job to prepare Canada's best juniors to play in the toughest road games. And those who win on an opponent's turf are prepared to handle things way out of their control—like a fan in the crowd blowing a referee's whistle.

Pat Flatley has his legs taken out from under him in Canada's disappointing 5–2 loss to Sweden.

1984

NYKÖPING
THE FIRST CHANCE
TO PLAY FOR CANADA

DEAN EVASON

J. J. Daigneault, flanked by linemate Lyndon Byers, crashes the net in Canada's 6–0 trouncing of West Germany. Canada's third straight victory put them in a strong position for a medal.

I was lucky enough to play for Canada in the world junior championships. I was even luckier to get a chance to pull on a red and white sweater and play for our country years after. A fair number of players from the world junior program do go on to play in the Olympics and world championships. I don't think that anyone, though, has had quite the experiences I've had. "Unusual" would be one word to describe them. "Unforgettable" would be another.

It's hard for me to express how much just getting an invitation to try out for the WJC team meant to me when I was 19. I was playing on a very good team in Kamloops and I was having a pretty solid season, but I never considered myself more than a good junior player. I was honoured to get the invitation, but I went to the camp without a lot of expectations. I didn't even really give a lot of thought to my chances of making the team and going to the WJC. Everything just happened so fast.

I was one of the last players selected to the team and a lot of things had to fall into place for me to make the cut. Some things were beyond my control. A big one was Mario Lemieux deciding not to play in the tournament even though he had been on the WJC team the year before. Even with Mario out I figured I was on the bubble. I had a couple of goals in the last exhibition game before the final cut and

that probably sewed up a spot for me. I ended up on right wing beside two pretty talented offensive players, Russ Courtnall and Dave Gagner. My role was to look after the defensive end and allow Russ and Dave to use their skills.

Our coach was Brian Kilrea—who, as everybody knows, is the only major junior coach in the Hockey Hall of Fame. Brian was the ultimate old-school hockey man. He wasn't so worried about systems and strategy—he just demanded that we play hard and encouraged us to have fun. I loved playing for him. I was used to the "hardcore" coach—I played for Bill Laforge in Kamloops and he had the same approach to the game.

So much of the WJC in the round-robin format rode on a good start. We didn't get one and ultimately that's what really hurt us. We lost our first game 4–2 to the Finns, who ended up with the silver medal. Four straight wins came after that, though, against the United States, Switzerland, Germany, and Sweden. We felt we were really coming together as a team and had a shot at winning the tournament when we went into a showdown with the Soviet Union.

The Soviets were the defending champions and we had a lot of respect for their talent. We thought they were the best team in the tournament, but we were confident we could stick with them. There was a bit of a scene before the game. We knew that they played head games in the warmup—at the end of their skate, they'd go up to centre ice and stare down the opposition, like you'd see a boxer do as the ref is giving him instructions before a bout. Brian Kilrea told us to give it right back to them. So when the Soviets stood at centre ice and were giving us dirty looks, we stared right back and held our sticks at head level. We let them know that we weren't going to be intimidated.

I remember it being a great game. We gave as good as we got and managed to take the Soviets off their game. Gary Leeman and John MacLean gave us a 2–0 lead in the first period. The Soviets tied it up in the second period—the second goal was by Nikolai Borschevsky, who ended up playing for the Toronto Maple Leafs years later. Kirk Muller gave us another lead but we couldn't hold on. We outshot them 37–30 and that's a fair representation of the game. We outplayed them but they got away with a 3–3 tie.

We took the result hard. We didn't have a shot at the gold and the best we could do was a bronze going into our final game against Czechoslovakia. Our attitude was gold or nothing, and after playing our best game against the Soviets we played our worst against the Czechs, losing 6–4 after taking a lead into the third period. The Czechs went away with the bronze and we came home empty-handed. Kilrea and his assistant Terry Simpson pushed us as hard as they could, but we weren't motivated. It was strictly our fault.

Russ Courtnall ended up being our leading scorer: seven goals and six assists in seven games. John MacLean picked up seven goals as well. I had six goals and three assists and probably was playing better then than I ever had before. Playing in the WJC was a real turning point in my hockey career. It gave me confidence going forward and took me places I never imagined.

I ended up playing 13 years in the NHL, over 800 career games, and I'm proud of my career. Still, I wasn't a threat to play on a Canada Cup team. I was a professional but not an all-star. I had to fight to make my spot on the roster every season. Years when my team didn't make the playoffs, I didn't get invited to play for Canada at the world championships. I made my peace with the idea that I'd just have that one shot to wear the maple leaf. By the summer of '96 it looked like my NHL career was winding down—Calgary had bought out my contract and all I had was a couple of tryout offers, nothing concrete. I had a chance to make some money playing pro in Europe. And that's when I got a call from Andy Murray, who was coaching the national team for Hockey Canada that season.

I knew Andy from growing up and playing in Manitoba as a teenager. He told me that he had a very young team and asked me if I'd be interested in being a player–assistant coach, a veteran who could help him out. He couldn't offer a lot of money—I think it was about $15,000 for the season—but at least I had a chance to play and maybe an NHL team would notice so that I might get another shot. I'd had such a good time playing in the Program of Excellence, even with the fourth-place finish at the WJC, and I took that into consideration.

I took the job with Andy and it was a great experience to play wearing the maple leaf—but then midway through the season I got an offer to play for an American Hockey League team and maybe get a final shot at the NHL. When I told Andy, he told me that he needed my help. If I stuck it out the rest of the way, he promised me a spot on the team that would play in the world championships at the end of the season—that I'd be playing alongside all the NHLers who'd join the team that spring. It was another chance not just to wear the maple leaf but to do it with a world title on the line, a chance to get the gold that got away 13 years before.

On that Canadian roster at the 1997 worlds there were a bunch of future Hall of Famers, including Mark Recchi, Rob Blake, Chris Pronger, and Jarome Iginla—all guys who had won gold at the world juniors. There was only one player who wasn't on an NHL roster. Me. It was an honour when they named me captain and a thrill when we won the gold. If it hadn't been for the experience I'd had in the Program of Excellence, I might have made a different decision when Andy offered me the player–assistant coach job. And I would have missed out on the greatest hockey experience of my life.

I played only one more season after that, a winter in Europe. I feel like my career started and ended wearing the maple leaf.

1985

HELSINKI
THE ONLY SHIFT ON THE WING

STEVE MILTON

With a gold medal
on the line against
Czechoslovakia,
Bob Bassen couldn't
completely duck under
a head shot in open
ice to make a play.

Jeff Jackson had never been so happy to be stuck on the bench.

Late in the afternoon of New Year's Day 1985, Jackson, who had just killed a penalty and was, admittedly, "really sucking wind," was told by Team Canada head coach Terry Simpson to take a breather while his regular linemates Brian Bradley and Adam Creighton were joined for a shift by a relatively unknown Saskatoon Blade named Wendel Clark.

"It kind of worked out," Jackson recalled with a laugh.

Indeed. It worked out to the point that Canadian international hockey history was made and permanently altered.

It was the last day of the 1985 world junior championships at the Helsingin Jäähalli (Helsinki Ice Hall), and Canada was trailing favoured Czechoslovakia 2–1 with less than seven minutes remaining in their final game. There were no playoffs in those days, so the round robin among the eight nations would determine the winner of the tournament—which Canada had won only once before, and had never won in Europe.

Going into the game, Czechoslovakia and Canada were undefeated, each with five wins, and a tie against Finland. Canada possessed a solid edge in goal differential so required only a tie to become the first Canadian team of any kind in 24 years to win a world championship in Europe.

Brian Bradley, here skating in open ice against Czechoslovakia, switched from one wing to the other when Wendel Clark took his single, yet unforgettable, shift as a forward.

Czechoslovakia had arrived in Helsinki as tournament co-favourites along with Finland and Russia. Canada was rated no higher than fourth, partly because that's where they'd finished the two previous years with much more high-profile rosters. Canadian hockey fans might not have heard of any of the Canadian kids before they went to Helsinki, but they knew all about them by the end of the first day of 1985.

Clark and John Miner of the Regina Pats were the two swing players on the team, defencemen who would play forward when the situation dictated. Simpson felt Clark's heavy shot might come in handy with a faceoff in the Czech zone to the right of the goalie who'd been stoning the Canadians, Dominik Hasek.

Simpson had Clark and Bradley flip-flop wings, with Clark and his left-hand shot playing to the right of centre Adam Creighton and closer to Hasek. Off the draw, Creighton pushed the puck ahead and Bradley moved forward to gain control.

"I hadn't played forward much, except in minor hockey, so I wasn't always sure where to go, and that was my first shift of the game on the wing," Clark recalls. "I saw Adam push the puck behind their centre, and headed right to the net. Then I pulled back from their defence to give myself a bit of space, and Brian fed me from the side. And I one-timed it."

Right into the history books.

The quick shot beat Hasek, triggering a furious final six minutes and 13 seconds during which Czechoslovakia blitzed Canadian goalie Craig Billington, looking

for the winning goal that separated them from their first-ever gold medal. It never came.

"Hasek was really good," Creighton said. "But Billington absolutely stood on his head."

After the Canadians survived a faceoff and frenzied attack over the final 20 seconds of the game, they knew they had won the gold medal, and celebrated accordingly—but it wasn't absolutely official. There was still a night game between the Soviet Union and Finland, and if the Finns won by eight or more goals they could finish first.

"And we knew those teams were too good for that," Clark recalled. "But we still had to stay and watch, just to make sure. It was really rare in international hockey then for Canada to be up on goal differential, but that was Craig Billington's goaltending. We took a lot of penalties, as we always do over in Europe, but Billy saved us. We allowed only one power-play goal all tournament, and that was the goal differential right there."

Unfathomably, Billington didn't make the tournament all-star team, but he did win the IIHF Directorate Award as best goaltender.

Billington, of the Belleville Bulls, and his backup from Michigan State, Norm Foster, had been the centre of a mild, but public, controversy during the pre-Christmas selection camp when they made the team and Patrick Roy was cut.

Dan Hodgson, here on a breakaway against West Germany, chipped in with five goals and two assists in seven tournament games.

"They left a lot of guys off the team who became Hall of Fame type of players, like Patrick and Gary Roberts, and some NHL players like Mario [Lemieux] and [Kirk] Muller weren't sent back," said Creighton, who was loaned to the juniors by the Buffalo Sabres, as was Bobby Dollas by the Winnipeg Jets. "That may be why we weren't considered very highly. We weren't expected to win by anybody, but on the team we expected to win."

Clark pointed out that in the fall of 1984 there weren't the advanced, and electronic, scouting techniques there are today. There was no under-18 national team and no summer training camp, and the Canadian Amateur Hockey Association had relied heavily upon Simpson, head coach of the Prince Albert Raiders, to know the western players, assistant Ron Lapointe of Shawinigan to be familiar with the Quebec players, and general manager Sherry Bassin of the Oshawa Generals to keep tabs on the Ontario players.

"And they went with their gut feeling," Clark said. "We were a kind of no-name team but there were a lot of guys who eventually made the NHL. Out of 20, I'll bet 16 played in the NHL for more than a cup of coffee."

His guesstimate is bang on: Every player on the 1985 team spent time in the big leagues, accumulating a collective total of 209 seasons, and 10 players had NHL careers that lasted 13 years or longer.

"The reason we were able to do so well was that no one on that team had an ego about ice time or being the star," Jackson recalled. "Wendel was going to be a high first-round draft pick, maybe even first, but he told the coaches that he'd do anything to make the team."

And the coaches told him that "anything" meant playing both defence and forward. It also meant cutting his shaggy hair. He agreed immediately to both conditions.

After a team-building training camp and exhibition games in Scandinavia, the Canadians arrived in Helsinki still unsure about their chances. The Czechs had the tournament's best player in Michal Pivonka. "I thought for sure Pivonka would be the next one to score 100 points for 10 seasons in the NHL," Clark said. They also had the best goaltender in Hasek. The Finns were led by the two Esas: Esa Tikkanen, who had played some junior hockey in Regina, and Esa Keskinen, who would set a tournament record for assists over the next 12 days. And the Soviets had history on their side as winners of the previous two tournaments, and six of the first eight.

"When you're going into the tournament now, you know a lot about the other teams, but we really didn't know anything," Clark said. "The teams from behind the Iron Curtain, the Russians and the Czechs, you'd watch them practice and the way they moved the puck … and you weren't sure how you'd do against them. The European and North American systems hadn't melded yet, and it was a completely different style of play with all that puck movement, difficult to get used to, especially on the big ice.

"But it's the way we play, our style of game, which won us that tournament."

Canada had plenty of role players, striking the template for future national teams, and what they may have lacked in marquee power they made up for in physicality. Whenever they needed the big hit, they got it.

Simpson set a calm but determined atmosphere, Lapointe was more fiery and an instigator—before the Finn game he told Tikkanen, "We're coming to get you Esa, we're coming to get you"—and general manager Bassin, choosing his moments carefully, lit the emotional fire.

And the players, having trouble adjusting to Finnish food, "were living on Coke and chocolate bars," Creighton said with a laugh.

Their diet might have been sketchy, but their play certainly wasn't.

After beating Sweden with surprising ease 8–2 to open the tournament, Canada clobbered Poland 12–1 on Christmas Day, and dispensed with West Germany 6–2 on Boxing Day. Then, in their first stern test, against a U.S. team that included Mike Richter, Eric Weinrich, Craig Janney, and Brian Leetch, Canada was forechecked mercilessly and fell behind 4–3 after two periods. But in the third period Simpson switched to a two-man-deep forecheck, and 28 seconds in Clark tied the

Claude Lemieux, left, and Dan Hodgson, right, celebrate a goal in their 8–2 rout of Sweden in the tournament's opening game.

Wendel Clark, seen here skating toward his celebrating teammates, scored what turned out to be the gold-medal-winning goal. Months later, he would be the first overall pick in the NHL draft.

score. Nearing the middle of the third period Creighton scored twice and Stéphane Richer once within a span of 3:18, and Canada won 7–4, going away.

That created a four-way tie for first, with the USSR, Czechoslovakia, Finland, and Canada all at four wins. Their games against each other would determine the medals, and the championship.

Canada's fifth game was against the two-time defending champion Soviet Union, "and we were very psyched up for sure," Clark recalls. Sherry Bassin did a lot of the psyching, during a rollicking pre-game speech in which he called on his players' patriotism and evoked images of his own family history of persecution in Stalinist Russia.

"He's probably one of the best motivational types I've ever heard," Clark said, still in awe. "For that age group, especially."

"I think Sherry even went into the Russia room and reamed them out, too," Jackson said. "I remember him starting on the plane on the way over, and keeping it up all tournament, the motivation, telling us that this was our chance, showing us his ring from '82.

"And it was just us. There was no entourage like there is today. No TV cameras, and just one reporter from Canada who was there for the whole tournament. One reporter. Kids today wouldn't believe that."

The CBC's Fred Walker called the games on radio, but only two were on TV. Yet as they continued to win, momentum and interest was building back in Canada— unbeknownst to the players in an era long before cellphones, the internet, and twenty-four-hour international sports TV networks.

One of those televised games was against the USSR. To counter the puck-savvy Soviets, Simpson put together a line of Clark and Bob Bassin plus Jim Sandlak— who had originally been cut, but was summoned to Europe when Dave Goertz was injured before the tournament.

"We were all very physical and we hit them," Clark said, "all over the rink."

The bang-'em-up principle worked perfectly, in large part because of Billington and the short-handed units. The Soviets were knocked off their game by big hits and fell behind 2–0. Then Canada managed to kill six straight penalties and finish fast, scoring three times in less than two minutes in the third period to win 5–0. Finland and the Czechs tied, leaving Canada as the only team with a perfect record.

Finland was next, and Tikkanen, never a shrinking violet, predicted a home side victory on New Year's Eve, especially since Canada's towering defenceman Jeff Beukeboom had been hurt against the Americans and would miss the game. But it ended 4–4, setting the stage for Canada vs. Czechoslovakia the next day.

"It was before the Iron Curtain fell, so they had both the Czech Republic and Slovakia to draw players from," said Creighton. "They were very skilled, and they had Hasek. We didn't know much about him. But he was very good."

Craig Billington matched Dominic Hasek save for save in the biggest game of his career.

And so was Billington, as the Canadians had to kill five penalties and Czechoslovakia only two. The Czechs opened the scoring in the second period, but Sandlak tied it with five minutes to go in the frame. Pivonka, the dominant forward in the tournament, scored at 12:23 of the third period and a confident Czechoslovakia began thinking gold.

But just over a minute later, Simpson had his brainstorm, and sent Clark out for his only shift of the game at left wing.

"When I first saw Wendel I couldn't believe how tough he was for a young guy and how hard he could shoot that puck," Creighton marvelled.

The last shot Creighton saw Clark take that week gave him and his 19 teammates the gold medal.

"We had no idea how excited everybody was back in Canada," said Clark, who was the NHL's No. 1 overall draft choice six months later, and played only forward in the league, partly because of that goal. The die was cast when scouts had seen him play up front with such impact in Helsinki.

"There were huge crowds to greet us at the airports when we got home. But when I got back to Saskatoon I went straight from the airport to the team bus, for that hard three-game swing through Alberta with my junior team."

Putting his goal and those 12 days in historical perspective, Clark said, "It was one of the most pivotal world junior tournaments ever because TV was just getting into carrying the games and Canadians saw us beat Russia and tie the Czechs. Canada became the best just when the tournament was coming back to Canada the next year. So the country had a lot of pride in that. And they sold a lot of tickets in Hamilton because of it."

1986

HAMILTON
THE LUCKIEST BREAK FOR LUC

STÉPHANE LEROUX

Playing for Canada at the WJC was a big step up for ninth-round draft pick Luc Robitaille, but it set him on course for scoring records, awards, a world championship, and a Stanley Cup down the line.

During his Hall of Fame career they called him Lucky Luc. You could make a case that the luckiest break Luc Robitaille ever got was a chance to play for the Canadian team at the 1986 WJC.

Unlike most players who end up on the Canadian roster at the tournament, Luc Robitaille wasn't a high draft pick. The Los Angeles Kings selected him 171st overall in 1984. Those who have been first-rounders arrive with high expectations and often a lot of publicity. For Robitaille, he came in through the back door.

When his name wasn't among the 44 players originally invited to the national team's 1985 summer camp, Robitaille was disappointed. Then Luc got lucky. As it so often turns out, one man's misfortune spells another man's big break.

"Pat Burns, my coach with the Hull Olympiques, contacted me in the middle of July, a few days before the start of the camp, and asked me if I was in shape," Robitaille says. "I told him yes, of course. He then went on to tell me that that was a good thing because I was to likely replace Stéphane Richer at the national junior team's camp."

Richer had injured himself during the summer and that injury gave Robitaille a chance to show what he was capable of in front of Terry Simpson, who was back as head coach of the national team for a second year in a row after winning gold in the previous season in Finland.

So Robitaille showed up at camp with a knife between his teeth, determined to impress the team's management staff. His play was a revelation to the Canadian team's staff.

"I was the best scorer during the intra-squad games at the summer camp and gave them no other choice but to invite me back to the final camp in December."

Robitaille's play was also a revelation to the team that had drafted him. At the Canadian team's camp, Robitaille outperformed Los Angeles first-round draft pick Dan Gratton, who was selected by the Kings 10th overall in 1984. Luc was lucky to get an invitation, but outperforming Gratton was no fluke. Robitaille would end up scoring 668 goals in his 20-year NHL career and Gratton only seven in his cup-of-coffee stint.

Robitaille's play in the QMJHL merited his selection to the team: he had registered 36 goals and 63 assists in only 33 games when he made the trip to the Canadian team's camp. Still, his big break almost came undone on the eve of the WJC. Just before the Canadian team's camp was set to start, he suffered an ankle injury during a regular-season game in the QMJHL. Robitaille did his best to hush up the fact that he was less than 100 percent. "I wanted to be part of that experience so badly that I wasn't going to let a minor injury force me to abandon it all."

Robitaille was among the 20 players selected by Terry Simpson. His selection over Tony Hrkac, a member of the Olympic team coached by Dave King, caused quite a stir at the time, especially since Hrkac had played well with the national team

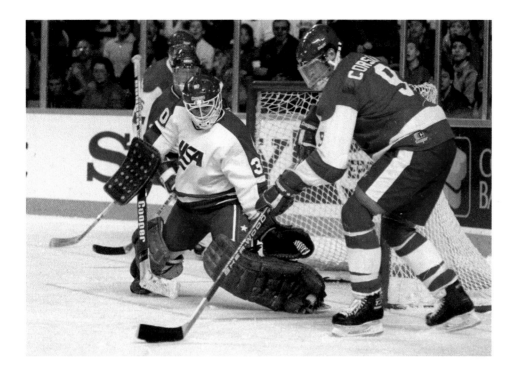

that was preparing for the 1988 Olympic Games. It also turned out that Robitaille was the only Quebec league player on the team. Two other Quebeckers, Alain and Sylvain Côté, were also on the WJC roster, on loan from their respective National Hockey League teams.

The WJC was a bigger stage than any Robitaille had played on to that point in his junior hockey career. Adding to the excitement was the fact that the tournament was being held on Canadian soil for the first time since 1978. A huge crowd at Hamilton's Copps Coliseum cheered for the Canadian teenagers, who started the tournament with a 12–1 pounding of Switzerland. The one-sided nature of the game didn't take anything away from Robitaille's excitement.

"I had never experienced anything like it at the time," Robitaille said. "It was a great experience for me to play for my country even though I wasn't on the ice often, being part of the fourth line. Playing for Canada at age 19 was incredible," he said.

The Canadian team went on to win its next four games. On January 2, Canada and the Soviet Union, tied for first place with identical records of 5-0-0, were to play for the gold medal because there was no medal round at the time. The sixth game was going to be the ultimate confrontation. The Soviets had a decided edge over Canada in WJC experience, with 10 players back from the bronze-medal winners the previous year.

"In 1986, playing against the USSR was a big deal," Robitaille said. "We didn't really know the Soviet players and there was without a doubt a lot of nervousness

Shayne Corson brought muscle up front for Canada and led the team in goal scoring with seven tallies in seven games.

Craig Billington emerged as the starting goaltender and carried the team to five straight wins en route to the pivotal game against the Soviet Union.

and a great atmosphere in the locker room. We had big, physical players like Shayne Corson, Jim Sandlak, Terry Carkner, and that was part of our game plan to use this to our advantage and intimidate the opponent."

Corson, the best Canadian scorer in 1986, sent the Copps Coliseum crowd to its feet in Hamilton when he beat Evgeny Belosheikin, the Soviet goaltender, at the seven-minute mark of the first period, but it was to be the only such moment for the crowd: the USSR won the game 4–1. "We played a very physical game, but we had a lot of penalties and that just cut our legs from underneath us," said Robitaille. When he harkens back to that game against the Soviets, he says the disappointment feels as fresh as if it happened yesterday.

Robitaille and his teammates had to settle for silver. Still, the experience was a catalyst to a breakthrough in his play.

"When I returned to play with the Hull Olympiques, everything seemed easier," he says. "I had just spent a month with the best junior players in the world and my confidence had been given an incredible boost even though we didn't win the gold medal. I had the impression of being so much faster than my opponent."

Robitaille won the QMJHL scoring title in 1985–86, the Guy Lafleur Trophy as the playoff MVP, and the President's Cup with the Olympiques before losing the Memorial Cup final to the Guelph Platers. Lucky Luc, who was inducted into the Hockey Hall of Fame in 2009, was also chosen as the CHL player of the year after his breakout season in 1986.

Robitaille went on to represent Canada on two other occasions, at the 1991 Canada Cup and at the 1994 world hockey championship. "I always loved to represent my country. For me, it was not about representing the QMJHL or Quebec—I played for Canada and I was extremely proud of it."

The Los Angeles Kings had closely followed the 1986 WJC and realized they had lucked into a born scorer. "The impression I made at the WJC helped me so much when I arrived at the Kings' camp the following season," Robitaille said. "I felt that I had a chance to make the team even if I was only 20 years old."

Robitaille did a lot more than make the team at age 20. That season he scored 45 goals with the Kings and won the Calder Trophy as the NHL's rookie of the year.

The 1986 tournament gave the hockey world a glimpse of another future 50-goal scorer and Hall of Famer, Joe Nieuwendyk.

Luc Robitaille won a gold medal with the Canadian team at the world championship in '94, and he'd end up hoisting the Stanley Cup with the Detroit Red Wings eight years after that. Yes, he's disappointed that it was "only" a silver at the WJC in Hamilton. But when he's asked how he went from a ninth-round pick to the Hockey Hall of Fame, he points to the WJC as a turning point. He couldn't have anticipated that someday he'd make the Hockey Hall of Fame, but he came away from Hamilton with a medal and the confidence that he was going to make the NHL with more talent than luck.

1987

PIESTANY
THE 33-MINUTE GAME

GARE JOYCE

Goalie Shawn Simpson gave away at least 60 pounds to the Soviets' backup netminder Vadim Privalov during the infamous bench-clearing brawl at the 1987 WJC, but he didn't shy away.

I wasn't in the arena when Canada played the Soviet Union with a gold medal on the line in the final game of the 1987 world junior championship in Piestany, Czechoslovakia. I experienced that game like most people familiar with it: I watched it live on television and in replays for years after. Two decades after the fact I wrote a book about the game and ended up talking to almost all who played on the Canadian team and many who played on the Russian side. I talked to many others, including the widow of the Canadian coach and the assistant coach on the Canadian team, Pat Burns. I talked to those who broadcast the game for CBC, Don Wittman, Sherry Bassin, and Fred Walker. And I talked to a linesman who saw trouble coming and a novice referee whose failure to take charge led to the disqualification of both teams from the tournament.

It was indisputably the worst moment in the history of the Program of Excellence, and one of the most important. I was at some level obsessed by the game and it drove me to write a book about it. I guess I was trying to figure out how, as the late Don Wittman put it in introducing the broadcast, Canadians were "guaranteed a medal even with a loss," and yet they skated off empty-handed even though they scored two more goals than the Soviets. The game became the source of endless debate and editorials. Some argued that the Canadian teenagers had disgraced the country.

Pierre Turgeon, Theoren Fleury, and Everett Sanipass went to Czechoslovakia with hopes of bringing home a gold medal—they still were favourites to win the championship midway through their final game in the round robin.

Some argued that the Canadian teenagers had been put in an impossible position and hung out to dry. Maybe both were true, and maybe neither fully explains how and why it happened. Or didn't happen, I suppose. If you went by the International Ice Hockey Federation history of the tournament, it was never played. When I went to the IIHF for the game sheet in the archives, they told me it hadn't been saved.

The linesman, a Finn named Peter Pomoell, had worked in many world championships and recognized that the situation was a recipe for disaster: take a bunch of hot-blooded Canadian teenagers, mix with a Soviet team that was already eliminated from the medals, and toss in a referee, Hans Rønning of Norway, who had never refereed a major international game. "I asked him, 'Do you want my help on calls—majors, misconducts?'" Pomoell recalled. "Rønning said, 'No, I'll call my own game.' Canada vs. the Soviets … those two teams produced the best hockey

Virtually every Canadian and Soviet player was caught up in the brawl. Even before the benches emptied, the game was hot-tempered and rife with cheap shots.

but they were also the toughest games to work. I knew this; maybe Rønning didn't. If Rønning had spoken to the captains and coaches before the game or during the game … maybe it could have been avoided."

That was exactly what Canadian Amateur Hockey Association executive Dennis McDonald asked IIHF officials to do: Instruct the referee to speak with the teams before the opening faceoff. "The first thing I thought about was the tournament in Hamilton the year before," McDonald said. "He worked a few smaller games in Hamilton and he was the lowest-rated official there. He was out of his league—just not ready or qualified to work a game like that."

The game was a riveting one for as long as it lasted—which was exactly 33 minutes and 53 seconds of playing time. The score at that point was Canada 4, Soviet Union 2, with a pair of goals by the diminutive Theoren Fleury and single markers by Dave Latta and Steve Nemeth. With the possible exception of Fleury, Canada's best player was Jimmy Waite, a young goaltender thrust into service when the projected starter

Finnish linesman Peter Pomoell knew before the game even started that an inexperienced referee and the Soviets' elimination from medal contention were going to make the final game of the round robin challenging for on-ice officials.

Shawn Simpson went down with an injury earlier in the tournament. The game was wide open. It was also mostly untamed. Instead of trying to establish control of the game early with penalty calls, Rønning ignored slashes, cross-checks, elbows, charges, and face-washes from the very first shift. With the line of Fleury, Everett Sanipass, and Mike Keane on the ice with seven minutes to go in the second period, a line brawl broke out.

If you go to YouTube you can find footage of the game's end, an old-fashioned bench-clearing brawl. The 15 minutes of mayhem look like they were lifted from a barroom scene in the last reel of an old western. You can't see who left the bench first, though those in attendance told me that it was a Soviet player, likely Evgeni Davydov. You can see Rønning, with a dozen scraps going on in front of him, stuffing his whistle in his pocket like a sheriff putting an empty gun back in his holster. And you can see him ducking into the corner to watch frontier justice play out and then helplessly skating off the ice to get out of Dodge. At one point

Theoren Fleury (under Pavel Kostichkin) was on the ice with linemates Mike Keane and Everett Sanipass when the fight broke out.

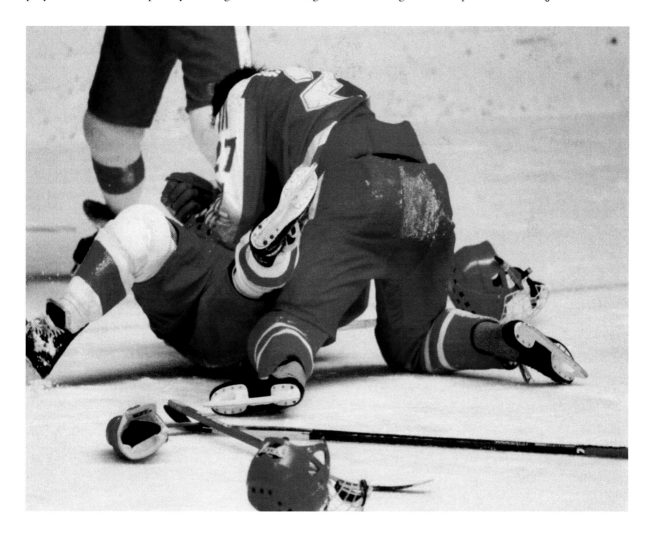

Polish linesman Julian Gorski tries to break up a fight between Everett Sanipass (left) and Sergei Shesterikov. Eventually, referee Hans Rønning led his linesmen off the ice and watched the brawl from the sidelines.

officials in the arena ordered that the lights be turned out, and Czechoslovakian soldiers waited for the two teams to punch themselves into exhaustion or unconsciousness.

Dennis McDonald held out hope that, even if the game was ruled a forfeit, the Canadian teenagers would be allowed to hold on to third place in the standings and bronze medals. Instead, it was the rawest of deals. The IIHF decided to throw Canada and the Soviet Union out of the tournament and void their previous results.

Even with this perfect storm of circumstances, a blood rivalry and an overmatched referee, it shouldn't have turned out the way it did. Many people absolved the Canadians of any responsibility because they weren't the first over the boards. Those who defended the Canadian team said it was a simple matter of self-preservation. Still, it did go well past the point of self-defence. "It was a tough tournament for me and I didn't have any chance to contribute," said Shawn Simpson, who, at 150 pounds, took on and pinned the Soviets' 225-pound backup goaltender at centre ice in what wasn't the most violent fight but the most comical one. "Maybe I was just getting out my frustrations in the fight."

Like Simpson, at least a few players from the Canadian team seemed to enjoy themselves once the chaos started. It would have turned out differently if many Canadian teams from different years were in the same position. The Canadian team that went to the 1987 world juniors was a younger team than those previous. They didn't lack for talent. Brendan Shanahan would go on to an NHL career that will land him in the Hockey Hall of Fame. Pierre Turgeon and Glen Wesley would go on to play well over 1,000 games. But they were 18 and had yet to be drafted. Theoren Fleury was a year older but had been so little thought of that he hadn't been drafted the previous June. It was the only team in the history of the Program of Excellence to hit the ice without a single returning player. In retrospect, a few experienced returnees in the lineup might have steadied a rocky ride. Might it have changed things and allowed Canada to skate away with a medal? Possibly.

In the aftermath, blame was laid at the feet of Bert Templeton, a veteran major junior coach. To put it kindly, he was a tough-love type of guy, so much so that Pat Burns, feared by his players wherever he coached, was good cop to Templeton's bad cop. After the forfeiture and disqualification from the tournament, Templeton was criticized for losing control of his players. But at least some of the players were on a program of their own. "We became sort of a rebel team," Shawn Simpson said. "We broke curfew and a bunch of us got trashed. We were the Bad News Bears and that's how we played and acted the whole tournament. [We were] a bunch of knuckleheads."

In fact, before the Soviet game, Bert Templeton was receiving praise from the media. Thanks to Templeton's coaching, the young Canadian team had improved with each game and, arguably, overachieved in being in a position to win a gold medal. The Canadians stumbled at the start of the tournament, tying Finland 6–6 in a sloppy effort and then falling to the host Czechoslovakians 5–1. A sound 6–2 win over the United States was a turning point and set the stage for a dramatic 4–3 win over the Swedes, most credit due to a breakout performance by Jimmy Waite.

All the good work went for naught, and in that way it was awful for the players. It tarnished the image of the Program of Excellence. The team had strayed a long way from the discipline that Murray Costello and Dennis McDonald saw as a foundation of the program. And yet, Canada versus the Soviet Union in Piestany was a hugely important game in the Program of Excellence's history. It showed exactly what was at risk when that discipline was lost or abandoned. It wasn't a coincidence that the most undisciplined and infamous moment would be followed a year later by a glorious win with a team that played smart and poised hockey in even more hostile circumstances. The team that went to Moscow a year later understood the risks of any lapse in discipline, as have all the teams that have represented Canada in the tournament since.

1988

MOSCOW
THE SWEETEST PAYBACK

FRANK ORR

Goaltender Jimmy Waite, one of four returning players from the Canadian team disqualified in Piestany, exacted a measure of revenge in Moscow. Waite's inspired performance sealed both the win over the Soviets and the gold medal.

I was a young sportswriter six months into my first newspaper job in Cornwall, Ontario, back in November 1957. I bought my own train ticket and paid my way into Maple Leaf Gardens for an exhibition game between the Soviet Union's national team and the Whitby Dunlops. It was the Soviets' first tour of North America and the Dunlops, one of the best amateur teams ever assembled, gave up two early goals but roared back for a 7–2 victory.

I didn't miss too many instalments of the game's fiercest rivalry over the next generation or two. In 1966, again at Maple Leaf Gardens, I covered a game between the Soviet nationals and the Toronto Marlboros, a strong junior team further fortified by a teenager from the Oshawa Generals, Bobby Orr. The Marlboros lost the game 4–3 but Orr was brilliant, rushing through the Russians repeatedly and giving a portent of a great NHL career. In 1972, I was in the arenas for the first four games of the historic Summit Series. The 1975 New Year's Eve game between the Red Army and the Montreal Canadiens, the 1976 Canada Cup, all manner of tournaments and exhibitions: Canada versus the Soviet Union was a recurring theme in my career. If you're writing about hockey, it's hard to lose with us versus them.

It wasn't until late 1987, however, that I made my first trip to the USSR. And it wasn't a case of being parachuted in for a game or two. It was a five-week jaunt

"In my entire hockey career, I never saw goaltending as good as Jimmy [Waite] was in Moscow," Theoren Fleury said. Waite was aided by a defensive unit that featured Eric Desjardins, on loan from the Montreal Canadiens.

to cover, first, the pre-Christmas Izvestia Tournament involving the top teams for the 1988 Olympic Games in Calgary—Canada, Russia, Finland, Sweden, and Czechoslovakia. In a surprise, the Canadians won the gold medal with a narrow win over the Russians in the concluding game. As he had done with the Canadian junior team back in 1982, coach Dave King had his team at the Izvestia well-prepared for the countless attempts by the Europeans, notably the Czechoslovaks and Russians, to incite them into retaliation penalties with assorted stealthy fouls.

That provided the perfect lead-in for the junior championship in Moscow. In the wake of Piestany, the Canadian team was selected carefully for of course skill, but almost as important, for the discipline to ignore the irritating attempts by opponents to draw penalties.

Undoubtedly, their best move was bringing back one player who covered himself in glory until chaos reigned in Piestany: goaltender Jimmy Waite of the Quebec Major Junior League's Chicoutimi Saguenéens. In Moscow Waite played in all seven games and surrendered a meagre 16 goals. Waite was outstanding in all games but absolutely brilliant in Canada's 3–2 win over the Russians in the pivotal game of the tournament. The Russians held a 40–16 margin in shots on goal, 17–4 in each of the second and third periods.

"In my entire hockey career, I never saw goaltending as good as Jimmy [Waite] was in Moscow, especially in that game against the Russians," said Theoren Fleury, captain of the '88 team. After being part of the Piestany debacle, Fleury went to Moscow a year later looking for redemption and got it.

That Canadian team had three other players back from Piestany—two defencemen, Greg Hawgood and Chris Joseph, and goaltender Waite. The Russians had four returnees, including their exceptional stars, forwards Alexander Mogilny and Sergei Fedorov, both of whom became all-stars in the National Hockey League.

"The Russians had a high skill level led by the offensive excellence and exceptional speed of Mogilny and Fedorov with Valeri Zelepukin not far behind," said Canadian head coach Dave Chambers. "Our scoring was not as explosive but more balanced and our defencemen, especially Greg Hawgood (Canada's leading tournament scorer with a goal and eight assists), were intelligent offensively.

"Our advantage was that all our forwards, even the high scorers, could play both ways. We used four lines through much of the tournament with no fall-off in quality or production."

Reflecting years later, Chambers felt the game against Czechoslovakia was important in Canada's gold-medal journey. As they often did against Canadian teams, the Czechs played a sneakily aggressive game with countless little spears, jabs, hooks, and elbows, and then staged elaborate dives when the Canucks retaliated with muscle. The Canadian teenagers spent much of that game shorthanded and, as he was throughout the tournament, Waite proved to be their best penalty killer in a 4–2 win.

"We learned the hard way that in international hockey it's almost always the retaliator, not the instigator, who gets the penalty," Chambers said. "We had a lengthy meeting after that game, one of the few we had, and you could feel the entire team vow to take all the baloney they threw at us and skate away from it. The players did for the rest of the games."

Against Russia, Canada opened with a strong first period and a 2–0 lead on goals by Fleury and Trevor Linden, a poised 17-year-old who finished off a dazzling rush by Hawgood.

In a familiar pattern for Canuck junior teams in international play, they didn't press the advantage in the second period. Instead, they concentrated on defensive play, which gave the Russian speedsters the chance to get their high-speed, quick-transition game into high gear. A goal by Harije Vitolinish at 6:55 gave the Russians a big lift and it seemed the Canadian lead would not last.

Defenceman Marc Laniel, a staunch defensive presence throughout the event, restored the two-goal margin with a slapshot from the point at 11:45. But the lift to

Theoren Fleury (wearing the captain's C) had been in the eye of the storm in Piestany, but he emerged as a leader on the disciplined 1988 championship team.

the Canadians didn't even last a shift. Less than half a minute later Zelepukin got the goal back and again put the Russians on the attack.

With almost half the game to play, the fans at Luzhniki Arena anticipated a batch of goals from their star shooters. But Waite showed the main quality of all great goalies: the ability to be unbeatable at a crucial point in an important game.

"It was as if Jimmy [Waite] decided there was absolutely no way he was going to allow the Russians to tie that game," Canadian assistant coach Ken Hitchcock said. "The Russians threw everything but the Kremlin at him and he never cracked."

While Waite did make several difficult stops against Mogilny and Fedorov, the Canadian forwards did strong defensive work against the Russian aces. Little centre Rob DiMaio led the man-to-man shadowing, a defensive job that was his specialty in an NHL career that would last 17 seasons.

In the third period, the Canadians were effective in keeping the Russians on the outside in their zone, away from the high-percentage shot area. But Waite made

seven difficult stops, five in the last 10 minutes, one a breathtaking split-pad save on Stanislav Ranfilenkov.

But in the last six minutes of the game, Canada actually carried the play to the Russians.

"We had an idea by then that Jimmy wasn't going to allow them to score another goal," winger Warren Babe said. "It was a big lift and we took it to them a little but carefully. That eased things a bit."

"We didn't want our guys to hang back quite as much as they did but when the Russians got momentum, their great passing made forechecking risky because of their breakout plays," Chambers said. "That forced us into a bit of a defensive shell to guard against odd-man rushes. Overall, we did a good job against them, a smart, straightforward approach. But, in the end, the kid in goal made the difference."

Waite somewhat reluctantly acknowledged that he had faced difficult shots.

"Some saves were quite tough to make," he said. "But my confidence was good

Canadian players in Piestany poured over the boards to join the ugly brawl, but a year later they hit ice to celebrate Canada's first major triumph in Moscow since the 1972 Summit Series.

and I was pleased with the way I played. When we got ahead, I figured that if I played good, we could win."

Through the tournament, Waite's laid-back approach was both a source of wonderment and encouragement to his teammates. "The rest of us would be all wound up tight, ready to head for the rink at noon for a night game, and Jimmy would go to his room, stretch out and have a snooze," said centre Joe Sakic. "I asked him if he ever worried about anything and his reply was that he didn't because worrying never did any good."

While the victory over the Russians had every trapping of the tournament championship match, Canada had two games to play against West Germany and Poland, which they won easily to claim the world title.

Fleury, the 5-foot-5, 150-pound captain, had played the tournament—in fact, the entire season as Western Junior League scoring champ—with a burning desire, inspired by the Piestany incident. His lead-by-example intensity inspired his mates to duplicate it. He and Rob Brown tied for the team goal-scoring lead with six.

"For a whole year, including many sleepless nights, I thought only about how the Russians took away something very special that belonged to me—a world championship gold medal," Fleury said. "Now that we have it, a big load is off my back. It has bugged me for a year—really badly, too, sometimes."

The victory was a career milestone for all 20 players on the roster, boosted by a strong team feeling that developed quickly at the selection camp before the trip to Moscow. "It was all for one because that's how it had to be for a shot at the gold," Sakic said. "The camaraderie was terrific and there were no little groups going their own way. That's why it was really sad when we got back to Canada and went our own ways."

Centre Mark Recchi was an important two-way player in the tournament. "I remember very well the empty feeling when the team got to old Mirabel Airport in Montreal and the guys all went to their own teams," Recchi said. "We had met a really big challenge and we would never have the chance to do it again. But what happened in Moscow will never be forgotten by any of us. All through my NHL career, I'd be, say, lining up for faceoff, look up and see a Theo Fleury, Joe Sakic, Trevor Linden, or Adam Graves, any of the Moscow guys, looking at me. We both would give a little nod or smile that said, 'Hey, you old dog! You and me did something really special one time.'"

The Canadian roster was built on the evaluation of CAHA director of scouting Dave Draper. He started the construction process at the '87 midsummer four-nation (Russia, Czechoslovakia, Sweden, Finland) junior tournament in Estonia.

"We knew then the type of teams four top contenders were building and the style of team we had to send to be competitive," Draper said. "Maturity in all areas was a prime necessity after Piestany and, with the tournament in Moscow, culture shock was a big factor with different living accommodations and food. We brought a solid, mature group of young men who also could play some hockey. They did Canada and themselves proud."

Head coach Chambers, who had much international coaching experience, was on sabbatical from his job as director of athletics at Toronto's York University.

The low-key Chambers made restraint his theme and Hitchcock, a hard-driver from the Kamloops Blazers, and easygoing Jean Begin, from the Drummondville Voltigeurs, were the ideal "bad cop–good cop" duo as assistant coaches.

Given the many NHL successes of the alumni from '88, you could make an argument that this was the best-ever Canadian junior team. Of the 20 players on the roster, 18 played at least a few games in the NHL. Six (Fleury, Sakic, Recchi, Graves, Linden, and Eric Desjardins) played more than 1,000 games. Five played on Stanley Cup winners.

Since '88, several members of the team expressed their surprise that two key parts of the Moscow effort—goalie Waite and defenceman Laniel—did not have distinguished big-league careers. Waite played 191 NHL games in 10 different stints over 11 seasons plus good minor pro stretches, but never relocated the brilliance of Russia. Laniel never played an NHL game in a six-year pro career.

"Over the years I've met guys from the Moscow team and we shake our heads when they think how good Jimmy was in that tournament and how he struggled in the NHL," Recchi said. "Marc Laniel? How could a guy who was so solid in his own zone, such a smart player with size and skill, not do in the pros what he did so beautifully in Moscow?"

There is no easy answer for the question, like so many others in the game. Nonetheless, the Canadian juniors that year had an answer to a powerful Soviet team: Jimmy Waite. In the toughest road game in the sport, he played as well as any goaltender I had ever seen. I would have paid my own way and bought my ticket to see it.

1989

ANCHORAGE
THE RUNAWAY TRAIN

TOM WEBSTER

Rob Cimetta and his teammates went to Alaska as defending champions, but faced the greatest team the Soviets ever sent to the world juniors.

My chance to coach the Canadian junior team came two years after I had to miss out on the tournament. I was named as an assistant coach on the team that went to Piestany, but after I had worked with the team at the summer camp the New York Rangers called me and offered me the head coach's job. I was coaching the Windsor Spitfires a couple of years later when I got the call from Team Canada to work with the team that was going to Anchorage as defending champion.

I thought our team played well and I'm proud of the job our players did. We went in wanting to put the team in a position to win a gold medal or any other medal. We were in that position down to the wire—we had four wins, a loss to Sweden, and a tie with Czechoslovakia going into our last game of the round robin. But we ran into a runaway train: the Soviets.

That Soviet team is probably one of the best that ever played in the world juniors and I'd say that there's never been a better line than Pavel Bure, Sergei Fedorov, and Alexander Mogilny in that tournament. Mogilny had an injury and wasn't even supposed to play in that game but he turned it on against us. We had managed to hang around in the first period, but in the second there were a couple of marginal penalty calls and Mogilny picked up a hat trick. That line was tough to hold off at even strength and impossible when you're playing short-handed.

Sheldon Kennedy, crashing the net against Sweden, was named Canada's captain and was one of two players returning from the team that won gold in Moscow.

We ended up losing 7–2. That left us with a 4-2-1 record in the round robin, tied with the Czechoslovakians, but they got the bronze by virtue of a better goal differential.

It was a tough way to miss out on a medal and a tough stretch for the program.

NHL teams were starting to change their approach with their young players. The kids that they drafted in June would go directly into NHL lineups the following October. In years past a few had made the jump—the exceptional prospects like Mario Lemieux, the top couple of 18-year-olds. But by the late '80s a lot of players were rushed into the pros. There were at least a dozen guys who would have been eligible for our team but weren't released back to us by their NHL clubs—Joe Sakic, Trevor Linden, Brendan Shanahan, and Pierre Turgeon, just to name a few. We weren't surprised by that and truthfully we didn't hold out much hope for getting those guys. It was just the way things were at the time.

I was lucky that my friend Pat Burns, whom I'd worked with in the summer camp a couple of years before, released Eric Desjardins back to us for the tournament. Eric, who was one of the real leaders for us, and Sheldon Kennedy were the only returning players from the gold-medal winners the year before. We might have had some benefit from a few more players who brought some more world junior experience to the team, but really it wasn't inexperience that cost us in

the end. We happened to run into one of the best teams that ever played in this tournament.

Going into the tournament we knew we didn't have a lot of high-end skill like the Soviets. We were going to have to look at rolling all four lines, taking a scoring-by-committee approach and having our players going in the dirty areas. I thought that our scout, Dave Draper, did a great job going out to find talent when a lot of the top young players we might have hoped to be available were sticking in the NHL. We all tried to bring something to the table in terms of the knowledge of players we'd invite to the selection camp. For coaches in our position, you want to keep tabs on the best players and try to get to know them in advance of the camps. Alain Vigneault was my assistant and he knew the players in the Quebec Major Junior Hockey League from coaching the Hull Olympiques. I knew those in the Ontario Hockey League and I went up to Michigan State to watch Rod Brind'Amour a few times—Rod was one player who really improved from the summer camp through to December. Dave Draper went across the country and we all shared our knowledge when we were putting together our invitation lists and tournament roster.

Because we were going to have trouble scoring, we had to play smart and avoid unnecessary penalties. It was a time when there was an eye-for-an-eye attitude

Mike Ricci, here backchecking against the Swedes, was luckier than most of his teammates. He was young enough to return to the WJC the following year for another shot at gold.

Goaltenders Gus Morschauser (pictured) and Stéphane Fiset gave a Canadian team depleted by the absence of tournament-eligible stars on NHL rosters a chance at a medal going into the final game.

among junior players, even really good ones. We had to separate them from that. The team excelled at that the year before in Moscow, and our players did a good job buying into an idea that some others might have had trouble with.

Wayne Halliwell, our team psychologist, did a really good job in helping get the message across to the team. He met with the players as a group and individually. We went through team-building exercises. He really helped get the players focused and aware that each and every shift is important in a short tournament like the world juniors. And, really, when you get the best junior players in Canada

Dan Lambert takes a spill in a loss to the Swedes that was a blow to Canada's medal hopes.

Reggie Savage, here with the puck behind the Swedish net, picked up four goals and five assists in seven games for a Canadian team that had to rely on scoring by committee.

together, almost all of them are going to respond to that type of direction and coaching.

It's a small world and it seems even smaller in hockey. After the tournament I went back from Anchorage to Windsor with Darrin Shannon, one of the leaders on that Canadian team and one of my players with the Spitfires. Later I was working in the Philadelphia organization when Rod Brind'Amour and Eric Desjardins were playing there and it made for a special relationship—you've shared an experience and gone to war with a young man in what was the biggest moment of his life to that point. Whenever I'd see players from the world junior team we'd always talk and have a laugh. I feel like I made a lot of friends through that opportunity to coach in the Program of Excellence.

I haven't coached for a few years now, but I've stayed active in hockey as a scout and I've seen the impact that Hockey Canada and the Program of Excellence have had on the game. The Program of Excellence has made tremendous strides over the years—we didn't always have the under-17 and under-18 programs to identify and work with the best young players, priming them for success at the world juniors. And the quality of hockey has just shot up. When you see players on Canadian teams at the world championships, at the World Cup, and at the Olympics, you're seeing players who have been put into a position to succeed because they've been made familiar with the challenges they are facing.

No matter who is on the roster, every Canadian team goes into international play expecting to win. Every loss stings, but to miss out on a medal because of goal differential was especially bitter for the 1989 team.

1990

TURKU
THE OUT-OF-TOWN SCORE

BOB McKENZIE

The 1990 edition of the Canadian team knew going into the tournament that it would have to rely on scoring by committee, and the players came through. Here, Stu Barnes celebrates a goal against Sweden.

It wasn't as if it was a moral dilemma, but I was a little confused on how to handle the information I'd just been given.

This wasn't anything that had been covered in my three years of journalism school and, to be honest, there hadn't been anything in my 11 years in the newspaper business that left me with a high degree of confidence on the "right" or "proper" thing to do. Besides, this was really my first foray into the world of broadcasting a live sports event, so who knew the protocol?

I certainly didn't.

There I was on January 4, 1990, in a frigid arena in Turku, Finland, wearing my royal blue CBC blazer as a member of the broadcast team for the 1990 world junior championship. The late Don Wittman was doing play-by-play up in the booth with legendary coach Scotty Bowman as the colour commentator, and Brian Williams was the host. I was a broadcast novice serving as the intermission analyst and self-appointed rinkside reporter once the game had started.

I had taken up a position at ice level right alongside the Team Canada bench, which is to say nobody booted me out of there. Today, they would fashionably call it "Between the Benches," but this was 1990 after all, and if I had decided to sit on the

Wes Walz slides the puck by the sprawling Soviet netminder in a 6–4 victory that kept the Canadians undefeated after their stiffest challenge. Even though they beat their old rivals, Canada would need a lot of help to capture gold.

end of the long and open bench area, I'm not sure anyone other than Team Canada head coach Guy Charron would have said anything.

Canada was playing its final game of the 1990 tournament, facing a talent-laden Czechoslovakian team led by junior scoring machine Robert Reichel, flanked on either side by man-child Bobby Holik and a big, baby-faced kid with flowing locks, Jaromir Jagr. When they dropped the puck to start that game in Turku, it was thought to be nothing more than the final match of the tournament to decide who would get the silver and bronze medals.

The Canadian team had wasted a big win over the favoured Soviet Union by losing to Sweden and tying Finland and was sitting with nine points, needing a victory over Czechoslovakia to get silver. The Czechoslovaks, meanwhile, had only one blemish on their record, a loss to the Soviets, and, with 10 points, a tie or a win against Canada would guarantee them silver. The Soviets, meanwhile, were in full control. Like the Czechs, they had 10 points, but they were playing Sweden in Helsinki at the same time as Canada-Czechoslovakia. No one thought it possible for Sweden to pull off an upset. If the Czechoslovaks beat Canada and the Soviets beat Sweden they would both finish with 12 points, but the Soviets owned the tiebreaker

with the head-to-head win over Czechoslovakia. And, with the initial reports out of Helsinki putting the Soviets out in front of Sweden, this Canada vs. Czechoslovakia tilt had the look and feel of a consolation game.

Maybe that was to be expected. The pundits had been concerned from the outset about Team Canada's defence, a not-exactly-star-studded unit of Patrice Brisebois, Kevin Haller, Dan Ratushny, Adrien Plavsic, Jason Herter, and Stewart Malgunas. And, sure enough, if not for an out-of-this-world netminding performance from Stéphane Fiset, Canada may not have been playing for a medal at all. It was a young team—half of the players, including 16-year-old Eric Lindros, who had scored four goals in the tourney, were eligible to play in the next year's 1991 WJC in Saskatoon. So a silver or bronze medal would not have been a surprise, or even necessarily a disappointment.

Nevertheless, Charron's players played hard that day. It was a terrific, up-and-down game. The Czechoslovaks jumped out to a 1–0 lead late in the first period on a Reichel goal, assisted by Jagr. But Canada came back strong in the second period. Mike Craig tied the game, and nine minutes later Newfoundlander Dwayne Norris put Canada ahead 2–1. Things got dicey in the third period when Canada took three

Finland gave Stéphane Fiset and his teammates all kinds of problems in their 3–3 round-robin tie. Although the Finns didn't win a medal in 1990—they wound up in fourth place—their strong play against Canada helped to sustain the tournament's drama right up until its final minutes.

straight minor penalties in a six-minute span, but Fiset stood tall with more of the tournament-long excellence that, even today, is considered one of Canada's most dominant goaltending efforts at the WJC.

Occasionally, over the course of the game, there were dispatches from Helsinki— and always the Soviets were comfortably ahead of the Swedes. The most recent had the Soviets up 5–3 in the third period. So Canada-Czechoslovakia remained a battle for silver.

But with about five minutes left in the game in Turku, I received word through my earpiece connecting me to the CBC production truck that Sweden had mounted a late-third-period comeback and, unbelievably, scored two goals, including a buzzer-beater at 19:59 of the third period. Final score: Soviet Union 5, Sweden 5.

The scene in the rink in Helsinki was said to be frenzied. The Soviet players were up on the dasher, ready to vault over the boards and celebrate their gold-medal win, when Swedish forward Patric Englund, set up by Nicklas Lidstrom, tied the game just as the buzzer sounded. Instead of swarming their goaltender, the Soviet players smashed their sticks on the dasher, cursed, and protested that the goal had been scored after time had expired. But the goal was ruled good.

Armed with that information, I could hardly contain myself. But I quickly, in my mind, did the math to be 100 percent. The Soviets finished the tournament 5-1-1, with 11 points. If the Canadians held on to their 2–1 lead against the Czechoslovaks, they would also finish at 5-1-1 with 11 points, but by virtue of beating the Soviets in the head-to-head matchup would get the gold medal.

Suddenly, right out of the blue, this silver-medal contest had become a gold-medal game with only five minutes to play.

And that's when I asked myself, How exactly do I handle this?

I was close enough to the Canadian bench to be able to tap one of the players on the shoulder and just tell him, "You better protect that lead because you'll win the gold medal if you do." But it struck me that a media member maybe shouldn't be interacting with players in the middle of a game and, had I done that, I'm pretty sure it would have resulted in some hysteria on the Canadian bench. I didn't want to be responsible for that.

But I'm not going to lie; I was fairly bursting to tell someone. This was huge news. It was exciting. I mean, I think that's why anyone in the media ever goes into the business in the first place—because they like to find out news first, before anyone else, and be "that guy" to tell everyone something they don't know.

There was a stoppage in play and I caught Team Canada head coach Guy Charron's attention and discreetly waved him over. He came down to the end of the bench, bent over, and I whispered in his ear, "The Swedes just tied the Soviets. The game is over. If you hold on to win this game, you win the gold medal. I don't know

Left: An unheralded blue line looked like one of the question marks hanging over the team when it left for Finland, but by the end Canada had allowed only 18 goals in seven games, half as many as they had scored. Here, defenceman Adrien Plavsic congratulates Eric Lindros on one of his four goals of the tournament.

if you want to tell your players or not. I won't say anything to them, but I thought you should know."

Charron's eyes lit up. If I recall correctly, he just said, "Really?" I nodded and he scooted back down the bench and immediately conferred with assistant coach Dick Todd.

More than 20 years later, Charron still marvels at how it all went down.

"I remember it being brought to our attention that the Swedes had tied the Soviets. I always thought it was Mats Sundin who scored the tying goal," Charron said. "It was you who told me? I didn't remember that part. I just knew we found out but the kids didn't know at that point and I talked to Dick [Todd] and [other assistant coach] Perry [Pearn] and we decided not to tell the players. They were playing the game. We didn't want to drop all that emotion on them—this is now a gold-medal game—and throw them all out of whack."

So the seconds ticked away and the magnitude of the little secret known by so few seemed to grow with every brilliant save Fiset made. It was high tension, to be sure, though at that point the players were oblivious to the stakes having been increased so dramatically.

But with about 90 seconds left in the game, during a stoppage in play, there was a public address announcement that the Soviets and Swedes had played to a 5–5 tie.

The players on both benches—Canada's and Czechoslovakia's—erupted. The Canadian players were celebrating their opportunity, all standing up, hooting and hollering and bouncing off each other with kinetic energy that you can't even imagine. That image is burned into my memory.

"What I recall is how garbled the P.A. was," said Team Canada winger Kent Manderville. "It was really hard to hear, but someone picked out that the Soviets and Swedes tied and it spread like wildfire all up and down the bench. It was crazy. We started the game thinking the best we could do was get a silver and now there's a very sudden realization ... we can win gold!"

The Czechoslovaks also rose up on their bench, more with grim determination and steely resolve than outright excitement, knowing a win over Canada would give them the gold and even a tie would create a three-way logjam with them, the Soviets, and Canadians that would require the calculators to come out.

Everything about the game had suddenly changed. It was the highest of high drama. All Charron was trying to do was maintain order, finish the job.

"It was crazy," Charron said. "When that announcement was made, the players went nuts on the bench. We had to try to stay focused."

Manderville said the striking memory of the final 90 seconds was that Reichel, Holik, and Jagr never came off the ice, and just how dominant they were.

"Those three guys were all-world in that tournament and Reichel was scary good,

Right: The Canadians protested this goal in their game against Finland, but it would later be the Soviets crying foul in their pivotal game against Sweden.

Stéphane Fiset, named the outstanding goaltender of the 1990 WJC, preserved a fragile one-goal lead against the surging Czechs in the tournament's final game.

so dangerous," Manderville said. "I was on the bench the whole time, but they just kept coming at us. It was electric, but it was scary, too. The time couldn't come off the clock fast enough."

Charron says he won't ever forget those final moments, how Fiset made some terrific saves. But for him, two things stand out.

"They had the puck in our end in the final minute but they never pulled their goalie," Charron said. "European teams and coaches didn't pull the goalie like we do. I thank heaven for that because this was a situation where you would want the goalie out for the extra skater. But they didn't do it. I was happy for that.

"Then there was a faceoff in our end late, I don't recall exactly how many seconds were left but it was to the right of Fiset. I had to decide who should take the faceoff. I had been using Stu Barnes for those faceoffs because he's a right-hand shot and I was using Kris Draper for the faceoffs to the left of Fiset because he's a left shot. Kris asked me if he could take the faceoff; he told me he could win it. I had Kris when I was coaching the Olympic team and I had a lot of confidence in him. So I had him take the faceoff—I know Stu Barnes was really disappointed it wasn't him—and Kris won it. We killed the clock. We won. I'll never forget it."

There was some talk in the immediate aftermath of the game that the Soviets were officially protesting the tie with Sweden—that the Patric Englund goal had been scored after time expired and they had video to prove it. But as Russian star Pavel Bure said many years later, "It was very close. Maybe it was 19:59, maybe it was 20:00, but there wasn't the technology then like now. The bottom line is the goal counted. We lost the gold medal."

"It's funny," said Charron from his Kamloops Blazers office, where he's been the head coach since the fall of 2009. "I'm not sure I realized then what a big deal the world juniors were. We wanted to win of course—Canada always wants to win—but I had been in the Olympics and I went into the junior tournament thinking it would be a good experience. I suppose now that the world juniors have grown to what they are, I know how important it is and how much it means to be a world junior champion in Canada.

"I have two pictures up in my [Kamloops] office. One is when I won the Memorial Cup with the 1969 Montreal Junior Canadiens and the other is from that 1990 world junior. I like to think those are things the kids who play junior hockey now can relate to. They are special."

Special, indeed. But for me, what I'll always remember—aside from figuring out whom to tell once I found out the Soviets and Swedes had tied and Canada was in a gold-medal game—is that some years a team wins a gold medal at the world juniors when it seemingly has no business winning one, and other years it loses when by all rights it should have won.

And it didn't take very long for history to repeat itself, right down to a Newfoundlander scoring the game-winning goal in a most improbable gold-medal victory.

1991

SASKATOON
THE SECOND LIFE

BOB McKENZIE

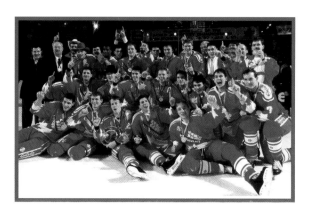

Goaltender Trevor Kidd came up with an impressive performance in Canada's 3–2 victory over the Soviets in the final game of the 1991 WJC.

The world junior championship has evolved from an annual tournament into a hockey phenomenon, especially in Canada. Though there have been many stages in that evolution, the 1991 tournament in Saskatoon, Saskatchewan, was a crucial catalyst.

It was the perfect storm in every way.

It was the first time Canada won the WJC on home ice. Hockey fans from Regina to Saskatoon—and all points in between, all over hockey's heartland—braved 10 days of –40°C temperatures to fill the rinks.

It was the first time TSN had televised the tournament—CBC previously held the broadcasting rights—and the first time all seven Canadian round-robin games were broadcast nationally. The tournament immediately became TSN's signature event, with a ratings bonanza of more than 1 million for what turned out to be the gold-medal game between Eric Lindros and Team Canada and Pavel Bure and the Soviet Union. It was unquestionably the launching pad that rocketed the WJC into the Canadian sporting stratosphere, making it what it has become now—the most highly anticipated and most-watched annual sporting event in Canada.

The images from January 4, 1991, remain strong to this day: The giant Canadian flag being unfurled at one end of a sold-out SaskPlace; Newfoundlander John

Slaney's unforgettable game-winning goal on the seeing-eye shot from the point in the final minutes to give Canada a 3–2 win.

For many, that goal and that tourney are synonymous with—or emblematic of—the WJC itself.

Fair enough—it really was something special. But those of us who were there and covering the entire tournament share a knowing smile at the remarkable set of circumstances that even allowed the Canada-Soviet game to become a gold-medal, winner-take-all showdown.

By rights, it never should have happened.

I was part of the TSN broadcast team that year. Jim Hughson and Gary Green did play-by-play and colour commentary, respectively. I provided pre-game and intermission analysis with Paul Romanuk hosting.

The 1991 tournament attracted more public attention than any previous WJC, and that can be attributed to one player: Eric Lindros. It was the Big E's NHL draft year, and by the holiday season he was at the centre of a full-blown media circus. At 18, he was possibly the most-discussed name in the game.

Peterborough Petes coach Dick Todd was the behind-the-bench boss that year, and he had a group that was considered a strong team but by no means an overwhelming favourite. Lindros was obviously the marquee talent, but he was one of seven returnees from the 1990 team that won gold in Helsinki. Still, there were question marks. Some wondered if Trevor Kidd and Félix Potvin were up to the challenge in net. And, as was the case in 1990, the somewhat generic defence: Patrice Brisebois, Jason Marshall, Chris Snell, Karl Dykhuis, Dave Harlock, a draft-eligible Scott Niedermayer (who played only three games), and Slaney. The blue line was scrutinized and, by some, doubted.

Making the odds of a repeat even longer was the strong competition Canada was facing. Bure was the electrifying phenom leading a strong Soviet team. Doug Weight led a talented U.S. entry and Martin Rucinsky, Ziggy Palffy, and Jiri Slegr led an impressive squad from Czechoslovakia.

Canada blanked Switzerland to start the tournament, hit a speed bump in a 4–4 tie with the U.S., but then reeled off comfortable wins over Norway, Sweden, and Finland to go 4-0-1 in their first five games. The Soviets, though, were perfect after five contests, having beaten the U.S., Norway, Sweden, Switzerland, and Czechoslovakia. With two games remaining for each of Canada and the Soviets, the arch-rivals looked to be on a collision course in the final game of the tournament.

But on January 2 in Saskatoon, Czechoslovakia beat Team Canada 6–5. Canada was trailing 4–2 in the second period but the dynamic Oshawa Generals duo of Lindros and Mike Craig went to work with three straight goals. Craig scored two goals and one assist, and Lindros one goal and two assists to give Canada a 5–4 lead midway through the third period. But the Czechs scored a power-play goal with less than five minutes to go and Rucinsky scored the game-winner with less than three minutes left.

That outcome was a disaster for Canada, because the next night in Regina the mighty Soviets were taking on a non-contender, Finland. A Soviet win seemed preordained—and if it materialized, the Soviets would clinch gold without having even played Canada.

"I think it's fair to say we thought we were done after that loss to the Czechs," head coach Dick Todd said 20 years after the fact from his retirement home in Florida. "That whole tournament was a struggle in many respects. Nothing came easy, and when we lost to the Czechs it was tough. There were a lot of things happening behind the scenes, some people who fell off the bandwagon. The atmosphere (after the loss to Czechoslovakia) wasn't very good."

Any time Team Canada fails to win, it doesn't take long for the sharks to circle, questioning everything from the selection of certain players to myriad coaching decisions and tactics. This was no exception.

Kris Draper went into the boards face first here, but he was face to face with Soviet star Pavel Bure in Canada's victory over the Soviet Union.

There could not have been any more doom and gloom in the Team Canada ranks than there was on January 3, leading up to that night's game between the Soviets and Finns at the Agridome, home of the WHL's Regina Pats. No one was giving Finland any chance at all.

TSN wasn't able to broadcast the Soviet-Finland game because it had other programming commitments that night, but the network, recognizing the significance of the game, dispatched Paul Romanuk and me to Regina to provide live updates over the course of the night into TSN programming.

It was wickedly cold that night in Regina. Team Canada sent advance scout Dave Draper to Regina for the game, but the rest of the team, including head coach Todd,

Canadian captain Steven Rice and his teammates had to wait for the results of the Soviet Union-Finland game to see if they would still have a shot at a gold medal.

stayed back in their Saskatoon hotel, hoping for a miracle from the Finns.

Team Canada winger Kent Manderville, a returnee from the 1990 gold-medal team that got an improbable gift from the Soviets a year earlier, recalls that January night like it was yesterday.

"We had the whole floor of the hotel to ourselves and everyone's doors were open and we were all just wandering around from room to room and through the hall," Manderville said. "It was like being a kid in a minor hockey tournament again, there with all your teammates, but we were waiting for the [Soviet-Finland] game to start. We were obviously down after losing to the Czechs but we hoped Finland might be able to pull off the upset. We were all gathered around the TVs, just watching TSN [for the updates]."

It turned out to be a night of theatre of the absurd.

Less than 14 minutes into the second period in Regina, the spunky Finns jumped out to a 4–0 lead on the Soviets, including two goals from Jere Lehtinen.

"We couldn't believe it," Manderville said. "We were going crazy but we also knew the lead wasn't safe, not with all the firepower [the Soviets] had, especially Bure."

There wasn't a huge crowd in the Agridome that night, but those who were there couldn't believe their eyes. I can recall the excitement building with each Finnish goal and the breathless TSN updates with Paul Romanuk, suggesting that maybe, just maybe, Canada was going to have an opportunity at redemption.

But the euphoria was relatively short-lived.

Less than two minutes after the Finns made it 4–0, the Soviets answered. Then, at 17:52 of the second, Bure scored to make it 4–2—and the sense of foreboding returned in a big way.

Less than five minutes into the third period, Bure scored again to close the Soviet deficit to one goal. He was literally taking over the game. He wasn't finished, and neither were the Soviets. Oleg Petrov scored at 11:08 to tie the game, and, 1:21 later, Bure got the hat trick and the Soviets were back in front 5–4. It was a tour de force by one of the game's most exciting players, as dynamic a 15-minute stretch of game action by one player as I've ever witnessed.

"It was like a roller-coaster ride," Manderville said. "We were so high when the Finns were up 4–0, out running up and down the halls between rooms celebrating, and we were so low when Bure scored his third goal. We figured that was it; it was over for us."

It certainly seemed that way. The Soviet defence included future NHLers Dmitry Yushkevich, Darius Kasparaitis, Sandis Ozolinsh, Boris Mironov, and Alexei Zhitnik. Up front, they had Bure, Slava Kozlov, Sergei Berezin, and Sergei Zholtok, among others. Now, after having been in a four-goal hole, it was unimaginable to think the Soviets would surrender their lead.

What happened next, though, truly qualifies as "you had to be there."

At 17:57, the Soviets took a too-many-men-on-the-ice penalty. The Finns pulled their goalie, playing six on four. The Soviets had changed goaltenders, from Sergei Zvyagin to Sergei Tkachenko, and the Finns were having a tough time mustering any real good scoring chances on their final power play.

But with less than 20 seconds to go, Finnish forward Jarkko Varvio backhanded a harmless looking bloop shot from the hash marks at the boards, to the right of Tkachenko—and the puck skittered between his legs and into the net.

If I hadn't been there to see it myself, I'm not sure I would have believed it. The Varvio power-play goal was scored at 19:45 of the third. Final score: Finland 5, Soviet Union 5. As was the case a year earlier at the 1990 WJC, the Soviets found a truly bizarro way to let Canada back into the gold-medal hunt.

"It was bedlam in the hotel," Manderville said.

"Just crazy," Todd added. "We were back in it. We had a chance."

"What I remember about all of that," Manderville said, "was the picture on TV of the Russian goalie, just sitting on the ice, all by himself, looking totally depleted."

What I remember is Pavel Bure, standing despondently during the post-game presentations on the blue line, his chin resting atop his gloves, which were on top of his stick—in sort of a forlorn Ken Dryden pose, staring off into space.

"I could not believe it," Bure said. "Honestly, I don't remember a lot of the details, it was so long ago, but I am sure I was thinking, how did this happen? That was two years in a row we did not do what we had to. We gave [gold] to Canada twice."

John Slaney's winning goal ultimately over-shadowed the unlikely events that led up to the title game. Victory was made sweeter by the fact that the Canadian juniors thought gold was likely out of reach just 24 hours earlier.

The despondent Soviets had to bus back north to Saskatoon after the game, with the now-gold-medal game the next night, while the Team Canada coaching staff strategized a game plan at the hotel in Saskatoon. The Canadian players, meanwhile, tried to calm themselves after the roller-coaster night of emotions, counting their blessings and trying to sleep.

Todd's game plan involved matching stalwart defensive forward Kris Draper against Bure. Draper brought a game and experience to the role, having been Guy Charron's go-to faceoff man in the final minute of the gold-medal game in the 1990 tournament.

As Bure recalled it, he didn't get much room in the final game against Canada.

"Was it Draper who was checking me?" Bure asked. "I didn't realize then that it was him. I do remember I didn't get as much room and as many chances in the Canadian game."

With Draper blunting the key piece of the Russians' offence, the game was a tense, tight-checking affair. With the score tied two-all and just over five minutes left in the third period, Slaney provided the magic moment that would become one of the most replayed goals in the history of the event. It was the second year in a row a Newfoundlander scored the game-winning goal for gold after a Soviet miscue opened the door for the big prize.

It's funny, though, what different people remember most about that 1991 tournament and that Slaney goal.

"What a lot of people don't realize is that the Soviet winger had flown their zone and was way out in the neutral zone looking for the breakaway," Todd said. "I saw the puck coming up the boards and I was screaming for Slaney to pull out and go back to get the guy in the neutral zone, but he didn't. I thought they were going to get a breakaway but John knocked the puck down, shot, and scored. It was a great play by him but I had been terrified he was taking a risk that was going to cost us. Funny how that goes."

Unquestionably, the 1991 WJC will forever be known as John Slaney's moment— but at the very least there should be a footnote for Jarkko Varvio and yet another improbable scenario paving the way for Canada to win gold when all had seemed so lost.

1992

FÜSSEN
THE FAILED CHEMISTRY EXPERIMENT

SHELDON FERGUSON

In a break from its usual approach to team building, Hockey Canada added Eric Lindros to the roster of the 1992 WJC squad at the eleventh hour. He led the team in scoring, but anything short of a gold medal would have been deemed a failure for the most celebrated junior player in Canadian history.

It really came down to one play, one call. There were less than 10 seconds left in our game against Sweden and we were in front 2–1. I could see the players on the bench, standing up, getting ready to celebrate. We were just a deep breath from a third straight victory to start the tournament. That breath turned out to be in the cheeks of the ref who blew a whistle on an icing call that brought the puck back into our end for a faceoff and a last chance for the Swedes. It was a real close call, too. I had seen a lot like it not get called.

The Swedes pulled their goaltender. It was Eric Lindros against Peter Forsberg on the faceoff. Forsberg won the draw and next thing you know the puck is in the net, past our goalie Trevor Kidd, who had been very solid for us. It wasn't his fault. You couldn't blame him. You couldn't blame Eric for losing the draw—he was out there against a heck of a player in Forsberg. It just happened.

It was a tie that felt like a loss. When I looked at the bench, I saw that all the energy that had been there just 10 seconds before was gone. When I watched the players after they came off the ice, I saw a team that was deflated. It was a turning point. I knew that it was going to be tough to rebound, especially in the format of

Paul Kariya went to Füssen as an under-age player. He would have to wait until the following January for gold in the WJC.

the tournament back then. There were no do-overs and a tie was just about as bad as a loss for your chances at getting the gold.

The team was hurting after that game and hurting worse after the game the next day: a 2–2 tie with the Finns. If we had a day off, maybe the team would have had a chance to refocus. As it was, that second tie took us out of contention for the gold medal and in those days it was the mentality that prevailed with Canadian players—we were there for the gold, not second or third place. I think the Program of Excellence has made real strides in getting the players away from the all-or-nothing thinking in a challenging situation in the years since, but that's how it was for our players in 1992. It was going to be all or nothing and, unfortunately, it turned out to be the latter.

If you look at our lineup and not the final standings, you'd think it was a very strong team, maybe even a powerhouse. We had a player who's going into the Hockey Hall of Fame, Scott Niedermayer, back from the previous year's team to lead our blue line, as well as a couple of other defencemen, Karl Dykhuis and John Slaney, who had played for the team that beat the Soviets for gold in Saskatoon. Trevor Kidd had played for that team. Eric Lindros was back—as an underage player he had been great for the team in Saskatoon and everyone expected him to be that much better in Germany. Martin Lapointe was another key player returning for a shot at a second gold. It looked like that experience would serve us well in '92.

We had a lot of talent beyond that. Paul Kariya was such a dynamic player. We had a couple of defencemen, Richard Matvichuk and Darryl Sydor, who would be the foundation of Dallas's blue line when the Stars won the Stanley Cup. We had tremendous size, too, averaging 6-foot-2 across our blue line plus Eric, Martin, and Turner Stevenson up front who would make other teams pay a physical price on our forecheck. The team had a lot going for it. There were such high expectations. And it went downhill so fast that it seemed like we didn't know what hit us until it was over. We ended the tournament with a couple of bad losses to Czechoslovakia and the former Soviet Union and finished sixth.

It's hard to pinpoint exactly what went wrong.

After the tournament some people wanted to pin it on Eric Lindros, but that's not fair or deserved. One player doesn't win a tournament for you unless it's a goaltender. He played well for us under the circumstances and he did that with so much pressure and publicity and hype surrounding him—far more than, say, Mario Lemieux or Wayne Gretzky had as teenagers. He was also fighting the flu when he joined the team. That's not uncommon for a player or two in your lineup at that time of year, but I don't think we'd ever had one of our frontline players hurting so badly during a tournament. It's one thing to have someone in a minor role play through it—a few shifts here and there. I think, though, that given his style of play and how

Having won gold playing alongside elite NHLers at the Canada Cup, Eric Lindros went to Füssen with unmatched and unrealistic expectations that he would singlehandedly carry his team to victory.

much we asked of him, it really dragged Eric down. He simply wasn't himself. And it wasn't just illness that weighed on Eric. He was in a very difficult position, too, that was part of a decision we made. Previously, the Program of Excellence had required all players to attend the summer development camp and the entire evaluation camp in December. Eric couldn't come to the summer camp—he was committed to the Canada Cup team, playing with the best pros even though he hadn't played an NHL game. And that winter, because he hadn't signed an NHL contract yet, he had joined the Olympic program. We brought him in late, only three days before we headed off to Europe. We named him captain, which only put more pressure on him. To an extent, we looked at him and his teammates looked at him, thinking, "Okay, Eric's here and he'll take over." We didn't put him in the best possible position to succeed, and we hurt our team chemistry by bringing in Eric, forward Kimbi Daniels, and Trevor Kidd so late in the process. In retrospect, would we have gotten a better read on Eric's illness and on his fit with the other teammates had he been with us all along? There's no way to know for sure—but we might have.

Some said that our coach, Rick Cornacchia, was guilty of favouritism in the way he dealt with Eric because he had been his coach with the Oshawa Generals. It just wasn't true. It was nothing that his assistant coaches Tom Renney and Gary Agnew would have sat still for. It's nothing that Hockey Canada would have tolerated.

Some years we benefited from some good breaks when we won gold. In Germany, we didn't really get a single one. But we couldn't pin it on bad luck. You have to give the other teams credit, too—it's a hard tournament to win and all those teams had very good players. That said, our team underachieved.

It was a bad tournament, but I think you can make a case that it was an important one for the Program of Excellence, maybe even a necessary one.

After the WJC, we analyzed what had happened in Füssen and came up with one major conclusion.

We did have an issue with team chemistry in Füssen. That really showed through when the team first faced adversity and never recovered. It was decided that we had to take what had been that team's flaw and make it a strength in our program going forward. We determined that we had to put a real emphasis on team building—Perry Pearn, who had been both an assistant and head coach of our world junior teams and a major contributor to the Program of Excellence, was a key guy in developing the team-building strategies.

I don't doubt for a second that we had the right players and the right coaches in Füssen. I believe, though, that we didn't do them any favours before the WJC. I'd love to take that same team back to the tournament and have another try. If we had everyone pulling together—everyone at the summer camp, everyone there for the evaluations in December, everyone through the team-building programs—I'd like our chances for gold in that field. I'd like our chances even more if the players had been through the under-17 and under-18 teams in the years before the world juniors.

It was my first year scouting for the Program of Excellence—I had worked as a scout for the Quebec Nordiques and as general manager of the Seattle Thunderbirds. The '92 world juniors was a tough introduction. That said, I think that Füssen taught us a lot about what it was going to take to win the world juniors. And it's no coincidence that after our poorest showing to that point, Canadian teams would bring home the gold the next five years.

1993

GÄVLE
THE BULLETIN BOARD

TIM WHARNSBY

Defenceman Joël
Bouchard coolly
controls the puck in
Canada's 9–1 rout of
the Russians. The
Canadian defence
faced a tougher test
against a high-flying
Swedish team featuring
Peter Forsberg.

The turning point in the 1993 world junior tournament in Gävle, Sweden, wasn't a goal, a save, or a hit. It was a bold prediction made by Sweden's star forward Peter Forsberg, who told reporters that his team had nothing to fear in playing Canada the next day.

The Canadian juniors were underdogs because of their youth and because the Swedish roster featured plenty of returnees from the team that lost 4–3 to Russia in the gold-medal-deciding game a year before. Forsberg centred wings Markus Näslund and Niklas Sundstrom on the most productive line in tournament history. The three would combine for 30 goals and 69 points in 1993 on a Swedish team that scored a remarkable 53 goals in the seven-game tournament.

A much less experienced Canadian team featured the top teenage prospects in Alexandre Daigle, Chris Pronger, Chris Gratton, Paul Kariya, and Rob Niedermayer. They would wind up filling the first five slots at the NHL entry draft six months later.

The young Canadians hadn't exactly instilled fear into the Swedes when they dropped an 8–5 decision to the host country in an exhibition game days before the tournament. It was an undisciplined effort that saw Sweden check in with seven power-play goals—impressive firepower considering that Forsberg sat out the game because of the flu. A few days later there was Forsberg rinkside, watching

the first period of Canada's tournament opener against the United States. The Canucks prevailed against their North American rival with a 3–0 win, but Forsberg wasn't impressed.

"They are not so good," he said. "We are going to beat them. We are a much better team. We are better skaters. They play tough, but it's a bigger ice surface and they're going to have problems with that. They may be good, but they are not so tough."

Forsberg underestimated the roly-poly figure that guarded the Canadian goal. His name was Manny Legace, and he turned in one of the most memorable netminding performances from a Canadian junior in the program's long list of stellar goalies.

Legace gave Forsberg and other tournament observers a hint of what was to come with his wonderful 31-save effort against the United States. His shutout was preserved with 35 seconds left when forward Brian Rolston rang a shot off the post on Legace's blocker side.

Winger Martin Lapointe was one of three players returning from the 1992 team that had fallen flat in Füssen.

"I remember kissing the post afterwards," recalled Legace. "My ears were ringing from that shot. He beat me. But that game was not only a big confidence booster for me and for the whole team. We couldn't have asked for a better result going into the big game against Sweden."

With Forsberg's remarks about what he believed to be an inferior Canadian team taped to the wall of the Canadian dressing room, hard-nosed centre Tyler Wright stood up and addressed his teammates before the Sweden game. Along with Kariya and Martin Lapointe, Wright was one of three returning players from the junior team that endured the debacle in Füssen.

Part of Wright's message was about how it all started to unravel for Canada in Germany after Forsberg beat Eric Lindros on a faceoff in Canada's end late in the game, which led to a tying goal in the dying seconds. Wright also had insight into what made Forsberg tick. The two had the same agent, Winnipeg-based Don Baizley, and they had become friends at the 1991 draft. Wright had trained with Forsberg the previous summer and Forsberg had also visited Wright at his home in Kamsack, Saskatchewan.

Wright's speech didn't have the impact he hoped for. Canada was badly outplayed, but because of Legace's determination the Canadian juniors were down only 1–0 after 20 minutes. Canadian head coach Perry Pearn blasted his teenagers in the first intermission. The harsh words did the trick. It was 3–2 for Canada after two periods and the kids hung on for a 5–4 victory.

It wasn't Wright's speech or Pearn's tirade that did the trick. It was Forsberg's braggadocio. "What [Forsberg] said definitely gave us a boost," Canadian defenceman Brent Tully said.

The usually circumspect Pearn took a not-so-subtle shot at Forsberg afterwards. "I would like to know what Peter Forsberg thinks about our team now."

Even in defeat, though, Forsberg didn't concede anything. "I thought we were a better team," he said. "But obviously they were the better team. We lost. Sure, I regret saying it now. But we are still going to win [the tournament] anyway. I hope I don't regret saying that. But I think Canada will lose at least one more game."

The Canadians did lose to Czechoslovakia in their final game in the round-robin tournament, but they had already locked up the gold medal by then. They had rolled over Russia 9–1 in a game that pitted Daigle against Viktor Kozlov, who was touted as a possible first-overall selection, two days after the sweet victory over Sweden. Then they escaped with a 3–2 win over Finland.

In the win over Finland, Pearn and Legace again played key roles. Pearn, who went on to the NHL as a long-time, valuable assistant coach in Winnipeg, Ottawa, New York, and Montreal, is a master tactician but was not known at the time for his motivational skills. In fact, he wasn't even first choice to coach the Canadian junior team that year. Alain Vigneault was originally named to head the coaching staff but had to resign in the summer when he accepted a position as an assistant coach with the Ottawa Senators.

In came Pearn, who had been an assistant coach to Guy Charron in 1990 and Dick Todd a year later. Both tournaments saw Canada win gold.

With Canada holding on to a slim 2–1 lead over Finland after 40 minutes, Pearn walked into the dressing room and cleared off the trainer's table. He then took off the 1990 world junior championship ring that he won in Finland and placed it on the table. Pearn didn't utter a word and left the room. He returned later to say: "This is what we came here to win, so let's go out there and do it."

He knew that with only Germany, Japan, and Czechoslovakia remaining on the docket, a win over Finland would lock up gold. When the final buzzer sounded, Canada improved

Defenceman Scott Niedermayer and four of his teammates on the Canadian roster would be the first five picks in the NHL draft months after the victory in Gävle.

to 4-0 with a 3–2 win. The shot clock indicated that Finland outshot Canada 60–38. The Hockey Canada staff kept its own stats and its tabulation was 45–23.

"I don't think I faced 60 shots," Legace said. "All I know is I was getting pretty tired."

Underneath his equipment Legace wore the threadbare t-shirt that he had pulled over his shoulders since his peewee days with the Don Mills Flyers, but he might as well have been wearing a Superman shirt.

"I don't think I was Superman," he said. "I just went there to do a job for my team and my country. I was just trying to do my best."

When 32 hopefuls gathered in Kitchener for the selection camp in early December, Legace was considered a long shot to crack the roster. His competition included Jocelyn Thibault, Norm Maracle, and Philippe DeRouville. At that time only DeRouville had been drafted, the previous June in the fifth round by the Pittsburgh Penguins. Thibault and Maracle were considered two of the top goalie prospects for the 1993 draft.

None of the four distinguished themselves at the selection camp, but Pearn and chief scout Sheldon Ferguson were first impressed by Legace in the summer at the evaluation camp. They liked how hard Legace competed and they had a hunch he would be the guy they could depend on.

"I just thought Manny was a big-game goalie," said Pearn, who went to grade school with Ferguson in Stettler, Alberta. "[Legace] is the type you want in there when you need a win. He is an extremely quick goaltender, who moves from side to side well. When you do that well in the international game, you will be successful."

Legace, a month shy of his 20th birthday at the time, was too good to be true on the ice and as humble as they come off the ice. He was so honoured to play for Canada that he stood ramrod straight as the national anthem played after each victory.

While Thibault went 10th overall to the Quebec Nordiques in the 1993 draft and Maracle was taken by the Detroit Red Wings five rounds later, Legace had to wait until the eighth round before the Hartford Whalers called his name. The native of Alliston, Ontario, spent a season with the national team and then toiled away in the minors for almost five years before he made his NHL debut with the Los Angeles Kings. He wound up winning a Stanley Cup with the 2001–02 Red Wings as Dominik Hasek's backup.

Before he could claim his WJC gold, Legace wound up beating Germany 5–2 to set up an anticlimactic gold-medal-clinching 8–1 win over Japan before a small crowd of 625 in Hudiksvall, a fishing village 130 kilometres north of Gävle. The Hudiksvall rink was a beautiful wooden structure built in 1989 and provided a

church-like setting for Canada's subdued celebration.

The Canadian juniors still had one more game to play against the former Czechoslovakia, which broke up into the Czech Republic and Slovakia at midnight on New Year's Eve. Legace gave way to DeRouville in the tournament finale that turned out to be a 7–4 loss for Canada.

But Legace already had locked up a spot on the tournament all-star team and top goaltender honours with his sparkling 6-0 record, 1.67 goals-against average, and .955 save percentage.

"Manny was by far the best goalie, and maybe the best player overall in the tournament," Wright said. "He did more than anybody on our team."

Many consider Manny Legace's performance in the 1993 tournament as the greatest ever by a Canadian goaltender in the WJC. His numbers (6-0 record, 1.67 goals-against average, .955 save percentage) have not been matched to date.

1994

OSTRAVA
THE PLUCKY UNDERDOGS

TIM WHARNSBY

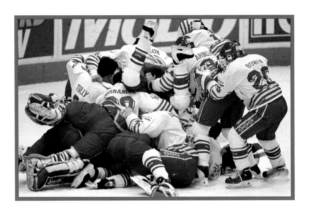

A narrow win over the Swedes in the final game of the round robin set off a wild celebration. Here, captain Brent Tully leaps into the arms of his teammates.

The depth of the Canadian junior program had never been tested like it was in 1994, when 10 junior-aged players had fixed themselves with addresses in the NHL or were trying to earn a spot on the Canadian Olympic team roster.

The total almost had been 11, but Olympic team head coach Tom Renney released Martin Gendron to the Canadian juniors. This was a welcome development, because Gendron, the Washington Capitals' 1992 third-round pick from Valleyfield, Quebec, was a prolific scorer who had checked in with five goals in seven games in the 1993 world junior tournament and would score six times for Canada in 1994.

The Winter Games in Lillehammer were a mere eight weeks away when Canadian junior head coach Joe Canale and his assistants Mike Johnston and Danny Flynn assembled in Kitchener for the selection camp. After the debacle in Füssen two years prior, the Canadian junior program had adopted a policy requiring all possible candidates to participate in the selection camp. This policy was intended to help team cohesion—on and off the ice—during the selection camp.

That made juniors Paul Kariya, Todd Warriner, and Brett Lindros unavailable because they were slated to play for the Olympic team hopefuls in the Izvestia Tournament in Moscow before Christmas, and they also were expected to see action on a six-game exhibition tour in Russia and the Czech Republic over the holidays.

Joe Canale was considered by some a controversial choice as the Canadian team's coach, but he left an indelible impression on his players.

The younger Lindros didn't end up accompanying Kariya and Warriner to Lillehammer because he didn't make the final cut, but in the end, whether or not Lindros suited up for Canada at the WJC did not matter. The seven junior-aged Canadians in the NHL were Alexandre Daigle, Chris Pronger, Chris Gratton, Rob Niedermayer, Jason Arnott, Mike Rathje, and goalie Jocelyn Thibault.

"We knew a lot would be said about who was not here, those 10 juniors playing in the NHL or with the Canadian Olympic team," said Canadian junior captain Brent Tully, who along with Gendron and defenceman Joël Bouchard were the only returnees from 1993. "In a way not having those guys was a good thing for us. It took pressure off us. The 22 players we had were excellent players, very capable of winning a gold medal. If we were looked upon as underdogs, then great. It was all that more sweet when we won."

This edition of the Canadian junior team had the perfect coach in Canale to lead the way. He overcame an episode of extreme adversity earlier in his life when his junior coaching career was just beginning, but he patiently persevered.

Back on February 20, 1978, Canale was a few months into his first major junior coaching job with the Shawinigan Dynamos when he was awakened by RCMP officers and arrested at his home on charges of trafficking narcotics in a Montreal coffee house that he had invested in.

Though Canale was later pardoned, his coaching career had taken a hit. A dozen years passed before brave Chicoutimi Saguenéens owner Jeannot Harvey took a risk and hired Canale, who rewarded that faith by steering the Saguenéens to their first QMJHL title and a trip to the 1991 Memorial Cup tournament in Quebec City.

"Joe was one of the best coaches I've had," said former Toronto Maple Leafs netminder Félix Potvin, who starred for Chicoutimi during that championship season. "He cared about us as people. But he also knew the right time to lean on us and push us."

Canale, who assisted Perry Pearn at the previous world junior tournament, continued to push the right buttons in Ostrava, Czech Republic, in 1994, and he left an impression.

"I was lucky enough to have Joe Canale as a coach for two gold medals," Tully said.

Canadian defenceman Chris Armstrong dumps Finnish centre Juha Lind in a victory that was likely the team's best game in Ostrava.

"As far I was concerned Canada should have had him coaching every year. But the way this one finished, it was definitely sweeter. You couldn't ask for a better finish."

Not only did Canale have Johnston and Flynn by his side, but Pearn was in Ostrava, too. He was coaching in Switzerland for Ambri-Piotta and was on a break. Pearn was there to help in any way he could. But despite the absence of some of Canada's best junior-aged talent, Canale had his team's title defence headed in the right direction after opening victories against Switzerland and Germany by a combined score of 10–3.

The third game of the tournament against Russia, however, was a different story. The Canadian juniors blew a 3–0 lead in the third period and starting goalie Jamie Storr was ineffective. So Canale made the move to backup Manny Fernandez for the next three games and the change had an immediate impact. Canada put forth its best all-around performance of the tournament in a 6–3 win over Finland.

"We definitely proved with this win we are one of the top teams in this tournament," said Canadian winger Anson Carter, who came to the forefront with a goal and an assist. "I'll admit we were down on ourselves after blowing a 3–0 lead to Russia. We doubted ourselves after that game. But now we have nothing but confidence. We're going to finish off these final three games with our best hockey yet and get that gold."

Canada beat the United States 8–3 and the Czech Republic 6–4 to set up a gold-medal-deciding game against Sweden on the final day of the round-robin tournament. All of a sudden the underdog Canadians were a win away from another championship.

When the Canadians arrived at Ostrava a couple days before the tournament began, they found themselves in a hardscrabble setting. Ostrava was a steel town and the arena was on its outskirts. If the streetcar across the street went left, you wound up downtown. If it turned right, a few blocks later you were right in the middle of a steel mill.

Jason Botterill, here fighting through a check, would end up with the shiniest medal collection of any player to come through the Program of Excellence. He won the first of his three gold medals in Ostrava.

There were security concerns. Ostrava is near the Polish border. Pickpockets and thieves had their run of the city's streets. Players were warned of the dangers and were kept under close watch. Storr's father Jim had a jacket lifted in a downtown restaurant. Flynn woke up one night in his hotel room to find an intruder that he scared away with a shout before any damage was done.

Because of these circumstances the Canadians were confined to one floor of the hotel that was right beside the rink. This turned out to be a good thing, because these teenagers quickly built cohesion, a togetherness.

"As a coaching staff we didn't focus on who could be on the team, but simply who wanted to be there," Johnston said. "When we met for the summer camp and again for our training camp in Switzerland just prior to the tournament, our number one priority was to build this group into a real team. We tried to drive home the message that even though we had no NHL experience and no stars, we could come together and be a team."

The Swedish team was staying at the same hotel as the Canadians. The young Canadians saw up close and personal just how confident the Swedes were. The Swedes strutted around, believing nobody could touch them. They had finished second in the previous two tournaments, and their lineup boasted high-end talent like Kenny Jonsson, Mattias Öhlund, Mats Lindgren, Niklas Sundstrom, Jesper Mattsson, and Anders Eriksson.

They looked at the Canadians like they were a bunch of no-names. Canale and his staff played the underdog card to motivate their team.

"We weren't even picked to win a medal," defenceman Bryan McCabe said. "Everyone had written us off because guys like Pronger and Kariya weren't made available to us. But I thought the coaching staff did a tremendous job in using it as a rallying point. We just used it as motivation and ran with it."

The Canadians, 5-0-1, had what they wanted—a shot at gold. A loss or tie did them no good against the Swedes, who had six wins in six games. Canada needed a win. In the off-day before the showdown, there was a noticeable change around the hotel. All of a sudden the confident Swedes didn't appear as sure about the outcome. They could see a determination in the Canadians.

"We had nothing to lose," Harvey said. "The pressure was on them because we weren't even supposed to win a medal."

The only decision left for Canale was his starter in goal. Fernandez wasn't sharp against the Czechs, so he went back with Storr. The move turned out to be golden. The Canadians jumped out to leads of 2–0 and 5–2 on goals from Aaron Gavey, Yanick Dubé, Jason Allison, and Gendron with a pair. But the Canadians didn't make it easy on themselves. The Swedes beat Storr twice in the third period to set up a frantic final minute.

Rick Girard embodied the breakneck commitment of the 1994 Canadian juniors. Here, he crashes the crease, literally, going headfirst over American Kevyn Adams and into the net.

Canada was short-handed and the Swedes pulled their goalie for a 6-on-4 advantage. Gavey made a sensational play when he intercepted a pass that would easily have been converted for the final goal. Then Rick Girard stripped Jonsson of the puck and scored into an empty net with six seconds remaining.

Every one of the Canadian players jumped off the bench to celebrate. Luckily, the on-ice officials decided against a delay-of-game penalty for the exuberant bunch. Instead, the final seconds were ticked off the clock and real celebrations began.

Harvey played with a painful hip injury, but exhibited tremendous grit. Girard persevered through a bothersome shoulder ailment. Tully underwent an emergency appendectomy in late October and had to play himself back into condition during the tournament.

"Being called a bunch of no-names hit a lot of us in the heart," Gavey said. "We wanted to prove we were good enough to win. We are proud of where we come from. We all worked hard to get here."

1995

RED DEER
THE DREAM TEAM

TIM WHARNSBY

Head coach Don Hay brought in forward Darcy Tucker (right) and defenceman Nolan Baumgartner from his Kamloops Blazers, the defending Memorial Cup champions. After adding a WJC gold, Hay, Tucker, and Baumgartner would lead the Blazers to a second consecutive Memorial Cup.

All eyes were on head coach Don Hay when he blew his whistle to begin the 34-player Canadian junior selection camp in Edmonton in mid-December 1994. The country was three months into the NHL lockout and the 1995 world junior championship in Red Deer could not have come at a better time.

Fans were starving for something to sink their teeth into. So there was Alexandre Daigle, Ed Jovanovski, Ryan Smyth, and Co. ready for the intense spotlight. The NHL was on hiatus and the tournament was being contested on home soil, where it matters the most.

The media dubbed the Canadians the "Dream Team." Theirs was a powerhouse squad even though out-of-work junior-aged NHLers Chris Gratton and Brendan Witt decided not to report to their junior teams in Kingston and Seattle and thus weren't eligible to play for Canada in Red Deer.

Either way, Hay detested hyperbole. He was a fireman and preached teamwork. He preached chemistry. He wanted players to buy into the team concept, not believe the hyperbole.

"I didn't like this Dream Team image," Hay said. "I don't think it was fair to the kids. Putting that label on it hurt them. We just kept stressing that there were a lot of good teams out there and they hadn't won anything yet."

The Dream Team idea was hard to ignore, however. Seven players already were under contract to NHL teams. Daigle was the first selection in the 1993 NHL entry draft and Jovanovski went first overall in 1994. Wade Redden was expected to be among the first two choices in 1995. In total, 17 of the 34 juniors invited to the camp were first-round NHL picks. Two more, in Redden and Brad Church (who didn't make the team), were drafted in the first round six months later.

On the final day of the evaluation camp, Hay made two controversial cuts: Jocelyn Thibault and Brett Lindros. Thibault had made 29 appearances for the Quebec Nordiques in 1993–94, but had seen limited action prior to the camp because of a shoulder ailment. The Lindros decision was a surprising development that the player didn't take well.

Asked if he was bitter, the younger brother of NHL superstar Eric snapped, "big time."

"I thought I played well enough to make this team—evidently not," Lindros said. "Donnie just said, 'Hey, you're more suited to the pro style.' There's no arguing with that. I'm pretty disappointed. He said he wanted a checker, and I checked. Now he wants more finesse out of me. I just don't know."

Hay remarked at the time that Lindros's skating held him back. "He has good assets, but we were probably looking for somebody that could skate a little better," Hay said. "More speed. In international games, speed is so important."

Once the roster was finalized, Hay had to keep his players from being distracted by the spotlight. This wasn't the only powerhouse team that Hay had coached. The previous spring he had won the Memorial Cup as the Kamloops head coach, but even more instructive were lessons he learned working as an assistant to Ken Hitchcock with the same club a few seasons before. That earlier edition of the Blazers had won the WHL championship to advance to the 1991 Memorial Cup, and though they were loaded with talent, they were the first team eliminated from the tournament. When they were asked for opinions afterwards as to what went wrong in Hamilton, the players remarked they weren't given much downtime and spent too much time sequestered in their hotel.

Hay made sure that wasn't going to be an issue in Red Deer. There were volleyball matches organized, walks in the park, and even an outdoor game of shinny was played prior to the tournament. Hay also had plenty of inspirational sayings plastered on the walls of the dressing room. One of the coach's favourites: "You can't count the days, you've got to make the days count."

"You have to pay attention to the player's mental state just as much as his physical

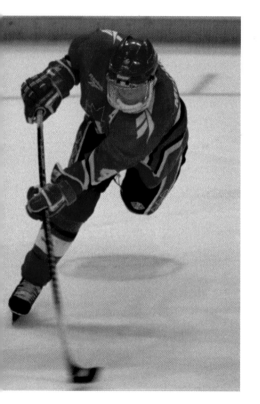

Defenceman Bryan McCabe contributed a big goal in a come-from-behind victory over the Czechs, the only stiff challenge the Dream Team faced throughout play in Red Deer.

skills," Hay said. "The mental part of the game is just as important. The motivation part also is key in a tournament like this where you have to refocus very quickly. In 1990 we went to the Memorial Cup and we had a pretty good hockey team, but it was like we were in jail all week and we didn't play very good."

Hay's Canadian junior team was very good in 1995. They opened the eight-team round-robin tournament with three lopsided victories, 7–1 over Ukraine, 9–1 against Germany, and 8–3 over the rival United States. But the games were about to become more difficult.

The Canadians travelled south to Calgary to take on the Czechs and escaped with a hard-fought 7–5 victory. Canada trailed 3–1 after the first period, but tied it up at 4–4 in the second period on goals from Bryan McCabe, Marty Murray, and Todd Harvey, only to see the Czechs go ahead 5–4 before the second intermission. Redden drew Canada even with four minutes remaining, then blueliner Jamie Rivers put Canada ahead for good with 2 minutes, 24 seconds left.

"The Czechs always gave us trouble and we were playing before a crazy crowd that night," Harvey recalled. "I remember the coaching staff told us to tighten up defensively and that there was to be no pinching from the defencemen. So Jamie Rivers pinches in all the way into the corner, picks up the puck, and scores."

The Canadian juniors went to Edmonton for a New Year's Day tilt against Finland and prevailed 6–4 to secure a medal. They returned to Red Deer for a game against Russia, which they won 8–5, though they didn't clinch the gold until 40 minutes after the final horn, thanks to Finland's late-game comeback to tie Sweden 3–3.

"To be honest, I thought the Finland-Sweden game was supposed to start in a few hours," said forward Jason Allison, who won a world junior gold medal for the second time. "Then I was undressing and somebody yelled it was 3–1 Sweden. I came out of the shower and some of the guys were yelling it was 3–3. It's great to win a second, but it would have been better winning it out on the ice against Sweden."

Jere Karalahti provided the heroics for Finland with his game-tying goal with 2:51 remaining. It was just another bizarre chapter in his life. Earlier in the tournament, he'd gone AWOL from the Finnish team after he met some new friends in a local bar and went off with them to party for a few days.

McCabe crashes the net in Canada's 8–3 rout of the United States. In their first three games, the Canadians lived up to the Dream Team hype, outscoring opponents 24–5.

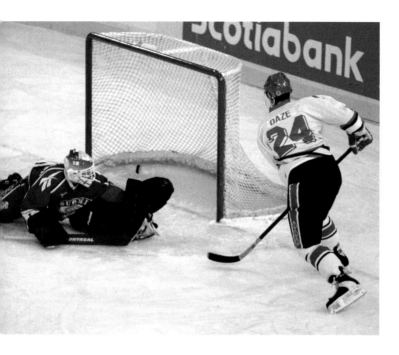

Winger Eric Daze was unheralded before the tournament but emerged as one of Canada's best players and a WJC all-star.

"Find out where Jere is staying, we have to send him something," Harvey yelled after the goal.

With the gold medal locked up, Canada went off to a country bar to celebrate. They had a day off before the tournament finale against Sweden. At stake not only was Canada's first perfect 7-0 record at a world junior tournament, but also the fact that if they could beat Sweden, Canada would do a favour for their new-found Finnish friends. A Sweden loss and a Finland win over Russia on the final day of the tournament would give Finland the silver medal.

Finland, however, was beaten 6–2 by Russia. Canada enjoyed a 4–3 win after Sweden made it close with goals 18 seconds apart with two minutes remaining in the third period.

For all the attention given to heralded pro prospects, two of the least-known players might have been the best during the tournament: Marty Murray and Eric Daze. Both were taken in the fourth round of the 1994 NHL entry draft. The Chicago Blackhawks chose Daze six spots before the Calgary Flames took Murray. Murray, a cousin of former Los Angeles Kings and St. Louis Blues coach Andy Murray, checked in with six goals and 15 points for Canada, while Daze scored eight times in seven games. His big outing came when he scored a hat trick against Russia.

"I just wanted to make the team," he said. "I would have never dreamed of scoring three against Russia."

The guy Daze beat out to make the Canadian roster was Brett Lindros.

"Going into the Edmonton camp [Daze] was probably fifth or sixth on the depth chart," Hay said. "He kept getting better and better. I thought he was one of the best players in camp. He put some right wingers out of a job. He had great hands for a big guy and he skated really well for a guy his size."

Daze was raised in Laval, Quebec, and played his minor hockey with Daigle. He mostly played with Daigle in the tournament, and off the ice Daze also enjoyed the company of the outgoing Daigle, who was thrilled about his linemate's success. "Everybody was focusing on me, but right now he's the centre point and he's got to enjoy it, too," Daigle said after the Russia game.

"I'm a shy guy and I don't talk a lot," Daze said. "[Daigle] talked to me a lot and brought me along with the rest of the guys."

Unfortunately, Daze's career with the Blackhawks was limited to 226 goals in 601 games because he was forced to retire after chronic back woes. While Daze was the biggest player on the Canadian roster at 6-foot-5, 205 pounds, the 5-foot-9, 168-pound Murray was the smallest.

But Murray, who grew up on a crop and cattle farm near Lyleton in southern Manitoba, not far from the U.S. border, had a tremendous amount of character. His passion for hockey ran deep. He would play for two teams some seasons in his youth—both his rural team and the nearby city team.

Murray ran up against the old not-big-enough stigma. But he was big enough and skilled enough to play 14 pro seasons on both sides of the pond, including 261 NHL games for the Flames, Kings, Flyers, and Hurricanes, and win a Calder Cup championship with the 2000–01 Saint John Flames.

"He has excelled at every level," Hay said after the perfect 7-0 run. "He's probably the smartest player I've ever coached and just has tremendous feel for the game."

That's one of the most remarkable achievements of the Program of Excellence. It's not just that Team Canada draws on the immense talent this country produces or showcases future stars on their way to professional stardom. It's that every year there will be a guy who may never be a household name or a millionaire, who nevertheless shines among those future stars on the brightest stage any of these young men have ever encountered.

Centre Jason Allison (right) was just one of a crowd of Canadian players who would jump directly to the NHL the following fall.

1996

BOSTON
THE BREAKTHROUGH FOR JAROME

GARE JOYCE

Jarome Iginla, who would go on to lead Canada to two Olympic gold medals, first burst onto the scene at the WJC in Boston. Just days before the start of the tournament, the Dallas Stars traded Iginla's NHL rights to the Calgary Flames.

The 1996 tournament will be remembered for many things but it won't be remembered by many hockey fans in Boston. The stands were virtually empty for most games, including the medal-round games. It wasn't entirely a lack of interest in hockey. *The Boston Globe* put citizens on alert for the storm of the century not once, not twice, but three times over the course of 10 days. The streets of the city seemed to be deserted, though someone might have been buried under a drift. "Find a Way" was adopted as the Canadian team's motto during its training camp, but for many on hand, finding a way to the arena was a challenge.

Those who were there or watched the tournament back in Canada remember the 1996 WJC as the coming-out party for Jarome Iginla. The Edmonton-born right winger put in arguably the best-ever performance by a Canadian forward in any under-20 championship and one that has been matched only a couple of times by individual players regardless of position or nationality. He led the tournament in scoring with five goals and seven assists in six games—but those numbers only hint at his impact. Whenever Canada needed a big play, Iginla was on the scene.

Today it's hard to think of Iginla arriving. It seems like he has always been there. There's a generation of hockey fans who can't remember a time when Iginla wasn't a fixture in the Canadian lineup. He was a leader in 2002, scoring two goals against

Jarome Iginla was a member of the Memorial Cup champion Kamloops Blazers when he was added to the Canadian roster. He led the team in scoring with five goals and seven assists in 12 games and was picked as the tournament's top forward.

the U.S. in the final in Salt Lake City when the Canadian men's team won its first Olympic gold in hockey in 50 years. Eight years later he dug the puck out of the corner and hit Sidney Crosby with the pass that set up Sid the Kid for the golden goal in the overtime victory over the Americans at the Vancouver Olympics.

In 1996 Iginla was making his debut on a major international stage, but NHL scouts knew all about him, having watched him with the two-time Memorial Cup champion Kamloops Blazers. He had been the 11th-overall pick of the Dallas Stars the previous June. Fans in Calgary would have recognized his name—the week before the tournament, the Stars traded him to the Flames for two-time 50-goal scorer and fan favourite Joe Nieuwendyk. Many of those fans were at first critical of the trade, but in Boston Iginla gave them reason to suspect he'd someday be the Flames' captain.

The Canadian Hockey Association had Iginla on its radar early. He'd played for Team Pacific, the bronze medallists from the 1994 world under-17 challenge in Amos, Quebec. Later that year he'd played in the national under-18 program,

leading the Canadian team in scoring in summer-tournament play in the Czech Republic.

He was known to the coach of the 1996 Canadian junior team. Marcel Comeau had coached his Kelowna Rockets against Iginla and the Kamloops Blazers. In fact, three of Iginla's Blazers teammates would also make the Canadian team's roster: two blueliners, team captain Nolan Baumgartner and Jason Holland, and left winger Hnat Domenichelli. Domenichelli had played across from Iginla for two seasons and, though they meshed seamlessly, they couldn't have been more different. Iginla, at 6-foot-1 and 190 pounds, was a power forward who rolled over and went through defenders, while Domenichelli relied on speed to slip in and out of traffic.

When players reported to the evaluation camp in Campbellton, New Brunswick, Comeau and Team Canada's management had a clear idea of the talent they were going to be working with. "We will have to be a disciplined two-way team and we will have to be opportunistic offensively," the coach said on the eve of the tournament. "We will not blow anybody out of the water. I think we have enough

Hnat Domenichelli, here on a scoring chance against Sweden in the final, played on Canada's top line with Iginla, his Kamloops teammate, and centre Daymond Langkow.

offence to get us there." Comeau had projected Iginla as a first-liner, the most likely source of that offence. Iginla was, Comeau said, "a real handful down low, too much of a handful for most anyone in the Western Hockey League." Playing with Domenichelli and gritty centre Daymond Langkow, he lived up to those expectations and far exceeded them.

Comeau did have his team pegged. The Canadian roster featured only a couple of forwards over 6 feet and more than 200 pounds. Iginla, Langkow, and Alyn McCauley were the only players up front who would end up playing any significant time in the NHL. After Iginla, the next forward who was slotted as a pure scorer was Jason Podollan, a 40-goal shooter with the Spokane Chiefs that season. Podollan didn't score until the semifinal, and he would wind up registering just one NHL goal in 41 career games. The team had to lean on Iginla for offence.

Iginla's numbers were impressive, but the idea that he was something special crystallized when Canada faced its stiffest challenge. In fact, after four fairly routine wins in the preliminary round, the semifinal against Russia was the first real challenge the Canadian teens had to stare down. These rivals ranked as the two best teams in the tournament—the best by far, really. That they met in the semis rather than the final might be misleading. The Russians lost their first game in Boston to the Czechs but gave every indication that they weren't showing all their cards early. They moved their phenom Sergei Samsonov from the fourth line only just before their quarter-final win over the Finns, a 6–2 rout. The Russians looked like a different team from the one that had lost to the Czechs, and Alexei Morozov raised his game to the point where he was challenging Iginla for the tournament's top forward honours. More than a few folks at the tournament figured the Russians were sandbagging and hoping to catch Canada by surprise.

Iginla's moment came in the third period against the Russians. Canada was clinging to a 3–2 lead despite being outshot almost two-to-one—the final shot numbers were 49 for Russia and 28 for Canada, and the defending champions were only in the game thanks to an impressive performance by goaltender José Théodore. The pivotal play came on a Russian power play. Though Iginla was the Canadian team's best offensive threat, he was also the first choice for the penalty kill, and he showed the opportunism that Comeau had ranked as necessary to gold-medal hopes. Morozov circled back into the Russian end to retrieve a loose puck. Iginla gave chase but Morozov had a couple of steps on him. It looked like Iginla was just putting token pressure on the Russian forward but would peel back into the neutral zone once Morozov took possession. When Iginla kept coming, Morozov thought he had a chance to slip by Iginla and leave him in his wake going back up the ice. Rather than making a safe play, clearing the puck and regrouping, Morozov decided to get cute—too cute, as it turned out.

Right: Defenceman Chris Phillips led a Canadian blue line that improved going into the medal round. The key game was a tense contest with the Russians in the semifinal.

Iginla had a good idea that Morozov was going to try to do something along those lines. Scouting the Russians' earlier games in Boston, the Canadian staff had spotted their tendency to make high-risk plays in their own end during power plays. Iginla and the Canadian penalty killers had read the scouting report and were put on high alert. "We wanted to pressure their power play, because we knew they liked to dipsy-doodle around a little in the centre ice area," Iginla said after the game. "We were looking for it."

When Morozov tried to flip the puck by Iginla, the Canadian forward snared it—blocking the puck in his mid-section, letting it drop to the ice, and then taking it in flight on the Russian goal. Morozov was caught leaning the wrong way and couldn't get back into the play. He could only watch as Iginla went in on Russian goaltender Alexei Egorov and beat him cleanly to make it 4–2.

Often, a goal coming against play—especially a short-handed one—might have been a soul-crusher, but the Russians continued to surge and Morozov scored a few minutes later to pull the Russians back within a goal. In fact, with 10 seconds left in the game, he almost fully atoned for his gaffe, setting up Ruslan Shafikov alone in front of the Canadian goal with Théodore out of position and helpless. Shafikov, however, fanned on the shot and before he could take a second stab at it Iginla arrived at the edge of the crease to lock him up.

With his 46 saves, José Théodore's performance would have been the big story in almost any other circumstances. This, however, was Iginla's night. It wasn't, however, the end of his heroics in Boston. Canada still had to beat Sweden in the final for the gold.

Since the WJC went to a playoff format, the '96 final stands among the most anticlimactic of gold-medal games. The Swedes had a few talented players, but they gave you the feeling they were just happy to have made it as far as the final. On the eve of the final, club teams in the Swedish elite league called back two of the three best defencemen on the juniors' roster. It would have been hard for anyone to like the Swedes' chances, including the Swedes.

The Canadian juniors weren't in their top form in the final. They had spent a lot of emotion in the semifinal and for 20 minutes allowed the Swedes to hang around. With the score tied one-all, Iginla again made a defining play that led to the winning goal. He didn't score it, but he created it with a smart read of the play and brute force. In a battle for the puck along the boards, Iginla knocked Swedish defenceman David Halvardsson reeling in the corner and then made a pass from behind the net to his centre Daymond Langkow. It wound up being one of Iginla's three assists in a 4–1 win. What's more, it sent messages. To his teammates, the message was that physical intensity was going to deliver them gold. To the Swedes, it was that you get in Jarome Iginla's way at your peril.

Iginla's wasn't the biggest hit in the game—honours for that would go to defenceman Denis Gauthier, who put an open-ice charge into a Swedish forward who had his head down. On impact, you could hear him grunt and groan even if you were halfway up the empty stands. Thereafter, the Swedes moved farther and farther out on the perimeter and almost out of the Boston area code—and by game's end, though trailing, they just rolled back into the neutral zone and were trying to keep the score relatively close.

Celebrating in the dressing room—and with his gold medal still hanging around his neck—Iginla said he hoped to be in the NHL at the start of the 1996–97 season. If he was going to be back in junior, he said, he wanted to help Canada go for a fifth consecutive gold at the WJC. "Having that maple leaf on our chests gives us more energy at times, being part of Canada's hockey tradition. When the going gets tough, it gives us a little extra, because when we were young we would watch Canada play and we always prevailed."

CHA executives weren't counting on his availability for Geneva. The Program of Excellence is a learning program, and Jarome Iginla's education, at least this part of it, was complete. They knew that they had seen a young man already primed for bigger things. If they had any illusions about that, Iginla's performance on his return to Kamloops obliterated them—he would end up scoring 79 goals in 79 WHL regular-season and playoff games and leading Kamloops to a third consecutive Memorial Cup championship. But it turned out he'd get a chance to wear the maple leaf on his chest sooner than he might have expected. In the spring of '97, after his rookie year with the Flames, Iginla was the youngest player selected to join Canada's team at the world championships—picking up a couple of goals, three assists, and another gold medal.

For Iginla, it has come full circle 15 years later. In that dressing room in Boston, after a game played in a vacant arena, Jarome Iginla talked about watching Canada play and prevail when he was young. He couldn't have imagined the influence he'd have down the line or his place in the program's tradition. The play Iginla made in the gold-medal game in Boston looked an awful lot like that pass to Sidney Crosby as he poured in on the American net in overtime in Vancouver. And when Jarome Iginla emerged as a star in Boston, Sidney Crosby was eight years old.

1997
GENEVA
THE RESILIENT OVERACHIEVERS
MIKE BABCOCK

Centre Alyn McCauley won his second WJC gold in Geneva. He was a key penalty killer and also set up linemate Boyd Devereaux's game-winning goal in the semifinal versus Russia.

Our team in Geneva wasn't the most talented team that Canada ever sent to the world juniors. We weren't especially talented at all. More talented Canadian teams have played in the tournament—and played well—and not won. I remember a reporter who had covered a lot of the tournaments coming up to me on Christmas Day and telling me that we weren't going to finish higher than sixth. I didn't think so, but I don't think that anyone looked at the team as a favourite for the championship or even a safe bet to win a medal. There was incredible pressure on the players after the program had won four straight championships. I know I felt it.

I wouldn't claim that my coaching "won" the tournament. What we had, though, were a bunch of young men who weren't the best pro prospects but knew how to play the game. We did have Joe Thornton, but that was before he was drafted first overall—he was the youngest player on our roster and he had limited ice time. We were lucky to have a few players who played their best hockey in the most important games of their career. We had players who were smart enough to figure out a way to win and had the nerve to step up when things got really tough.

I wouldn't claim that the coaches brought the team together. The leaders in our room brought us together. The one I'd point to first was our captain, Brad Larsen. He wasn't the most skilled guy but he worked hard and took charge in the room.

Goaltender Marc Denis started every game for the Canadian team and capped the tournament with a shutout victory over the United States in the gold-medal final.

He made sure that everyone was involved, that everyone parked his ego at the door. A player in the room, not a coach, has to deliver the message that team success is the only goal and individual accomplishments don't mean anything. Brad was the perfect one to deliver that message. He was comfortable standing up and talking to his teammates. He was in the centre of everything—he could put himself there but it was natural, not forced. If it was setting up a card game, he was dealing. If it seemed like some of the boys were down or maybe feeling left out, he was bringing them in. The role he took wasn't something you could ask someone to do or try to show him how to fill. When I came into the room, Brad was the one I looked to when I wanted to get a read of the team's energy and emotion. Brad wasn't a great pro prospect but he was maybe the most important player on that team.

Our road to the medal round wasn't easy. There were times when we didn't get calls that we were sure we deserved and other times we ended up on the wrong end with the referees—it was a quick education for our players that it's a different game when you're playing in Europe.

Then we had a couple of tough games in the opening round. We had been down 4–3 to the United States with about four minutes left and Peter Schaefer came through for us and tied the game. And then in our final game in the opening round, we had a one-goal lead in the last minute against the Czechs. We were on the power

play and had a chance to dump the puck into their end to ice the game. Instead, we turned the puck over, trying to force an unnecessary play.

The Czechs took the puck the other way and they beat our goalie Marc Denis with 10 seconds left.

We didn't get a bye into the medal round and those ties put us in against the Russians, a strong team, in the semis. But those two ties were good for us in the long run. They were good for building the team and getting us ready for the semis and then the final. Adversity made that team.

In the semis we were down 2–1 to the Russians after two periods, which would have been a tough spot but it was made a heck of a lot tougher when the ref gave Jason Doig a five-minute major for slashing. We lost Jason, our second-best defenceman behind Chris Phillips, and had a five-minute penalty kill. The funny thing was that the players weren't down in any way. They were sure that they were going to kill the penalty and get back into the game. I didn't need to try to pick them up or reassure them. They were really ready for this moment—all the time they had spent together in the weeks leading up to that point were going to pay off.

It really was an amazing thing. The Russians didn't get a shot during those five minutes. I was joking when I told the reporters after the game that the Russians killed off the major themselves—but, fact was, they weren't ready to deal with the

Christian Dubé, here celebrating with Brad Isbister looking on, was an important piece of the puzzle in his second trip to the world juniors.

advantage and we were ready to handle the adversity. Boyd Devereaux, who really hadn't played a lot early in the tournament, scored a couple of shifts into the penalty kill to tie the game. Boyd and Alyn McCauley were just great on that penalty kill and all through that game. Alyn set Boyd up with the winning goal midway through the period. It's a credit to the players on that team that, when things looked really tough for them, they had composure—even confidence that they were going to find a way to win.

Our kids had to come up with a clutch performance to tie the U.S. in the opening round, but in the final against the Americans they were a different team. They really had learned what they needed to do to win. Each player knew his individual responsibilities and everyone was confident that his teammates were going to do their jobs. Boyd and Alyn ended up being our two most important forwards in the medal round

and Boyd scored the winning goal when we won the final 2–0. Still, it wasn't any one player's show or one line's show. Everyone had a reason to feel his job was important, and that was how the team ended up being more than the sum of its parts.

A player who really represented the character of that team was Trent Whitfield, a winger who played for me at the time in Spokane. He wasn't invited to the national junior camp the previous summer. He has managed to play professionally for a long time and he had some injury problems that held his career back, but back in '97 he was a great junior. I didn't select him because I coached him in Spokane—in fact, in the team selection I recused myself when his name came up. On that team, though, he was a perfect utility forward. I felt like I could send Trent out—like Alyn, like Boyd—in the important situations. If the other team sent one of the top scorers out, I could send Trent to stick with him. If Trent was out on the wing and his centre was thrown out of the faceoff circle, he would come in and win the draw. He was like other players on that team—you could count on him to do all the little things right. If we had taken the 22 most talented players in major junior or the 22 best pro prospects he wouldn't have been on the team. But the Program of Excellence focuses on team building, finding players to fill roles, and Trent, as much as anybody on that team, filled his role perfectly.

Coaching that team was a tremendous opportunity for me. I'll admit that, at the time, I wasn't thinking about the opportunity as much as the pressure to win. I felt that, and everybody on the roster and involved in the program had to feel it. But in the years after, that tournament has had a huge impact on my career, like it has for other coaches who have taken Canadian teams to the WJC. My involvement with the under-20 program and the Olympic team has allowed me to meet and talk with and work with those coaches, and all of them have been generous to share what they've learned through their experiences.

For me, Geneva in '97 was an opportunity for personal and professional growth, and I know that others who have worked with these teams over the years feel the same way. I'm sure that it was an important educational experience for the players, too. I've stayed in touch with Brad Larsen—he's a coach now and he's going to be a great one. He might have picked up a thing or two from me, but I'm sure he picked up a whole lot more from his role as captain of a championship team. He learned about what it takes to win from his experience with a team that won the hard way.

Left: Cameron Mann, Jason Doig (plate aloft), and Daniel Brière (in flag cape) celebrate Canada's victory over the United States in the gold-medal game. The team's chances of getting to the final looked dim when Doig was assessed a major penalty at the end of the second period in the semifinal against Russia.

1998

HÄMEENLINNA
THE HUMBLING GAME

JESSE WALLIN

Forward Josh Holden holds up a Russian opponent in Canada's 2–1 quarter-final overtime loss. After that game, Holden, the team's leading goal scorer, was suspended along with defenceman Brad Ference and forward Brian Willsie for team discipline violations.

The Program of Excellence has given me great memories from victories and awful ones from the most humiliating defeat you can imagine. I learned a lot about the game from both.

I was named captain of the '98 team in Finland. Cory Sarich and I were the two returning players from the Geneva team. We had a great experience in '97 and we saw how the Program of Excellence could and should work. We had outstanding leadership in '97—from Mike Babcock, from our captain, Brad Larsen, and from other players in the room. Everyone bought in and had faith. Everyone took a lot of pride, and anyone who had to play a different role didn't hesitate—Alyn McCauley was one of the best junior players in Canada, maybe the best, and Mike asked him to play the third line. It wasn't a problem. He took it as a challenge and so did everyone else who was asked to do something different from what he was used to with his junior team. We all understood how hard it was going to be to win that tournament.

In '98 we had the talent to win gold again but things felt different, even before the tournament started. It just felt different. It's hard to put a finger on exactly why. It wasn't just one thing. We had an inexperienced group, but that wouldn't be enough to explain how things fell apart. We might have been the favourites in '98, and a lot of players on the team were more talented than players on the '97 squad. But in '98 there were cliques

Forward Matt Cooke sticks with a Russian winger in the quarter-final. Cooke would be knocked out of the tournament with a concussion.

on the team, just a different attitude overall. A lot of the players were focused on the wrong things. They were worried about themselves first and foremost, taking an I'm-on-my-own-page attitude. What happened on the ice was a by-product of that attitude and a loss of discipline off the ice as well.

When we left for Europe after the training camp I thought things would get straightened out, but I knew we were in trouble after the first period of our first game in the tournament. We were playing the Finns in Helsinki on Christmas Day, a real challenge. When we went back to the dressing room in the first intermission, I felt like we were still in a good position to win—the game was scoreless and we were as good as the Finns. But I was shocked by what I saw in the room—one of our players slammed his stick and helmet down and started complaining about not being on the power play. That just wouldn't have happened in '97.

We showed that we had a pretty talented team in that game. We jumped out to a 1–0 lead and Alex Tanguay scored to tie the game two-all in the third period after Finland had fought back. But the Finns scored a goal with less than four minutes to go and won 3–2. We almost tied the game again right at the end. Maybe things would have turned out differently if we had, but there's no way to know. The Finns ended up winning the tournament and we barely lost to them, even though they had twice as many power plays as we did and we were still supposed to be coming together as a team—supposed to be.

But we started to fall apart at that point. We lost to the Swedes the next game 4–0 and we didn't compete. At that point we started to take undisciplined penalties, retaliatory penalties. We spent a full period of that game shorthanded—a few minors would have been okay but we had unsportsmanlike penalties and roughing calls, penalties that really hurt us. We were taking retaliatory penalties right at the time when we needed to suck it up, take one for the team, and be disciplined. We had a couple of guys who were benched after taking completely unnecessary penalties. It was embarrassing.

It looked like we might get it together in our next two games to advance to the quarter-finals. First we beat the Czechs 5–0; then we beat Germany 4–1. My time

Centre Vincent Lecavalier, a 17-year-old scoring sensation with Rimouski in the QMJHL, was expected to be an offensive catalyst but registered only one goal and one assist in seven games.

It seemed that it couldn't get worse for Canada after losses to Finland, Sweden, Russia, and the United States. But the loss to Kazakhstan in the seventh-place game added insult to injury. It was Canada's worst finish in the history of the WJC.

on the ice ended in the German game. I broke a bone blocking a shot and I was in a cast and crutches the rest of the tournament. I learned the hardest way possible that you can't lead a team from the sidelines.

I wanted to win a gold medal in '98 even more than I did in '97. Winning it once made me want it more the next time. I had come back from a broken arm that I had suffered that fall in a car accident and I probably came back too soon, but that's how much I wanted to play in the world juniors again. It was agonizing not to be able to play. What I saw the rest of the way was a lack of commitment and there was nothing I could do about it.

In the quarter-finals we played the Russians in Hämeenlinna. It started out strangely. Our team had to wear the sweaters of the Hämeenlinna club team in the first period because we thought we were scheduled for red sweaters, not our whites. So we were the first and so far only Canadian team not to wear the maple leaf. Our white sweaters didn't arrive until the intermission. That was typical of the game and the tournament—everything just felt a little bit off. We still had a great chance to go ahead to the medal round. It was one-all at the end of regulation and Eric Brewer hit the post with a shot from the point in overtime. But with 30 seconds left in the first overtime period, there were a bunch of mistakes, a shift that was too long, a safe play that could have been made and wasn't, a pinch at the wrong time, and the Russians took the puck the other way and scored.

I thought that it could never get worse in hockey than that loss. Not even close. In the consolidation rounds, we played the United States first—a game that we should have been able to get up for, no matter what had happened against the Russians. But our team was really falling apart.

Two other guys were knocked out because of injuries and three more were benched for discipline reasons, showing up late and missing meetings. With a short bench, we lost to the U.S. and it never felt like we were in the game. It was humbling watching the Americans celebrate.

Again I thought that it could never get worse than that loss. Again I was wrong.

We didn't even show up for the seventh-place game against Kazakhstan. We should have been able to dominate that game, even with the injuries and a short bench. The Kazakhs even started their backup goaltender. I remember going into the dressing room and yelling at the guys between periods. I don't remember what I said, but it wouldn't matter now because it didn't make a difference then. It was a complete collapse. We lost 6–3 to a team that had half a dozen sticks in the rack by their bench and skates that didn't match.

I believe you learn something, as a player and later as a coach, from every experience you have with a team. I learned what was possible with the right attitude and discipline with the Canadian team in '97; I learned the risks of having the wrong attitude and a lack of discipline with the team in '98. I think things are different in a lot of ways today. The under-18 teams deliver players to the world junior teams who have a lot more international experience than back in the '90s. I was an example of that—I had none when I went to Geneva and there were players on our team in Finland in the same situation.

One thing that I learned as a coach in the Program of Excellence is that "discipline" doesn't mean rules and no fun. I worked as an assistant to Pat Quinn with the Canadian team that won the world under-18s in Russia in 2009. It was an amazing thing to see how Pat was able to get his message across and to instill in a team discipline without being draconian about it—it's not all bad medicine if you just make it a habit. A team with good habits doesn't even feel like it's working with a tough system of discipline. It's something I strive for with my junior teams in Red Deer these days. I wish it was something that we'd had in Finland in '98.

1999

WINNIPEG
THE COLDEST NIGHTS

DAMIEN COX

1999 CANADIAN NATIONAL JUNIOR HOCKEY TEAM

Goaltender Roberto Luongo was Canada's best player in Winnipeg. It turned out that great wasn't good enough to win the host team a gold medal against Russia in the final.

The indelible signature to the 1999 tournament was supplied by goaltender Roberto Luongo. Even in defeat, Luongo's remarkable efforts in nearly single-handedly capturing gold for Team Canada on a frigid January evening at the Winnipeg Arena set a standard only a handful of Canadian junior goalies have been able to match over the long history of the event.

With arch-rival Russia as the opponent it didn't turn out to be Canada's night, despite the relentless, screaming support of the sea of white, but it surely was Luongo's night. If not for Luongo, if it had been a goaltender who was only very good, the Russians would have run Canada out of the old barn under the giant portrait of Queen Elizabeth II that night, and ruined the sense that the home country had bounced back after the eighth-place finish at the world juniors the previous year in Finland.

"Roberto was our best player throughout the tournament," defenceman Robyn Regehr recalled. "But I thought he saved his best performance for that game."

That, of course, was exactly what Luongo was supposed to do. At the time, he was the highest drafted goaltender in the history of the NHL, with the New York Islanders selecting him fourth overall in 1997. He had been part of the Canadian junior squad that had suffered a shocking defeat to Kazakhstan in 1998. Luongo,

Fans gave the Canadian juniors the full "sea of white" support at Winnipeg Arena. The atmosphere in the building after the semifinal rout of favoured Sweden was in sharp contrast to the silence that followed Artem Chubarov's overtime goal in the final.

one of five returnees from the '98 team, was the focus of attention from the start. "I've heard all these things about him," said head coach Tom Renney. "Now I look forward to seeing them."

Every member of the 22-man Canadian team would eventually play in the NHL, but it wasn't a powerhouse, particularly offensively. That meant it was clear that if Canada were to rebound—"This Is for Pride" was the team's slogan for the competition—Luongo would have to lead the way.

Canada had won three of the four previous times the event was held on its soil, including four years earlier with a dominant performance in Red Deer, Alberta. But this was a bigger stage at a turning point in the history of the world juniors, when the event was looking to bigger cities and bigger arenas, and greater exposure around the world. The 10-team event was to include games in Brandon, Selkirk, Portage La Prairie, Morden, and Teulon, spreading the wealth of the international junior game around a province starved for big-time hockey. Still, the games and atmosphere in Winnipeg are what the players remember most.

"The fans in Winnipeg were fantastic," Regehr recalled. "I remember they were truly excited. They had the sea of white going, and it had been a few years since they'd lost the Jets so they were really excited to see hockey again in that way."

Renney, a CHA vice-president at the time, searched for chemistry as he formed his team, cutting five NHL first-rounders before settling on his roster. Mike Van Ryn was the captain, Daniel Tkachuk of the OHL's Barrie Colts was to be the top centre, and Brad Stuart of Rocky Mountain House, Alberta, had turned down an NHL contract from San Jose for one more year of junior hockey and a chance to fight for a world title. The roster featured skill possessed by the likes of Simon Gagné and defenceman Brian Campbell, but the team was defined by the grit of those who skated in front of Luongo—grinders like Tyler Bouck, Kent McDonell, Brenden Morrow, and Adam Mair.

A 5–3 pre-tournament victory over Russia in Kenora, Ontario, seemed to suggest that

Defencemen Andrew Ference and Mike Van Ryn (wearing the captain's C) were part of a solid blue-line corps that, along with Luongo's brilliance, helped push the final into overtime.

Renney had chosen well, but the opening game of the tournament told a different story. Slovakian hockey officials declined to invite their top two tournament-eligible players, Marian Hossa and Robert Dome, but those who did play against the host nation made it tough. Canada couldn't score a single goal on Jan Lasak in the Slovakia goal, stunning the fans at the Keystone Centre in Brandon. But Luongo wouldn't be beaten either, stopping 36 shots and leaving the impression that while Canada had certainly not shone, it had an ironclad insurance policy between the pipes.

"The whole tournament was that way for me," said Luongo, who had been traded from Val-d'Or to Acadie-Bathurst two days before leaving to join the national team. "I just remember being in a zone the whole time."

Canada's next game, against Finland, was expected to be a classic goaltending matchup, pitting Luongo against Mika Noronen, who had been brilliant the year before in helping the Finns win gold in Helsinki. Instead, it was a shootout. The Canadian offence burst to life, producing a 6–4 triumph. Tkachuk scored twice, his linemates Kyle Calder and Rico Fata each scored once, and Gagné found an empty net to put the game away. Luongo posted his second shutout two days later, 2–0 over the Czech Republic, to keep Canada unbeaten.

But after being beaten 5–2 on New Year's Eve by the previously winless Americans (led by Brian Gionta and David Legwand), Canada was forced into a quarter-final game and it seemed possible that for a second straight year, the national program might not produce a medal. The opponent was, once again, Kazakhstan, featuring Toronto first-round pick Nikolai Antropov, who had been part of the squad that had

upset mighty Canada 12 months earlier. This time, however, there would be no such upset. Gagné scored four times, Canada led 8–0 after two periods, and the final 12–2 score set up a clash with the Swedes in the semifinals.

Sweden—managed by two former New York Islanders, Stefan Persson and Mats Hallin—came in featuring the much-discussed Sedin twins, Henrik and Daniel, and a new attitude. "The days of the chicken Swede are long gone," said Hallin, the coach of the team. "We ain't backing down." Armed with that belligerent new attitude, the unbeaten and untied Swedes were heavy favourites. Canada hadn't beaten a team with a winning record, while Tre Kronor had

Russia's speed in transition forced the Canadian team to scramble back on defence in the gold-medal game. Here, Van Ryn tries to close the gap on a Russian forward.

scored 25 goals in four games and received 21 points from its top line of the Sedins alongside Christian Berglund.

Before a sellout crowd of 14,000, the game was emotional and physical from the start. Each team had a player ejected in the first period. Canada's Brad Ference was tossed for a heavy check on Gabriel Karlsson that saw Karlsson carried off on a stretcher, while Berglund was mistakenly given a game misconduct for high-sticking Tyler Bouck (as replays showed, it was actually Berglund's skate that had accidently clipped the Canadian forward). Even the coaches, Renney and Hallin, got into it, shouting at each other across the benches.

Sweden scored first, but then McDonell tied it in the second, Gagné scored short-handed, and Tkachuk put the third Canadian goal past nervous Swedish netminder Andreas Andersson. The rout was on. By the end, it was 6–1 for Canada, a spectacular result for a national squad that had looked flat for so much of the tournament but had come to life when challenged by the Swedes.

On the other side of the draw was Russia, a team with talented forwards like Maxim Afinogenov, Artem Chubarov, Roman Lyashenko, and Maxim Balmochnykh, and a CHL netminder in Alexei Volkov, who played for the Halifax Mooseheads. The Russians had lost the gold-medal game to the Finns in overtime the year before, and, while strong defensively, they didn't seem to have an overwhelming array of offensive weapons to throw at Canada. What they did have, however, was an emotionally spent opponent—spent from the intense battle against Sweden the night before.

"I felt the tank was empty by the six-minute mark of the first period," Renney said.

From the start, the Russians dominated the contest as they searched for their first world junior title in seven years. Luongo was all the Canadians really had in response, as their attack managed just nine shots over the first two periods. But the Russians could build only a 2–1 lead by late in the third thanks to Luongo's heroics. When defenceman Bryan Allen's knuckler skipped past Volkov with six minutes left, an overtime classic was at hand.

Again Luongo bared his teeth at the Russian attack, and by the five-minute mark of the extra session had stopped 37 of 39 shots. Moments later, Chubarov, who had scored in the first, grabbed a loose puck along the boards in the Canadian zone, cut to the middle of the ice, and let a shot go.

"He kind of fanned on it," Luongo said. "It was a bit of a knuckler, and I kind of whiffed on it. Then it hit the post and went in."

Disbelief immediately set in. This wasn't the fairy-tale ending the Winnipeg crowd had anticipated. Just as the Jets had packed up and left, Team Canada had arrived and come up with silver, but not gold. And yet Luongo defined the gold-medal game and the tournament. His heroic efforts in the final gave his exhausted team a chance to win.

Brenden Morrow and other Canadian forwards rocked Sweden with a punishing forecheck to get to the gold-medal game. By the final, however, the host team had run out of gas and faded, despite Luongo's heroics.

"It was 12 years ago, and so much has happened since then for me," said Luongo, recalling the '99 junior tournament. "The Olympics, world championships, I've had international experiences, and they've kind of taken over from that. Maybe it would be different if we had won."

Different, perhaps. More memorable, probably not. Anyone who was there will always remember that game, that performance, that cold night in Winnipeg when a hot goalie was nearly enough.

2000

SKELLEFTEÅ
THE WEIRD TIMES

DAMIEN COX

One of the players to win a surprise spot in the lineup was Michael Ryder, who played for Canadian coach Claude Julien's Hull Olympiques.

Distant and remote. A land without light. Foreboding. Hardly the place most teenage boys want to spend New Year's Eve.

Yet perfect for an unexpected shot in the dark. Or a save.

Going overseas to challenge for the world junior hockey championship, of course, had always required a special effort for Canadian national teams. Problems from simple homesickness to illness to bad food to poor behaviour had, on occasion, tripped up the junior nats, often making the job of winning gold more difficult.

And then there was the 2000 WJC in northern Sweden.

Shared between the cities of Skellefteå and Umea, it was a trip for 22 Canadian hockey players to one of the least exotic parts of Sweden at a time of year when simple daylight is at a premium. Sometimes the sun shines for only a few hours a day just south of the Arctic Circle, producing a gloomy holiday season for the unprepared.

"We basically had three hours of light per day," recalled Claude Julien, the head coach of that Canadian team. "We told the guys to leave the lights on in the hotel room, because that's where you got your energy from. Whenever it was light outside we'd go for a walk and really tried to utilize the light as best we could."

Far from home, in the dark and without big-time reinforcements from NHL teams, Team Canada needed no more obstacles, particularly with the defending gold-medal-winning Russians having brought another strong team, and with the Swedes featuring the Sedin twins, Daniel and Henrik, for their third straight attempt at winning a world junior medal.

But there was one more obstacle, at least a psychological one. As the end of 1999 approached, the world was engulfed with concern—mass hysteria, really—over the so-called Y2K problem, or the Millennium Bug, as it was popularly known. Whether it was a global hoax, as some claimed, or an international problem ameliorated by hundreds of billions of dollars of pre-emptive planning remains a debate. But before the clock struck 12 on December 31, 1999, there was at the very least great uncertainty across the world. Would nuclear plants be tripped up by the problem of computers having used two digits to designate years for so long rather than four digits? How would the world banking industry be affected? Would the lights go out in Skellefteå, already one of the darkest places most of the Canadian hockey players had ever visited?

"It was New Year's, 2000, and it was a big sacrifice for our guys to be there," said Julien. "That was something unique. Everybody was waiting for all the computers in the world to shut down, thought the world was going to end." As it turned out, it was more like the Comet Kohoutek than catastrophe, and the world experienced only a

few minor problems. In gloomy Skellefteå, 2000 was brought in with champagne, "Auld Lang Syne," a spectacular fireworks show—and nothing out of the ordinary.

For Julien that was helpful, since he was already dealing with anything but an ordinary Canadian team.

For starters, it was a squad that featured 16-year-old defenceman Jay Bouwmeester, the youngest player to ever skate for a Canadian national junior team. And the next youngest? That was Jason Spezza of the Mississauga IceDogs, who was on the roster as well. These were two magnificently talented kids, to be sure, but their presence was very much the result of an absence of returning players and the reluctance of most NHL teams to lend their eligible players to Canada for the event.

So, no Vincent Lecavalier, Mike Fisher, Jonathan Girard, Simon Gagné, Robyn Regehr, or Rico Fata, some of whom had been available the year before when the Canadians weren't quite good enough to beat Russia at the '99 world juniors in Winnipeg.

Oddly enough, the New York Rangers were willing to make Manny Malhotra available after declining to release him for the Winnipeg tourney. Malhotra had played for the junior nats two years earlier at the disaster in Finland, an eighth-place finish, so his experience was very useful. Montreal made available slick centre Mike Ribeiro, and the New York Islanders sent big Mathieu Biron, a godsend for Julien given that not a single member of the '99 defence corps was back.

Julien departed from convention with his selection of two 16-year-old phenoms, defenceman Jay Bouwmeester and centre Jason Spezza, to that point the two youngest players ever in the Canadian juniors' lineup.

Only backup goalie Brian Finley and forward Tyler Bouck were back from the defending silver medallists, with a third returnee, Blair Betts, unavailable due to injury.

The back end featured future NHLers like Bouwmeester and Barret Jackman, but also players like Matt Kinch, Joe Rullier, and Kyle Rossiter who would not go on to significant NHL careers. This, Julien understood from the outset, was not going to be one of the strongest, most talented teams Canada had ever sent to the world juniors. The team wasn't even particularly big, which meant the heavy-hitting style of the previous year's squad would not be repeated.

"We had to really dig deep without the talent Team Canada is used to having," said Julien. "But we had a lot of hard-working guys." Julien had been an assistant coach under Tom Renney on that 1999 team and previously a Memorial Cup champion, and perhaps he was also a fellow shaped by destiny to be a head coach. After all, 16 years earlier he and Gord Donnelly had been traded by the St. Louis Blues to the Quebec Nordiques for the rights to coach Jacques Demers.

Having been traded for a coach, perhaps it made sense Julien would in turn trade his holidays for a chance at coaching for gold. The team would have been even smaller had the diminutive Mike Comrie not been the last cut. Up the middle there

Maxime Ouellet had the bulk of the work in net but in the bronze-medal game, Julien opted for his backup Brian Finley.

was Brad Richards, Brandon Reid, and Ribeiro, while Malhotra would centre a checking line. In goal, Finley made the team, but was challenged from the outset by Maxime Ouellet.

If there was a player expected to be a star, it was University of Wisconsin sniper Dany Heatley. On a team filled with players already drafted, or too young for the NHL draft, Heatley was already being watched very closely by NHL talent scouts as a potential top pick in the 2000 draft.

After being crushed by the Swedes in a pre-tournament game, the Canadians started the round robin with Ouellet in goal and beat the Finns 3–2. Stuck in the toughest of the two pools, it was clear Canada couldn't afford to struggle in the early going or the team would risk finishing out of the medals. Ouellet then delivered a 34-save performance against the Czechs, pushing Canada to 1-0-1 after two games.

Spezza, meanwhile, was a big story, and not for his play—it was Julien's decision to hardly use him at all that became a daily source of speculation and rumour. The IceDogs centre had been shifted to right wing behind Michael Ryder, Chris Nielsen, Jamie Lundmark, and Mark Bell, had played only two shifts against Finland, and then didn't play at all against the Czech Republic.

Even Switzerland's stick work couldn't hold up Brandon Reid or his teammates, and Canada cruised to an 8–3 victory.

A 1–1 tie with the Czechs set Canada on course for second place in Pool A and a semifinal meeting with the Russians.

Bouwmeester played a little more, but it was clear the two 16-year-olds were not going to be featured pieces on this Canadian junior team, one that had scored five goals in four games (two pre-tourney, two round robin).

"Sure, it's hard to sit on the bench when we're only scoring one goal," said Spezza, who had tallied 38 points in 28 games with Mississauga to that point in the OHL season. "I don't know why [Julien] won't play me."

The fact that the crowds for most of the games ranged from small to pitiful, an enormous contrast to the enthusiastic sellout throngs the previous year in Manitoba, added to the sense that this was not going to be a year to remember at the world juniors, for Canada or any other country.

After getting some offence going against Slovakia in a 4–1 win, the Canadians finished the round robin with a 1–1 tie against the United States, stoned by Philippe Sauvé in the American net and once again shown to be a team without a great deal of firepower. Eric Chouinard was the only Canadian to beat Sauvé as the Canadians headed for a quarter-final game against the Swiss.

That turned out to be not much of a challenge for Canada, and the big news came in the other quarter, with the United States ousting the Sedins and the Swedes by an embarrassing 5–1 score on their native soil. In three world junior events, the Sedins had come away with no medals, and in big games against Russia and the U.S. in the 2000 event, the twins had been held pointless.

Against Russia in the semifinals, Heatley scored, as did Matt Pettinger. But the Russians led the whole way despite being outshot 25–20, including 14–6 in the third, and Canada was forced to play for bronze. It was not a predicament Canada was used to being in, and when it had happened in previous years, teams hadn't fared well—not surprising given the national mantra that only gold mattered.

Still, the players argued that this was different. "We've travelled a quarter of the way around the world and we don't want to go home with nothing," said Malhotra, who already knew the empty feeling of playing in the world juniors and not winning a medal.

It would be a North American clash in the bronze-medal game between the U.S. and Canada, a precursor to the major junior battles that lay ahead between the two countries in future tournaments. Ouellet had started all the games, but Julien turned to Finley for the bronze game, hoping he might deliver something special.

The 4-1-2 Canadians fell behind 2–0 after a period, and still trailed by a goal going into the third before fighting back and forcing overtime, then a shootout. Two years earlier in Nagano, of course, a Canadian Olympic team led by Wayne Gretzky had lost to the Czechs in a shootout, and since then the term, let alone the actual exercise, had been looked down on by many Canadians as a gimmick, something not quite hockey.

Yet here it was staring Julien in the face, and without a particularly skilled offensive team at his disposal. But what he had came through. First, U.S. winger Andy Hilbert missed, and then Lundmark scored. Pat Aufiero scored on Finley, but Reid put another one into the U.S. net past Sauvé. Big American winger Jeff Taffe missed, but Heatley found twine, putting the Americans in a do-or-die position with Boston University winger Daniel Cavanaugh lined up at centre.

The 2000 WJC gave hockey fans their first chance to see high-scoring University of Wisconsin winger Dany Heatley, who would be the second pick overall in the 2000 NHL entry draft.

"I tried to make them all deke," said Finley afterwards.

Cavanaugh deked, to his backhand. Finley stuck out his right pad and Canada had bronze—bronze that, given the team, the conditions, and the darkness, seemed to gleam like gold.

"The one thing we wanted was to at least get a medal, and we did that," said Julien. "The States was a big rivalry, and we wanted to make sure we came up with a medal on that day." A bronze medal for Canada.

And the world didn't end.

2001

MOSCOW
THE THIRTEENTH FORWARD

TERRY KOSHAN

Winger Raffi Torres brought his hard-hitting game to the WJC in Moscow. His one-timer won the bronze-medal game in overtime against the Swedes.

Often, veterans of the Program of Excellence will drop by and speak to young players in the formative stages of their careers with Hockey Canada—not only about the demands that come with the crest on the front of the sweater, but also about the accompanying privilege and the organization's rich history.

Those guys over in the corner? Well, they might be a former coach talking to the current one, offering salient pieces of advice.

Stan Butler took everything in when he spoke with Mike Babcock, who had coached Canada to a gold medal at the 1997 world junior championship in Geneva. In major junior and NHL play, those who would be the 13th forward or 7th defenceman on the depth chart would be sitting up in the press box on game nights. But with expanded rosters in international hockey, a 13th forward and a 7th defenceman aren't castaways. They're on the bench and on call, ready to jump the boards on a second's notice.

"I told Stan you have to trust those guys, and if you trust those guys, in big moments they can be good for you," Babcock said. "And if those players happen to be the guys you know really well, that is a benefit. I just knew that when I coached that team, it was an important part of the process.

Maxime Ouellet played well for Canada through to the semifinal, but he struggled in the loss to the Finns that sent the team to the bronze-medal game.

"You know if they don't play one shift, everything is rosy and they are with you."

Babcock's extras who became integral in 1997 were centre Trent Whitfield and defenceman Hugh Hamilton, two players he coached in Spokane in the Western Hockey League. Both Whitfield and Hamilton ended up playing bigger roles than even they might have imagined.

Butler was mindful of Babcock's advice when he assembled the roster for the team that would go to Moscow for the 2001 world juniors. For his 7th defenceman Butler took Jay Harrison, whom he coached on the Brampton Battalion in the Ontario Hockey League. For his 13th forward he took Mike Zigomanis, the captain of the Kingston Frontenacs. Butler had never coached Zigomanis, but he had coached against him. He knew that Zigomanis was carrying a full load of courses at Queen's University and had been nominated for the league's academic excellence award. Butler and Zigomanis shared hockey roots, both coming out of the Wexford minor hockey association.

"I had known Michael for a long time," Butler said. "I had always admired him as a player."

It's true that in the world juniors, players are experiencing things they never have before. For some, they're hearing for the first time in their career that they're not going to be getting a regular shift. Zigomanis was winding down an excellent junior career with the Frontenacs when Butler chose him for the squad that was going to Moscow. The 19-year-old had put up 94 points in 1999–2000 with Kingston and was a second-round pick of the Buffalo Sabres. In other words, if hockey was going to be a living, Zigomanis had a long hockey career ahead of him.

He could not help but bristle a bit when Butler told him he wouldn't be starting among the 12 forwards.

But the feeling didn't take long to dissipate.

"I was playing a lot in Kingston and to go into that extra-player role was a change," Zigomanis said. "You are one of the 22 players going over there, and that is an accomplishment."

Of course, Zigomanis had no idea at the time how his career would unfold. He also could not say what would happen in the next couple of weeks.

But he had not been designated as the extra forward just because he had the fortune of knowing the head coach. "When you're talking about Ziggy,

Canada's leading scorer in the 2000 tournament, Val-d'Or forward Brandon Reid, was back for a second shot at the gold in Moscow.

you're talking about a team player," said Barry Trapp, who was the head scout for the program at the time and as such spent months travelling the country, watching more hockey games than most people do in 10 years.

"If there was a choice between taking a highly skilled player who had no character and one who might not have been as skilled but had lots of character, I would take the second guy. I would always have room on my team for a Zigomanis."

As the tournament started, Zigomanis had sporadic shifts—today, he says that if he had enough time to think about it, he could recall each one.

Canada won two games, tied one, and lost one in the preliminary round. A 5–2 loss to Finland in the semifinal meant Canada's medal hopes rested on a bronze, not a gold, or even a silver.

The Canadians had been dealing with various illnesses over the course of the

Jay Bouwmeester clears U.S. forward Kris Vernarsky from the front of the Canadian net.

Sweden blunted the Canadian offence though 60 minutes of the bronze-medal game. Here, Brandon Reid gets muscled off the puck.

tournament, but even those who stayed healthy had to feel a bit off. This was before Hockey Canada sent a chef to the championship to feed an eager bunch of teenagers. The food in Russia, Butler said, fell well short of what his players were accustomed to in Canada.

Though the players had no desire to travel back to Canada without a medal, their final game—versus Sweden, and with the bronze medal to be awarded at the end—did not start with much intensity. It was clear that Butler's team needed energy, and quickly.

Zigomanis, despite his lack of ice time, had produced a goal and an assist to that point. "You don't think about [getting few shifts] at the time," Zigomanis said. "It was one of those things where you just have to live in the now. I still try to do that in every game. You build off your past shifts. But you can't reminisce about your shifts and what you did wrong and what you did right. You are only as good as your last shift, and you have to give it everything you have on your new one. That is how I took that tournament—do everything you can when you are on the ice."

Butler recalled what he told Zigomanis, and would give the same message to Jay McClement a year later. "You are one injury away from getting more ice time, or you are one play away from a coach getting fed up with a player and putting you in a spot," Butler said. "At least you are on the bench. You can't get on the ice if you

Another player returning to the Canadian lineup, Mike Cammalleri would get going against the Swedes to claim his second bronze medal.

are not on the bench, and one thing I always tried to tell guys in those roles, that you are dressed and on the bench, which means there is a chance you will play."

Not long after the game started, Butler sensed that the trio of Jason Spezza, Raffi Torres, and Brad Boyes required a change. Off came Boyes and in came Zigomanis. Zigomanis and Torres had played minor hockey together, so there was another connection that made the transition a fairly simple one. Butler's switch worked. Zigomanis, after only a couple of shifts, tied the game in the second period.

The line was effective through regulation, but so was Swedish goalie Henrik Lundqvist.

Overtime, however, did not last long. Butler's new-found strong line was on the ice for a faceoff in Sweden's end barely a half-minute after the sudden-death period began.

Stan Butler was faced with what has proven to be the most unenviable task for a Canadian coach in international competition: rallying the troops for a bronze-medal game.

"I remember Spezza was struggling in the circle all game, and I went to him and said, 'Are you going to win the draw or not?'" Zigomanis said. "'Because if I take it, I am going to win it.' And he looked at me, and he had a little fire in his eyes, and he said he was going to win it. He won the draw and put it right on Raffi's tape. I went to the net and screened, and we went home with some hardware."

Torres's one-timer rocketed into the top corner of the net and Canada had a 2–1 victory at the 37-second mark. If Lundqvist saw it, he had no time to react.

"Every player wants to play and they want a regular shift in the tournament and they want to make a difference," Zigomanis said. "For me, it was better late than never. I was just happy to be out there."

In the end, the trust that Butler had in Zigomanis, the trust that Babcock had said was essential in that 13th forward, was paid back. In a big moment, Zigomanis was good for Butler.

Zigomanis was one of two Canadian players—Brandon Reid was the other—who was not on the ice for any goals against in Canada's seven games. Zigomanis's mark of plus-5 was tops on the team. And though he played on the wing, when Zigomanis was summoned to the faceoff circle, he won 10 of the 13 draws he took.

"He adapted," Butler said. "There never was a thought that he was a bad player, but you have to decide who will be that 13th forward. It was him, and there were a lot of kids released from that team who would have liked to have had that opportunity."

Fortitude wasn't the only factor in Zigomanis's positive handling of the initially limited role. In teammates such as Boyes, Torres, Mike Cammalleri, and roommate Mark Popovic, Zigomanis had people close by to whom he could talk about his role.

"I had known him for a while, and he was just thrilled to be there," Brad Boyes said. "Whatever he was given, he took advantage of it. He played well in that tournament."

"It was a tournament I had watched growing up," said Zigomanis. "I used to get up with my dad on those early mornings and turn the TV on. To actually be there, to win a medal—it felt like a gold medal to me—was a great experience. It was better to win the bronze than the silver, because you go out winning."

The pockets of ice time that Zigomanis had in Russia were to

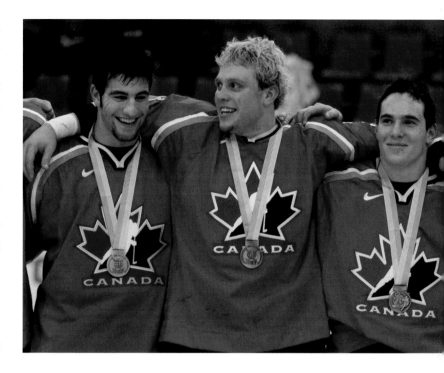

be reflected when he became an NHL player. Zigomanis spent the majority of the 2010–11 season with the Toronto Marlies of the American Hockey League, but previously he had stints with five NHL teams.

"I think it helped me out in the long run," Zigomanis said of his world junior experience. "I learned to play with limited ice, and most of my 200 games in the NHL have been between five and eight minutes. It was a good test for me and it was something I was able to apply to my game [in the professional ranks]." At his home, Zigomanis has a collection of his personal hockey memorabilia. In one frame are the bronze medal, his sweater, a program, and a puck.

Upon the players' return to Canada, pictures of Zigomanis with his medal appeared in the *Toronto Sun* and the *Toronto Star*. Before he rejoined his teammates in Kingston, people on the streets of Toronto recognized him.

Not bad for a kid who began the tournament as the 13th forward.

"I had a lot of adrenaline in that tournament, a lot of energy and the crowds in Moscow were great," Zigomanis said. "I can tell you it is something I will remember forever. I was there."

After playing sparingly as the thirteenth forward, Mike Zigomanis (left) finally got to contribute on the bronze-medal-winning overtime goal by Raffi Torres (centre). Mike Cammalleri is at right.

2002

PARDUBICE
THE TEST OF DISCIPLINE

TERRY KOSHAN

The youngest member of the Canadian team in Pardubice, high-flying Rick Nash had his first of many opportunities to play for Canada in major international tournaments.

Brian Sutherby couldn't count the times he had been jostled after a whistle over his junior career. A shove, maybe a stealthy elbow or slash—they were all part of the game. A few times after a whistle he had dropped his gloves to defend himself or send a message or both.

But only once, during the 2002 world junior championship in the Czech Republic, was Sutherby spit on.

"The first thing that came to me was shock," Sutherby said. "I couldn't believe it happened."

The Canada-Russia hockey rivalry has had dozens of intense chapters. Sutherby lived one. More than nine years after Russian forward Alexander Svitov spat in Sutherby's face during a round-robin game at the 2002 WJC, there's no hesitation when Sutherby recalls the incident.

"We were up 5–2 late in the game, and there was under a minute left," Sutherby said. "There was not really a hit or a slash or anything, but we came together after the whistle. He spit on me, and it landed just above my upper lip. I turned away, and when I looked back, he was long gone. I think I said something to the referees and looked over at their bench, but nothing happened."

Flanked by Mike Cammalleri (left) and Jay Bouwmeester (centre), Brian Sutherby faced the ultimate test of discipline in two games against Russia.

Sutherby was livid. He struggled to keep his composure after the game when fielding questions from reporters. Not retaliating, he said, was "probably the toughest thing I ever had to do in my life." Sutherby was so visibly shaken that assistant coach Marc Habscheid had to corral the 19-year-old in the dressing room and try to settle him down.

For Sutherby, there was no option other than to pretend Svitov hadn't just crossed one of those imaginary hockey lines that have been in place for decades.

From the initial moment that Hockey Canada takes teenaged players under its wing—whether it's in preparation for the world junior or much earlier, when players are gearing up for the under-17 championship, or at any other point—the importance of properly representing the country is emphasized. So too do the players have to accept that retaliation or acting out is selfish. If one isn't willing to check his personal agenda at the dressing-room door, chances are he won't make it out of a selection camp and he won't be missed by the coaches or those who do make the team.

"Everyone talks about the pride, but they often look past the sacrifices that go into what it takes to put that sweater on," said Jay Harrison, another member of the 2002 world junior team. "This tournament is the pinnacle of your junior career. The discipline has to be dead on. And what Brian did, to not retaliate, was a prime example. There was something a lot bigger going on there."

It's not just the coaches who drive home that defining message in the Program of Excellence. It's a theme delivered early and often by Hockey Canada. Harrison recalled that prior to an under-18 tournament, former Canadian juniors Mike Van Ryn and Manny Malhotra spoke to the team, and what they emphasized was playing for the crest on the front of the sweater.

The learning process for Sutherby involved a couple of incidents during the exhibition games in the days prior to the 2002 tournament. Sutherby had made the team; he was a strapping forward who had earned a spot on the Washington Capitals' roster coming out of training camp, but was returned to Moose Jaw of the Western Hockey League after playing in seven games for the Capitals.

In short, Team Canada was counting on Sutherby and he wasn't going anywhere, no matter what transpired in Canada's exhibitions.

On two occasions, though, Stan Butler, Canada's head coach, had to summon Sutherby for one-on-one meetings.

"I had elbowed a kid from Finland and I think I punched a guy in a game against the Czech Republic in the exhibition games," Sutherby said. "Butler had to pull me aside and [emphasize] what was at stake."

In Butler's mind, it was crucial that Sutherby know the entire landscape of the world junior tournament

"Brian was going to play a big role on our team," Butler said. "He was on a line with Steve Ott and Jarret Stoll, and they were going to play against the best line of the other team. When you play against the top line, one of the things you can't do is take penalties.

Scottie Upshall, here giving a Swedish opponent a rough ride into the boards, was just one of the Canadian players who understood that you can play with an edge but also with discipline.

"Not so much for Stoll, but for Sutherby and Ott, we had to change their game for international hockey, and make sure they understood that the game would be called a little bit different. They were key players and we needed them on the ice."

When Sutherby later did not respond to Svitov, it was hard proof that the message had been ingrained.

"I was as angry as I have ever been, but I was not going to put myself above anybody else," Sutherby said. "It was a difficult situation for me because I don't back down. I mean, it was a gob of spit on my face. I wanted to react in a much different way."

Though Sutherby had never been spat on before, and it has not happened to him in a professional career that has stretched over 10 seasons and included more than 460 NHL games, it's not entirely surprising that Svitov let fly. During the 2001 world junior, he was ejected twice from games and led all players with 58 penalty minutes. In 2002, Svitov still was playing off the same page. He again led all players in penalty minutes, this time with 43, and one game after spitting at Sutherby and getting away without a penalty, he jumped a Swiss player and was suspended for two games.

After Sutherby told the media about the spitting incident, reporters went to Svitov to get his version of the story. The Russian tuned out their questions, but he didn't try to deny that he did it.

Sutherby would love to relate that everything turned out well in the end. Yet that's not quite what happened.

After the Canadians beat the Russians in the round robin on December 29, 2001, both teams advanced to the gold-medal game. Canada led 2–1 after the first period but allowed three goals in the second and wound up losing 5–4. Sutherby had to watch a gold medal be placed around Svitov's neck, knowing that he'd lost the chance to exact revenge—not that he would have anyway.

"I had zero intention of doing anything stupid in that game, no matter what the score might have been," Sutherby said. "It was not on my mind at that point. What he had done was sickening and it ate me up inside, but my focus entirely was on winning.

"And then to lose to them ... I didn't shake his hand. I couldn't."

The hockey gods wanted to play around with Sutherby one more time. As the Canadians gathered in their hotel lobby the next morning to make the long trek home, the Russians straggled past, still wearing their gold medals after a night of celebration.

"You could tell by the look in his eyes that Brian was still angry," Butler said. "I just had to remind him that the way he handled the thing was classy. Something could have got pretty ugly."

As it was, Sutherby figured he and Svitov would meet again one day in the National Hockey League. And they did. But this story, for Sutherby, doesn't have a happy ending where he was able to make it clear to Svitov he had not forgotten.

Svitov was the third pick overall by the Tampa Bay Lightning in the 2001 entry draft, but soon provided evidence that high-end picks don't always become top-notch NHLers, let alone have lengthy careers. Svitov didn't have discipline on the international stage as a teenager, and though he had skills in abundance, he played just 179 games in three seasons with the Lightning and Columbus Blue Jackets.

Sutherby and Svitov squared off against each other just once in the NHL, during the 2002–03 rookie season for both.

"There was one game where I went after him and it looked like something was going to happen, but Chris Dingman jumped me from behind and that was it," Sutherby said. "I figured I would have lots of opportunities to get him back. You know, I still think about it a lot, especially at Christmas.

"It's something I will never forget. If I ever play him again, I will let him know that. But I don't think it's going to happen."

Goaltender Pascal Leclaire registered a sparkling .937 save percentage in five games, but Canada failed to protect a two-goal lead against the Russians in the gold-medal game.

At the time, Svitov said through a translator that he did not worry whether Sutherby would respond one day in the NHL "because first we both have to make it." Almost a decade on, Svitov has become a veteran of the Kontinental Hockey League, not having skated in the NHL since 2007.

In Butler's mind, when Sutherby turned away from Svitov and did not physically attack the Russian in 2002, there was no greater example for future teenagers who have earned the privilege of wearing Canada's colours. What's true, though, is that many would have applauded had Sutherby not turned away.

"What happened there was a disgusting act, and was something that should never be tolerated in hockey," Butler said. "Brian took away his personal feelings to do what was best for the team and for the country.

"I think what you have to understand is that when you put a Team Canada jersey on, the standards are higher for you to begin with, even to get a chance to try out for that team.

"That's what separates the type of people who wear the Hockey Canada jersey. They do whatever it takes to be successful, but if that means putting aside anything personal, they do it time and time again."

Brad Boyes was one of the offensive leaders for a Canadian team that beat the Russians handily in the preliminary round but couldn't seal the deal in the final.

2003

HALIFAX
THE QUIET ROOM

BRENDAN BELL

Defenceman Brendan Bell (here skating against the Czechs in the opening round) said Canada had a relatively easy route to the final in Halifax but knew that the Russians were going to be a stiff challenge.

We were leading Russia 2–1 at the end of the second period in the final and we were playing in front of a crowd that was 100 percent behind us. We hadn't lost a game. We weren't ever in too much trouble during our run to the gold-medal game. And our goaltender Marc-André Fleury had been lights-out all tournament long. People in the stands in Halifax and those who were watching that game on television would have thought that things were going our way when Scottie Upshall scored a power-play goal in the second period to give us the lead. They would have been confident of a win and a gold medal for Canada, the first one that the program would have won at home in eight years.

But when we went back to the dressing room after the second period, hardly anyone was talking. It hadn't been that way for other games. We always talked a lot, had a lot of fun, and kept things loose. Not this time. We had a lead but we also knew that this was anybody's game. Ours was a good team that played better as the tournament went along, but we also knew that the Russians were a really strong team and they were coming on. We could tell that they had a surge left and we had to be ready for it. We also knew that this was the last time all of us were going to play together. We had 20 minutes to bring everything to a close and we knew that

we didn't have anything locked up at that point. We'd been hanging on at the end of the second period.

Looking back at the 1983 WJC, we didn't have the high-end skill that a lot of other Canadian world junior teams have had over the years. We had thought that Jason Spezza was going to be on the team, but he was in the NHL when Team Canada sent out the invitations to the evaluation camp. Derek Roy was probably our best scoring threat. We weren't going to run up scores against teams in this tournament. We knew that in order to win, we had to play a tight, grinding game with guys like Jordin Tootoo making teams pay the price on our forecheck. We beat the U.S. 3–2 in our semifinal and knew we were going to have to win a close game like that in the gold-medal finale. And we had a goaltender who could win those types of games. In the summer, we thought that goalie was going to be Dan Blackburn, but the New York Rangers decided to keep him on their roster that season. No one thought it was going to be Marc-André Fleury back in the summer, but he turned out to be not just our youngest player but more importantly our best one.

We couldn't have been better prepared than we were before the final. For all of our games, our coaches—Marc Habscheid and his assistants Mike Kelly and Mario

Centre Kyle Wellwood, in an opening-round game, scores one of the most spectacular goals in the history of the tournament, sliding on his right hip through the slot and firing the puck by the Czech goaltender.

Durocher—were giving us detailed scouting reports on the opposition. Everything was broken down and we all knew our roles and what we had to do to be successful. The coaches and scouts would be working opponents' games; at practice we'd watch video. Everything that matters was covered—it was a football mentality, and we dissected opponents as much as possible. It was my first experience with that kind of NHL-quality advance work and I'm sure it was for a lot of the others on our roster. I thought it was great. We were working with an amazing amount of support. And Marc, Mike, and Mario knew everyone on the roster really well. During the summer and in the tryout camp, they were watching us and talking to us all the time, on and off the ice.

It was a funny thing—we knew how strong the Russians were, but fans probably didn't. The Russian group played their round-robin games in Cape Breton and there weren't even highlights of the games on television. They didn't play in Halifax until their semifinal game against the Finns. But we had seen them on video and we knew what they were capable of.

The media had focused on Alexander Ovechkin during the tournament and before the final, and that was understandable because everyone had projected him as the first pick in the 2004 NHL

Winger Pierre-Alexandre Parenteau scored 12 minutes into the first period of the final to give Canada a 1–0 lead against the Russians.

draft. But as good as he was, Ovechkin skated on the Russians' third line. They had a lot of big and talented guys up front. And with the scouting reports, we knew what we were up against.

The Russians just came with so much in the third period. I was playing beside Steve Eminger on the blue line and we had worked together all through the training camp and the tournament. We were on the ice when the Russians scored the tying goal about four minutes into the third period. Their top line, Igor Grigorenko, Andrei Taratukhin, and Alexander Perezhogin, came down on us on a three-on-two and a pass squirted through to Grigorenko, who put it past Fleury. Yuri Trubachev scored what turned out to be the tournament-winning goal with nine minutes left in regulation. Over those last minutes we struggled to get anything going. We just couldn't mount any offence at all and ended up with only four shots on goal in the third period. That wasn't going to get it done. Our best wasn't good enough—that's all there was to it. It ended up being 3–2, but, really, it didn't feel like a one-goal game in the third period.

It was hard to watch the Russians celebrating on the ice after the game and we were hugely disappointed. That said, I still think of the world juniors in Halifax as my best experience in the game. The support we got from the fans there was amazing. I've played in front of bigger crowds in the NHL, but none louder or more enthusiastic. Even away from the arena we had a sense of the energy and excitement in the city, and I think our team fed off that. It really didn't begin and end in Halifax. Everyone talks about how this team comes together over a few weeks for the tournament, but that's not the whole story. I had played with Steve Eminger, Derek Roy, and others with the Ontario under-17 team back in 2000. I had played with a bunch of guys who were on our roster at the summer under-18 tournament. And there was the summer development camp. You get to know the other players pretty well over the course of that time, and even those players who come up from other parts of the country work within the same sort of system. You don't start preparing for

Pierre-Marc Bouchard (left) celebrates after setting up Parenteau with the opening goal in the gold-medal game.

this tournament in the tryout camp. The process begins when you get the call for the under-17s. And it doesn't end at the tournament either. I've stayed in touch with a lot of the players on that team—any time we've played against each other in the pros we've met up in the hallways of the arena after the game. It's a different feeling than you might get with teammates from the pros. With those teammates you may never have been part of something big. But in the Program of Excellence, all of us who played shared something very special. We played for our country, and had the added bonus of playing *in* our country. It's maybe a little like being war veterans—at the risk of sounding overdramatic: we went to war. Everyone in that room before the third period of the final knew that we would be tested like never before. We went through something many people can only imagine. Words on a page can't express the tension we were feeling at that moment or the disappointment of watching the Russians come away with their gold medals. I've been lucky enough to play for the Canadian team that's gone to the Spengler Cup the last couple of years. Any time Hockey Canada calls, I'll answer.

Matt Stajan and other Canadian forwards struggled to skate through the stronger Russians. Even though the Canadians carried a one-goal lead into the third period, they knew the Russians were surging.

2004

HELSINKI
THE UNLUCKIEST BOUNCE
STÉPHANE LEROUX

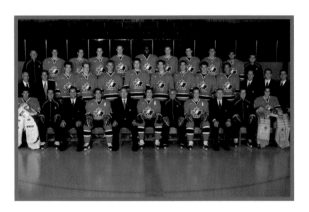

Standing beside a disappointed Derek Meech during the medal presentation after the gold-medal game, Marc-André Fleury was for the second year in a row the most prominent player for the Canadian juniors, albeit for the most heartbreaking reason.

January 5, 2004, is a day that Marc-André Fleury would like to forget. That's the day Canada's star goalie went between the pipes in the WJC gold-medal game against the United States. More than that day or that game, there was a moment, a play in the third period—something that seemed routine, even inconsequential in the lead-up; something that was over in a split second. That moment is what the goaltender wishes he could erase from his bank of memories. Many Canadian hockey fans feel that way, too. So do all of Fleury's teammates who were on the ice, or on the bench, in Helsinki at that moment. But it haunts Fleury like no one else.

The funny thing is, people seem to have forgotten everything leading up to the play. Let me refresh your memory and throw that awful moment into context.

At the beginning of the third period, the Canadian team, under the guidance of head coach Mario Durocher, was ahead 3–1 over the United States in the final game thanks to two goals by Nigel Dawes and one by Anthony Stewart. Canada seemed to be in complete control of the situation and on its way to winning its first WJC gold medal since 1997. Nothing should have been taken for granted—Canada had seen third-period leads evaporate during the final games of the previous two tournaments.

Still, neither of those teams had looked as dominant as this one. No team they had played in the tournament had come within three goals of Team Canada, and

they were coming off a 7–1 thrashing of the Czechs in the semi-finals. Though the Americans had been medal favourites heading into the tournament, in Mike Richards, Jeff Carter, Dion Phaneuf, Brent Seabrook, Ryan Getzlaf, and of course Sidney Crosby, the Canadian team was loaded with guys who could step right into the NHL. If there was one thing these players should have had after two periods, it was confidence.

"I remember that the mood was calm in the locker room in the second intermission," said Durocher, who had been an assistant coach under Marc Habscheid at the 2003 championship in Halifax 12 months earlier. "The only thing that we reminded the players, especially our defencemen, was to be on the lookout for the stretch pass beyond the red line, a rule with which our players weren't familiar at the time compared to the American university players."

No one expected what happened next to the Canadian squad, especially to the 19-year-old Fleury. The Pittsburgh Penguins had drafted him with the first overall pick largely based on his impressive performance as an underager in Halifax the year before. The Penguins then tried to rush Fleury onto the NHL roster, where the youngster sometimes struggled, in the fall of '03. As the promising young star

With a 3–1 lead going into the third period of the championship game against the United States, it looked like Fleury and his teammates were going to bring gold medals back to Canada for the first time since 1997.

started to fade in the big league, the Penguins ended up loaning him to the WJC team in the hope of getting him work and boosting his confidence.

And it seemed to be working. Playing against the best junior-aged players in the world, Team Canada had allowed only five goals in the five games heading into the final against the Americans. And after two periods, the much-touted Americans had managed only one.

In the Americans' dressing room before the third period, coach Mike Eaves was trying to rally his squad, and looking for offence. He decided to shuffle his lines in the last frame, putting Ryan Kesler with Zach Parise and Steve Werner on his top line. Eaves's second line would feature his son, Patrick, along with Drew Stafford and Patrick O'Sullivan.

The changes paid immediate dividends.

Less than five minutes into the third, O'Sullivan scored on Fleury, and reduced the lead to one goal.

A little more than two minutes later, Ryan Kesler finished off a play started by defenceman Dan Richmond—one of the long stretch passes the Canadian coaches had warned their players about in the intermission.

Panic then set into the Canadians' play with the score suddenly tied at three.

"Marc-André became extremely nervous, much like every member of our defensive squad," Durocher said. "I thought of taking a time out after the third American goal in order to calm things down, but a commercial break was imminent and I thought that we would be able to regain our composure then. I wanted to keep my time out for the end of the game in case we needed it."

If he had a chance to do it over again, Durocher would almost certainly have done it differently.

The United States continued to pressure the Canadian defence, and then—with 5:12 to go in the third period—came the play, the one that haunts the coach and his players. And no one more than Marc-André Fleury.

With the puck lying near the crease, and open ice in front of him, Fleury made what looked like the safe play—he leaned into a shot to fire the puck out of the Canadian end. But instead of clearing the zone, the puck hit defenceman Braydon Coburn in the chest.

Then, with Fleury out of position at the top of the crease, and his defencemen too far away, the team could only watch helplessly as the puck somehow bounced into the net.

Hockey is a game of bounces, and this one cost Canada a gold medal.

Patrick O'Sullivan was credited with the goal and suddenly the Americans were leading 4–3, their first lead of the game. O'Sullivan would never score a bigger goal with less effort.

Two photos from the shocking sequence on the Americans' winning goal in the gold-medal game: Marc-André Fleury came out his crease and tried to clear the puck, but it bounced off defenceman Braydon Coburn. Despite his best efforts, the goaltender could only helplessly watch the puck roll across the goal line.

"Marc-André and I were confused as to who should play the puck," said Coburn after the game. "I thought that he wanted to play the puck but he only wanted to clear it away from the front on the net."

Over the last five minutes of regulation, the Canadians tried desperately to find a tying goal but time wound down. For the first time in WJC history, the United States had won gold.

After the game, Marc-André Fleury was inconsolable. He felt that he had let the entire team down after it had played brilliantly throughout the tournament. In the seven years since, Fleury has won a Stanley Cup and an Olympic gold, yet the memory of Helsinki is still clearly painful. And that's perfectly understandable: This had been the biggest game of his life up to that point, a chance to make good after carrying a team that was just 20 minutes away from gold the year before. "That play is now part of hockey history," Fleury said. "Every time a similar situation arises, TSN brings out the footage as part of a montage of the worst blunders. I have no choice but to live with it for the rest of my career."

The hard times for the teenager from Sorel, Quebec, didn't start or end there. After the WJC tournament, Fleury returned to the Penguins. Later that month, after 12 losses in his last 13 NHL games, Fleury was reassigned to the Cape Breton

Through two periods, Fleury and his teammates were almost unchallenged, thoroughly outplaying a U.S. team that featured Ryan Kesler. The only time the Canadians trailed in Helsinki was during the last 5:02 of the gold-medal game.

Jeff Tambellini (number 19) and captain Daniel Paille create havoc in front of American goaltender Al Montoya.

Screaming Eagles. Upon his return to the junior ranks, Fleury had a good run, going 8-1-2. "I always believed in Marc-André Fleury," said Pascal Vincent, his coach at the time. "He was so good and he had done so much for us since the age of 16 that I knew he would bounce back."

However, during the playoffs, Fleury faltered—and, after three straight losses to Chicoutimi, Vincent had to give the No. 1 job to Martin Houle. So a goaltender who had been Canada's No. 1 for the last two WJCs ended his junior career sitting at the end of the bench at the Centre 200 in Sydney, Nova Scotia. The Screaming Eagles, who had finished second overall with 103 points, lost in five games to the Saguenéens, who had ended the season 28 points behind them in the standings.

It should have been the end of the torment for Fleury, but it didn't even stop there. Pittsburgh assigned Fleury to the Wilkes-Barre/Scranton Penguins in the American Hockey League, but coach Michel Therrien had him start only one game in the playoffs, a game that he lost.

If 2004 had been the ruin of Marc-André Fleury, it would have seemed cruel, if not tragic. Eventually, though, Fleury got his game back on the rails and more. Not only would he go on to win a Stanley Cup with the Penguins, but it was his incredible, acrobatic save on Detroit's Nicklas Lidstrom in the dwindling moments of Game 7 that preserved Pittsburgh's one-goal lead and won them the Cup. It was the kind of heroic save goalies dream of making, at the biggest moment of his career and the perfect time for his team.

If anything could erase the memory of that botched clearing attempt in 2004, it was that save. Mario Durocher thought Fleury took too much blame back in Helsinki. "Sidney Crosby and Ryan Getzlaf both missed great opportunities to put the game out of reach of the Americans at the beginning of the third period," he said. "When the score was 3–1, those goals would have broken the Americans' back."

There were so many good things that came out of the 2004 WJC. Jeff Carter and Dion Phaneuf were named to the tournament's all-star team and Nigel Dawes ended up the top scorer with six goals and five assists. In six games in Helsinki, Canada scored 35 goals and allowed only nine. During those six games, Mario Durocher's team trailed during only eight minutes and 42 seconds. All that is easy to forget.

What people remember is what still weighs most heavily on the mind of the goaltender who watched helplessly when his clearing attempt ended up in the back of his own net. You needn't shed a tear for Fleury, though. There had been many remarkable performances by goaltenders en route to the world junior championships—by Jimmy Waite, Manny Fernandez, Marc Denis, and José Théodore, among others. In the narrowest of victories they managed to avoid the unlucky bounce that burned Fleury. In his two world championship tournaments Fleury had come away with silver, steeping himself in glory but for that awful moment. The other goaltenders with whom he'll be compared do have gold medals, but he alone has a Stanley Cup ring.

2005

FARGO
THE POWERHOUSE

ED WILLES

Corey Perry had doubts about winning a place on the Canadian roster. He ended up playing on the wing beside the two best-known players in the lineup: Sidney Crosby and Patrice Bergeron.

It wasn't exactly a secret at the time, but Corey Perry knew the makings of something special were there with Team Canada at the 2005 WJC.

He just didn't know if he'd be a part of it.

Starting with the late-summer camp in Calgary, Perry, along with the other invitees, all fought for a spot on the deepest, most talented Canadian team in the history of the world junior championship. That team was stocked with the players from the impossibly rich 2003 draft, many of whom had played for Canada in the '04 tournament in Helsinki. The NHL lockout that year ensured half a dozen players who'd normally be playing in The Show—centre Patrice Bergeron had already played a full season with the Boston Bruins, for pity's sake—would be made available to Team Canada.

True, Perry had some credentials of his own. He was coming off a 113-point season with the London Knights, he'd been a first-rounder in that '03 draft, and he'd been a late cut of the '04 team. But all that résumé earned him was an invitation to the selection camp in Winnipeg—which is why, when the phone rang on cut-down day, Perry's first thought was, "This can't be happening again."

Turned out it wasn't. Turned out Perry would play a role on the best-ever team in the history of the WJC.

But there was a price to pay.

"I thought I was getting cut again," says Perry. "Then [head coach Brent Sutter] called and said, 'Do you want to be the 13th forward? If you do, you have to cut your hair.'

"That was a sacrifice I was willing to make."

It wouldn't be the last time someone took one for that team.

The kids from Grand Forks have since morphed into a collection of the game's greatest stars—and, less than a decade after their starring turn in North Dakota, their accomplishments continue to stagger. Six players from Sutter's team would win a gold medal with Team Canada at the 2010 Winter Olympics. The graduates included Sidney Crosby, generally regarded as the game's greatest all-around player; Perry and Ryan Getzlaf, who'd win the Stanley Cup in Anaheim as 22-year-olds; and

Centre Mike Richards played with a physical edge that keyed Canada's dominance of the field leading up to the medal round.

Mike Richards and Jeff Carter, who'd help form the nucleus of the Philadelphia Flyers that made the Stanley Cup final in 2010. The blue line featured Shea Weber, Dion Phaneuf, Brent Seabrook, and Braydon Coburn. Six of the players on that roster went on to become captains of their NHL teams. As a group, they were talented. They were mature. They were focused. And, for all that, their greatest achievement was not in meeting the great expectations which had been placed on them.

It was in exceeding them.

"The biggest thing is we started in August with a highly competitive camp," said Sutter. "There was one goal and one goal only and that was to be a totally dominant team. We wanted to make sure the players understood the coaches were very serious about the way we wanted them to play. They got the message and it just carried on from there."

And everyone connected with that team shared the feeling.

"We were kids but you kind of realized what we had," said Perry. "That was a stacked team.

"We had that feeling going into every game. Brent had a game plan for us in every game and we didn't take anyone lightly. We didn't want to be scored on. That

was our whole mindset. Grind things out. Then guys started scoring. We were just running teams out. That was the kind of team we were."

Perry, as things transpired, had an interesting time of it all the way around with that team. That year, Team Canada featured 12 veterans from the '04 team that lost the gold medal in Helsinki to the United States on Marc-André Fleury's infamous clearing gaffe late in the third period. Canada had also gone seven years without a gold medal, and that drought, coupled with the returnees, ensured motivation wouldn't be a problem.

Then again, this group didn't need a lot of help in that department. At the August camp in Calgary, Sutter divided the players into two teams, then watched as Phaneuf and Colin Fraser, who were teammates with the Red Deer Rebels, dropped their gloves in one of the first scrimmages.

"That's the kind of team it was," the coach said.

By the time the December selection camp rolled around in Winnipeg, the competition was even more fierce and Perry found himself battling a handful of players, including Eric Fehr of the Brandon Wheat Kings, for the final forward spot. In that final inter-squad game Perry scored three goals, which punched his ticket for Grand

The Canadian blue-liners didn't just shut down opposing forwards—they punished other teams for simply trespassing. Here, Dion Phaneuf decks a Swedish forward in the opening round.

Forks. In the pre-tournament schedule, he then received a battlefield promotion when Jeremy Colliton, a rugged, two-way winger with the Prince Albert Raiders, suffered a knee injury. Colliton would come back and play one game for the maple leaf in Grand Forks before he was scratched from the tournament. Perry would move up and take his place.

His linemates? Crosby and Bergeron.

"You couldn't ask for much more than that," he says.

"Through that process there were a couple of players who were right there," said Sutter. "It came down to Corey and a couple of others in the last exhibition and Corey just took it to another level."

Which also pretty much describes what happened with the team.

Following the selection camp, the group repaired to the Manitoba resort town of Gimli, where they celebrated Christmas at the home of former NHLer Ted Irvine. Irvine, as it turned out, is the father of professional wrestler Chris Jericho, and Jericho and some of his wrestling colleagues made a video wishing the junior team good luck.

Thus fortified, the team travelled to Grand Forks and, in their four round-robin games, they beat, in order, Slovakia, Sweden, Germany, and Finland by a combined score of 32–5. Perry, Bergeron, and Crosby would form the nominal No. 1 line, but

Patrice Bergeron was in an unprecedented position in Fargo: He made his debut in the WJC after having played a full season with the Boston Bruins and having won a gold medal at the senior men's world champi-onships in 2004.

the dropoff from their unit to the rest of the lineup was imperceptible. Getzlaf centred a line with Carter and Andrew Ladd. Richards played with Anthony Stewart and a bit with Nigel Dawes. The fourth line, such as it was, consisted of Stephen Dixon, Clarke MacArthur, and Fraser and they played a huge role throughout the tournament.

"I never looked at who was our 13th forward or our first line," said Sutter. "I looked at it as we had a unique group and they were going to determine who was going to play and how much they were going to play.

"They just kept getting better and better. It was exciting to watch. We didn't match lines too much. On that team, we didn't have to."

Still, the Perry-Bergeron-Crosby line led the way, offensively at least. Bergeron topped the team in scoring, Crosby was second in goals with six, and Perry recorded seven points in the six games. Bergeron and Crosby remain close friends from that experience.

"Good players don't always play well together," said Perry. "But we just clicked and it happened pretty quickly."

Following the round robin, Canada would get its biggest scare of the tournament, relatively speaking, in the semifinal game with a 3–1 win over the Czech Republic. But even that score was a tad misleading. Czech goalie Marek Schwarz, the tournament's all-star 'keeper, stopped 39 of the 42 shots sent his way while his teammates mustered a puny 11 shots at Canadian goalie Jeff Glass. (It became a running joke in Grand Forks when Hockey Canada officials brought Glass out for post-game media scrums. By the end of each night he'd faced more hard questions than he had testing shots.) The win over the Czechs set up the gold-medal game against the Russians. Again, motivation wouldn't be an issue.

The Russians were led by Alexander Ovechkin and Evgeni Malkin, who had been taken first and second respectively in the 2004 draft. They had also dismantled a strong American team—Ryan Suter, Drew Stafford, Phil Kessel, Ryan Callahan— 7–2 in their semifinal game.

Before the gold-medal game, Ovechkin, who was playing in his third WJC, heard his name mentioned as he walked by a TV monitor.

"What are they saying?" he asked a media type.

"They're saying Canada is going to play the Bergeron line against you with Phaneuf and Weber," Ovechkin was told.

"Good luck," he sneered.

Luck, however, was the last thing the Canadians needed. Luck was something Ovechkin was going to run out of before the first intermission

By the time the final rolled around, Grand Forks had almost become an unofficial Canadian city. Hockey-mad fans from Winnipeg and environs had made the three-hour trek down the highway for the entire tournament, making each Canadian contest

Corey Perry, here skating against Germany, says head coach Brent Sutter kept the team "on an even keel and made sure everyone checked their ego at the door." Ego might have been the only thing that could have stopped the 2005 team.

a virtual home game. The final would be played in front of another rabid, red-clad sellout crowd of just under 11,000 at the magnificent Ralph Engelstad Arena.

They got their money's worth. In the first period, Ovechkin was hit by, in order, Crosby, Phaneuf, Richards, and Bergeron. He then came out for one shift in the second period before he excused himself for the evening.

Getzlaf, meanwhile, scored 51 seconds in and the Canadians drove Russian starter Anton Khudobin from the game early in the second period. The Canadians, in fact, were leading 6–1 midway through the second when they finally took their foot off the gas.

That suited the Russians, who were playing like they wanted the night to end as quickly as possible. When they'd won gold in Halifax two years earlier, the Russians trash-talked the host team during and after the final. Ovechkin and his teammates would go out quietly and peacefully this time.

"We went out and dominated physically," said Perry. "Guys knew what they wanted and we didn't stop. We just kept going and going."

Then the final horn went. Then it all started to sink in.

The Canadians had done to the tournament field what Genghis Khan did to Asia Minor. Over the six games of the tournament they outscored their opposition 41–7, allowing an average of 17 shots on goal per game in the process. They took apart the mighty Russians, holding Ovechkin and Malkin off the scoresheet while allowing just 11 shots on goal over the first two periods. They were never seriously challenged in the gold-medal game or the tournament. They set out on a mission. The mission was accomplished to the fullest extent possible.

"The kids were focused and they were prepared," said Sutter. "They just wanted to get better and it was great to watch them come to the rink every day. They knew what they wanted."

OK, this team didn't exactly need a master coaching job, but Sutter laid out a plan for them four months before the tournament and received the maximum buy-in from every player on the roster.

"He kept on us," said Perry. "He didn't want our heads to get too big. He kept us on an even keel and made sure everyone checked their ego at the door and played for their country, not for themselves. He's a tough guy to play for but he gets the best out of players."

And there was a lot to get out of that group. Bergeron, who led Canada and the tournament in scoring with 13 points, was named the tournament MVP but it could have gone to Carter, who had seven goals, or Getzlaf, who had 12 points and played a huge two-way game. Phaneuf, Carter, and Bergeron were named to the tournament all-star game. Crosby could have been named. Weber didn't record a point but played with Phaneuf on the fearsome shutdown pairing. And, for all that, the most impressive thing about this team was the whole was still greater than the sum of those considerable parts.

The real measure of the team, moreover, is still being counted. The next season, 12 of Sutter's players would step into the NHL. And no one imagines that the legacy of this team ended in Vancouver, when Olympic golds were draped around the necks of Crosby, Bergeron, Richards, Weber, Seabrook, and Perry. No other team so fully lived up to the Program of Excellence's central objectives: in the short run, to win the world junior championships, and in the long run, to prepare the country's best players to compete in major international tournaments, the Olympics foremost among them.

"It's crazy when you look at the guys on that team and what they've been able to do at a young age," said Perry.

Crazy? Maybe. But what that team accomplished in Grand Forks was real enough.

2006

VANCOUVER
THE BEST FRIENDS

ED WILLES

Luc Bourdon (pictured at the 2008 tournament) heard cheers at Vancouver's GM Place, the arena where he had hoped to play for the Canucks.

As is often the case with close friends, the pair was a study in contrasts.

Kris Letang was a city kid from Montreal. Luc Bourdon was from the tiny fishing community of Shippagan on New Brunswick's northeast coast. Letang was a little more worldly; a little more certain of himself and his place. Bourdon, for his part, was just taking his first steps into the bigger world and learning about the possibilities that awaited.

On the ice it was a similar story. Letang was an undersized defenceman who compensated for his lack of mass with skill and an outsized hockey sense. Bourdon was a thoroughbred, a size-and-speed blueliner who played on instinct and impulse.

"When he hit guys, he'd just destroy them," says Letang.

So, superficially at least, they didn't have a lot in common. But it was a funny thing. From the moment they met at a summer camp in 2004, before they joined the Val-d'Or Foreurs, Letang and Bourdon discovered something about each other that made all their differences seem irrelevant.

"We were great friends from the first time we met and it grew," says Letang. "We used to hang out after every practice. We had races. We shot pucks. We tried to push each other. That's the way I remember Luc: how passionate he was; how much he loved the game and I was the same way."

But Letang has another memory of his friend; a memory so pure and powerful that it gives him comfort when he thinks about Bourdon, who died in a motorcycle accident near his hometown on May 29, 2008. At the 2006 world junior championship in Vancouver, they were part of a Team Canada that put together one of the most improbable runs in this country's history at the WJC. A year after a super team had demolished the field in Grand Forks on the way to a gold, head coach Brent Sutter would mould a far-less-celebrated group of players into a team that didn't have the star power of the '05 squad but was just as efficient.

Canada would win all six tournament games, blasting Russia and Evgeni Malkin 5–0 in the final to capture gold before a sellout crowd of 18,000-plus at GM Place.

Letang and Bourdon played every game in that tournament on the same defensive pairing. They were also on the ice together when the final horn sounded in the gold-medal game; friends and teammates forever. It's not an aspect of the Program of Excellence that draws cheers or shows up in newspapers or on sportscasts, but it's something that looms large for players in every lineup: when a team is brought together, the seeds of friendship are planted. The players share a special experience—living and playing together for a couple weeks in the summer, then gathering again in December for the most important games of their career to that point.

"It was just unbelievable," says Letang. "Everything. The crowd, the emotion. And I was able to share it with my friend."

"He had this charisma about him," Sutter says of Bourdon. "He was intense but he was also loose and guys were drawn to that. It was a terrible, terrible thing that happened. He had such a tremendous life ahead of him."

If ever a team was a reflection of its coach, it was the Canadian entry at the '06 WJC. The year before Sutter had won with a group that included, among others, Sidney Crosby, Ryan Getzlaf, Corey Perry, Jeff Carter, Mike Richards, Shea Weber, Dion Phaneuf, and Brent Seabrook. That team simply required a coach who could open the door to the players' bench.

The '06 team was different.

For starters, there was just one returning player—defenceman Cam Barker, who'd missed the latter stages of the Grand Forks tournament with mononucleosis. Many on the team were unproven and unheralded. There was no go-to star, no elite first line. There were no big scorers, no big reputations. There was, however, balance and quality throughout the lineup, and if Sutter didn't have a team that would overwhelm with firepower, he did have one that could wear down the opposition through its diligence and determination.

In the end, it was the perfect Sutter team—a "wolf pack" that was committed to the greater good and the coach's vision.

"They didn't have as much talent but our work ethic and leadership was just as strong [as the '05 team]," Sutter says. "It was exactly the same game plan. The guys were on a mission. They wanted to be as good as the team in '05. They wanted to be as dominant."

And if they didn't earn any style points along the way, they met their goal. The Canadians would surrender just six goals in the tournament, shutting out Finland in the semifinal and the Russians in the gold-medal game. Goalie Justin Pogge, who was something of a surprise selection over Carey Price before the tournament, was the team's MVP for the tournament, but the larger story was the totality of Canada's team game and the work of the head coach.

Bourdon and his Val-d'Or teammate Kris Letang keyed a defence that surrendered only six goals in the tournament, capped by a shutout victory over Russia in the final.

"A lot of coaches could have won [with the '05 team]," Hockey Canada president Bob Nicholson said after the win over the Russians. "There aren't a lot of coaches who could have won with this team."

If there was a player who epitomized Sutter's grand plan it was forward Steve Downie, a fireplug who'd been a late invite to the Team Canada summer camp and who carried some baggage on to the squad. The season before, Downie had been involved in a much-publicized fight with Windsor Spitfires teammate Akim Aliu over a hazing incident. That summer he'd also been a first-round selection of the Philadelphia Flyers, and when Downie arrived at the camp, Sutter explained the way things would be on his team.

"Obviously there was so much going on with Steve," says Sutter. "Basically it was just getting him into a situation where he was really focused. I never had an issue with his emotional level. I just wanted him disciplined. We spent time with him on a daily basis and he was huge for us."

Downie would be named to the tournament all-star team, but this doesn't begin to tell the story of his contribution. Playing with Dustin Boyd and Blake Comeau in what passed for Sutter's first line, Downie was everywhere throughout the tournament. Against a strong entry from the United States, Canada needed a tie to win their group. Downie set up Boyd for the game-tying goal, then, with American goalie Cory Schneider pulled for an extra attacker late in the game, sent in Canadian

Andrew Cogliano picked up a pair of assists in the 5–0 gold-medal-game victory over Russia. Cogliano injected open-ice speed into Canada's offence by committee.

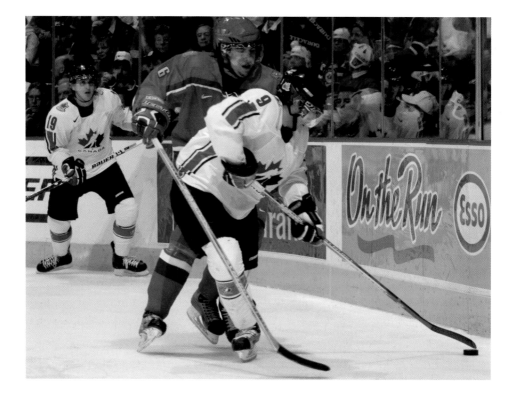

Defenceman Marc Staal thumped Evgeni Malkin in the gold-medal game. Staal and blue-line partner Ryan Parent shut down and thoroughly frustrated Malkin and the favoured Russians.

captain Kyle Chipchura for the game-winning goal about the same time as Team U.S.A.'s Jack Johnson was throwing a flying elbow at Downie's noggin.

None the worse for wear, Downie came back for the 4–0 win over Finland in the semifinal, then scored the first goal against Russia in the gold-medal game and drew back-to-back penalties in the second period that led to Canada's fourth goal.

The tournament final, in fact, would provide the canvas for Sutter's most enduring work in his two years with the Canadian juniors. The Russians were stacked. Malkin was among the best players, period, in the KHL. His supporting cast included Nikolai Kulemin, Alexander Radulov, Enver Lisin, and Ilya Zubov. The Russians had also demolished the Americans 5–1 in the other semifinal.

"We were facing a much stronger team with a superstar like Malkin," said Letang. "But it was a chance to show everyone what kind of team we had."

And they did every bit of that. Downie set the tone, blasting Russian rearguard Denis Bodrov in the opening minutes and taking a charging penalty for his troubles. The Russians would outshoot Canada 15–3 over the first 15 minutes of the first period but Pogge stood tall. Downie then beat Malkin behind the Russian net and sifted a roller through goalie Anton Khudobin to open the scoring. Less than two minutes later, defenceman Marc Staal picked off a pass in the neutral zone and set up Comeau for the second goal.

The Russians would have a goal disallowed early in the second and were still carrying the play when Michael Blunden scored a backbreaking third goal on the power play. Blunden would add another power-play goal. Chipchura would add the fifth goal with three minutes left and, in a celebration that presaged the gold-medal game at the 2010 Winter Olympics in the same arena, Canadian fans stood for the final two minutes of the game and saluted their young heroes.

"The whole focus was on winning the gold," said Sutter. "Everyone on that team was focused on that moment."

The summer before the WJC, the Vancouver Canucks had taken Luc Bourdon with their first pick, 10th overall, and there was considerable buzz about the young blueliner as the tournament opened. Bourdon had enjoyed an impressive training camp with the Canucks and almost made the NHL team as an 18-year-old. As it was, he became fast friends with the Canucks' Alex Burrows before returning to Val-d'Or.

He would be traded to Moncton during the WJC, where he played in the Memorial Cup that spring.

"We worked out together for a solid week," says Burrows. "That's really where we started to become great friends. He came from a small town and didn't know a

Michael Blunden (number 21 with stick raised) picked up two power-play goals in the second period of the gold-medal game. Russia had outshot Canada 15–4 in the first period, but Blunden's second goal made the score 4–0.

lot about the big city. I'd been around the team and I think he was comfortable with me."

Bourdon would enjoy a solid WJC. Staal was named the tournament's outstanding defenceman, but Bourdon was one of the focal points of the team. Choruses of "Luuuuc, Luuuuc" would rattle around the building every time he made a play. He would also be named to the tournament all-star team, and it seemed the WJC represented just the first of many memorable moments for the big blueliner in Vancouver.

"It was really exciting for him," says Letang. "It was pretty much his building. For him, it was a chance to show them he was going to be ready to play in the NHL. He was already a leader."

The next season, Letang and Bourdon would again win gold for Team Canada at the WJC in Sweden. The year after, Bourdon split the season between Manitoba and the Canucks while Letang played 63 games with the Penguins. Letang was with the Penguins in the Stanley Cup final against Detroit when he heard he'd lost his friend. Luc Bourdon had just turned 21 when he died.

Blunden (here hammering Sergei Shirokov) and his Canadian teammates surrendered scoring chances to the Russians through the first two periods but were the more physical team throughout the game.

"It's always fresh in my mind," says Letang. "It's hard when the month of May comes around. I try to think about him every day. It's something you don't forget."

So he keeps the friendship alive. Letang makes a point of talking to Bourdon's mother, Suzanne Boucher, a couple of times a year. He also sees her at the annual Luc Bourdon Golf Classic. Before he passed, Bourdon donated $10,000 to sports groups in Shippagan. Boucher has since established the Luc Bourdon Foundation to help students and athletes from the area.

Burrows, meanwhile, is also involved in the tournament. He and his wife, Nancy, remain close to Charlene, Bourdon's fiancée, who is attending medical school.

In the Canucks first game of the 2008–09 season, a permanent display honouring Bourdon was unveiled at GM Place (now known as Rogers Arena). As a video tribute played, Canadian recording artist Tom Cochrane sang "Big League" with bandmate Ken Greer. Vancouver fans then chanted "Luuuuc" one more time before the game started with the Calgary Flames.

Burrows would score twice in that game. After each goal, he mimed pulling an arrow from his back and shooting it into the sky. That was for Bourdon.

"He was my friend," says Burrows. "He'll always be my friend."

2007

LEKSAND
THE TENSE VICTORY

GARE JOYCE

Jonathan Toews (here taking a faceoff against U.S. rival Peter Mueller) did it all for Canada in the 2007 tournament, leading the team in scoring and notching three goals in the shootout victory over the Americans in the semifinal.

For sustained suspense, no single game matches it in the history of the Program of Excellence. Sixty minutes of regulation couldn't settle it, nor could 10 minutes of sudden death. The semifinal between Canada and the United States at the 2007 world juniors had to go to a shootout. And even the shootout had to go into overtime.

The cliffhanger was so dramatic that Canada's 4–2 win over Russia in the final seemed anticlimactic.

The images that are burned in the memories of most who watched the semifinal feature the two best Canadian players in Leksand, Sweden: Jonathan Toews and Carey Price.

Toews was in his second turn with the under-20 team. As the youngest Canadian player in Vancouver the year before, Toews served on the checking line and flew under the radar, picking up just a couple of assists. In Sweden, however, he centred the first line, worked the first power play and penalty-killing units, and was expected to do everything but drive the team bus. He was at something of a disadvantage—he was playing through a shoulder injury and his season at the University of North Dakota had been a disappointment to that point. Still, Toews led the Canadians in scoring with four goals and three assists in six games—none of his teammates had more than two goals. Still, what people remember most about Toews in that

Defenceman Ryan Parent was the loneliest player on the ice when the United States went on the power play in overtime of the semifinal game. Parent and blue-line partner Marc Staal reprised their roles from Vancouver as Canada's shutdown defence pairing.

tournament were three goals that don't show up on the stats sheet: the three goals that Toews scored on goaltender Jeff Frazee in the shootout victory over the Americans.

It seemed like the U.S., with players like Patrick Kane, Peter Mueller, and Kyle Okposo, had an advantage over Canada in the skills department going into the shootout. At the outset of the tournament, the conventional wisdom had been that the Canadians were going to be gritty, disciplined, and defensively sound but offensively challenged, that they could count on Toews for goals but would have to scramble to find others to chip in. That's pretty well how it played out when Canada went undefeated in the opening round. Toews keyed the most crucial win in that round, a 6–3 victory over the United States in which he scored two goals, the second being a winner on a penalty shot.

Before the semifinal, the Canadians were at risk of a false sense of confidence with that win and the Americans' unimpressive run through the opening round—a loss to Germany meant that the U.S. needed an overtime win over Sweden just to avoid heading to the relegation games. The Americans, however, saved their best effort and most effective play for this showdown against their rivals and, for the Canadian teenagers in the lineup and thousands of fans who travelled to Sweden, comfort gave way to anxiety.

After a close-checking and scoreless first period, the U.S. took a lead on a power play with an attempted pass by Taylor Chorney banking off Canadian defenceman Marc Staal's skate and eluding Price. The defending champions were still trailing by that single goal deep into the third period but pulled even on a power-play goal by Luc Bourdon with less than 8 minutes in regulation.

When the game went to four-on-four in the 10-minute overtime period, it looked tense. And when a high-sticking penalty to Kris Letang gave the U.S. a power play, it looked tenser still, especially from the penalty box where the fretful defenceman sat. Letang called it "the longest two minutes of my life." Coach Craig Hartsburg sent out his designated shutdown defencemen, Ryan Parent and Marc Staal, who were reprising their roles from Vancouver a year before. They had been teammates on the Ontario under-17 team and in the Canadian under-18 program. Parent and Staal were the blue line's bedrock and a good fit. Both hailed from northern Ontario, Parent from remote Sioux Lookout, Staal from Thunder Bay. Both played in the Ontario Hockey League, Parent for Guelph, Staal for Sudbury. It was a tough test for the two and the forward out there with the game on the line, Tom Pyatt, who had grown up playing with Marc Staal in Thunder Bay.

The American power-play unit (Mueller and Jack Johnson on the blue line and Patrick Kane and Kyle Okposo up front) controlled play for the entire two minutes and the Canadian penalty killers could neither get the puck out of their zone nor get close enough to the bench for a line change. Parent was completely stranded on the opposite side of the ice, 180 feet from the Canadian bench. Others might have panicked, but Parent, Staal, and Pyatt went about their business. "It was lonely out there," Parent said. "They had possession, but we could have got into trouble if we chased them and overcommitted. We were doing what we needed to do, pushing them out to the perimeter. Our job was to deny them the areas they had a chance to score from."

Over the course of the 10-minute overtime period, the Canadians never mustered a serious scoring chance and Price had to make 12 saves compared to two by Frazee.

The anxiety was ratcheted up during the shootout. Many players on the Canadian bench kept their heads down almost prayerfully when their teammates took their turns. Any prayers weren't answered in Canada's first two turns, with Frazee turning aside Steve Downie and Bryan Little. When it came to the Americans' second attempt, Mueller deked and beat Price. After he gave the U.S. the 1–0 lead, Mueller skated by the Canadian bench and gave a shrug with uplifted palms, as if to say that it was all too easy.

Thereafter, Jonathan Toews took charge. On the very next attempt, Canada's third, he wired a low wrist low past Frazee, the first of five consecutive attempts that would beat the U.S. goaltender. Because of the vagaries of the IIHF's rules on shootouts, coach Hartsburg could send out shooters for more than one attempt. He sent Bryan Little back out in the fourth round and this time he beat Frazee. In the fifth round, Toews picked the top corner. In the sixth, Andrew Cogliano's wrist shot again found the net. And finally, in the seventh round, Toews deked and beat Frazee—remarkably, it seemed like each of Toews's goals in the shootout was more sure-handed than the previous one. The last made it 5–4 for Canada, with the Americans owning the last shot.

Price needed to turn aside a shot and secure a berth in the finals. It was poetic justice that his save in the seventh round came on Peter Mueller. A high-scoring centre with Everett in the Western Hockey League, Mueller was a known quantity to Price. What's more, Mueller tried a move on Price that he had used on a breakaway in a WHL regular-season game. Like Toews, Mueller had scored in his first two attempts in the shootout and it looked like this third might slip through Price's pads,

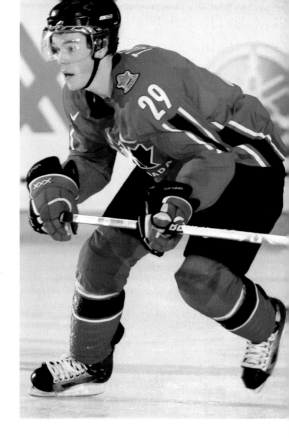

Toews was the undisputed leader of the 2007 Canadian team, but he had come into the tournament with a shoulder injury and had not enjoyed much success to that point in his season with the University of North Dakota.

but the puck disappeared into or under the goalie's pads within a hair of the goal line. Afterwards the Americans would protest that it at least merited video review, and some would claim it was in. No matter; Canada advanced to final against Russia.

"I can't put it into words," Price said. "Playing hockey, I usually don't get nervous. But this was really nerve-racking."

For Price, who gave up only seven goals in six games, the 2007 world juniors were vindication. He had gone to the evaluation camp in December '05 hoping to make the Canadian team defending the championship in his home province. Instead of a Team Canada sweater he was handed a bus ticket back to the Tri-City Americans. "I play for a team in the States so I didn't really even get to watch the tournament," Price said afterwards. "The one thing about getting cut is that you don't give up. I wasn't going to give up. I wanted to show the doubters. There are always doubters," he said. "They're out there."

Winger Darren Helm, here pushing a Czech opponent off the puck, brought strong two-way play and a physical presence to Canada's checking line.

Though he wouldn't name the doubters, it was clear to whom he was referring: Those who criticized the Montreal Canadiens for selecting him with the fifth pick in the first round of the 2005 NHL draft, and those who cut him from the Canadian junior team the year before.

Like any victory, the win over the U.S. wasn't a solo or even duo effort and it was full of subtexts, not the least of them Hartsburg's decision to go with Toews three times in the shootout, a strategy that would have been ruthlessly second-guessed if the outcome had been different.

There was still work to do. In the final the Canadian juniors would face a skilled and swift Russian team that had rolled over the host Swedes in their semifinal.

The defending champions came out in the first period as if on an adrenaline high carrying over from their shootout victory over the U.S. Again it was Toews who set the stage. Canada had jumped out in front 1–0 on a goal by Andrew Cogliano in the first period, but the lead didn't look safe at all. A few minutes before the intermission Toews drew a holding minor on Artem Anisimov and Bryan Little scored on the ensuing power play. On the next shift, with the Russians reeling, Toews scored the prettiest goal of the game, a roof-shot over goalie Semyon Varlamov's right shoulder, to make it 3–0 for Canada. Six minutes into the second period, Toews set up Brad Marchand to extend the lead.

After the fourth goal, the Canadians' energy level dropped. Toews said it was "natural to let up with a lead like that." It was also inevitable, given the frenetic pace of the game.

The second half of the game belonged to Price. The Russians beat him twice on

10 second-period shots, which on paper looks like a mediocre performance. It was anything but.

Late in the second period, he made the save of the tournament, one that will be up there with anything you see in any hockey season. Andrei Kiryukhin, the Russians' most dangerous forward, was parked off the edge of the crease, on Price's glove side. With Price kneeling and committed to the far post, the puck came over to Kiryukhin, who one-timed it. You could hear the air being sucked out of the arena, which was filled with Canadian fans who had travelled to Sweden. They were sure the Russians had scored once again. Kiryukhin seemed ready to raise his stick. And Danny Kurmann, the Swiss referee, was looking in the back of the net for the puck. Price was the only one on the ice and maybe the only person in the arena who knew he had it in his glove. "I couldn't look," forward Ryan O'Marra said. "I had my head in my gloves on the bench. I couldn't believe it when I looked up and heard the Canadian fans cheering." That save would have been reason enough to make the Russians believe it wasn't going to be their day.

After the medal presentation, Jonathan Toews and Carey Price stood outside the dressing room.

Toews was smiling—no, beaming—through the pain. He had a welt under his right eye, a cut across the bridge of his nose, and a patch of tender skin under one nostril where he'd had stitches removed days before. There was a big blotch of blood on the right sleeve of a sweater he has saved and never washed.

Carey Price was unmarked but subdued, keeping his emotions in check, as he did throughout. He had silenced Peter Mueller and the Americans and then the Russians. He almost meditatively took it all in, quiet satisfaction—his resolve issued from that silent bus ride out of Vancouver the year before.

The Canadian juniors stormed out to a 4–0 lead in the gold-medal game but had to hold off a surge from the Russians to secure the title.

2008

PARDUBICE
THE NARROW ESCAPE

DONNA SPENCER

Seventeen-year-old Steven Stamkos started out as a small part of the Canadian team's game plan in the 2008 WJC, but his smooth skating and smart defensive play earned him more ice time in the medal round.

Canada was distinctly lacking in humility upon the team's arrival in Pardubice, Czech Republic, for the 2008 world junior hockey championship. The players felt bulletproof.

Canada was riding an 18-game winning streak in the tournament. The golden run had survived a serious challenge the previous year in Leksand, Sweden. Most of the players on the 2008 team had thumped rival Russia a couple of months earlier in the Super Series, an eight-game set commemorating the 35th anniversary of the 1972 Summit Series. The Super Series was hardly super-competitive, with Canada outscoring Russia 39–13.

Head coach Craig Hartsburg preached to his players how hard it would be to win the country's fourth straight gold medal at the world junior championship. It was a tough sell, maybe an impossible one. He could see them nodding their heads and his words going in one ear and out the other.

"We knew at the start it was going to be a battle with young kids and a younger team," Hartsburg recalled. "The core group of kids went through that summer program without a real challenge.

"They had to experience that there were some good teams in this tournament and a lot better teams than the Russians in the summer."

Brad Marchand (number 17) was Canada's player of the game in the gold-medal victory over Sweden. Kyle Turris, about to take the faceoff, was the Canadians' leading scorer in the tournament.

One player who might have had a modicum of humbleness was Brad Marchand. He and defenceman Karl Alzner were the only two returning players from the previous year's squad.

As a veteran, Marchand was expected to be in the lineup again and put that experience to work. But coach Brent Sutter benched him in the final game of the Super Series for his lack of discipline and told Marchand he wouldn't play for Canada again if he didn't clean up his act.

Marchand was named to the team but still hadn't lost his swagger.

"After we dominated the Super Series, I think we thought we were going to walk through the world juniors," Marchand said.

Alzner, named the team's captain, felt the weight of the expectations created by three straight gold medals.

"Right away I felt a little bit more pressure because I didn't want to be the captain of a team that broke that streak," Alzner says now. "I know it's not a big deal, but to me it was."

This Canadian team was similar in makeup to the young squad that emerged victorious in Vancouver in 2006 despite having one returning player from the previous year. The 2008 group faced the additional challenges of taking it on the road to Europe and onto the bigger ice surface.

Three exhibition wins and then back-to-back shutouts against the host Czechs and Slovakia to open the tournament reinforced Canada's sense of invincibility. The players were so self-assured, the chatter in the dressing room between periods touched on non-hockey topics.

Their third game against Sweden was following the script in the Canadians' heads. They led 2–0 early in the third. What happened next was akin to a sucker punch in the solar plexus—and Canada would not recover easily from it.

When the Swedes had needed a 5–4 win over Belarus five years earlier to avoid relegation, it galvanized their hockey federation into examining what was missing in the development of their junior-aged players. Officials convened a summit conference to plot a new strategy. Better coaching for young goaltenders and fostering a more physical and aggressive game were identified as primary goals.

Those changes were manifested in the Swedish junior program by 2008. Sweden had 12 NHL draft picks on their WJC roster that year.

The biggest, fastest, and toughest Swedish team Canada had faced in years scored three unanswered goals starting at 5:14 of the third period to take a 3–2 lead.

Momentum swung hard to the Swedes on their second goal, when Tony Lagerstrom's shot from behind the goal line went off the back of goaltender Jonathan Bernier's skate.

Canada's Claude Giroux managed to tie the game at 16:18 with a power-play goal, but the Canadians were scrambling in the face of Sweden's pressure. Tobias Forsberg scored the winner for the Swedes with seven seconds left.

More than their inability to protect a lead, the Canadians were stunned by the discovery they had chinks in their armour.

When Alzner and assistant captains Marchand, Logan Pyett, Brandon Sutter, and Stefan Legein met with the coaching staff to analyze video the following day, they saw the room they gave Sweden's speed down the middle, breakdowns in coverage, missed backchecks, and turnovers.

While Canada generated more even-strength chances on offence than in their first two games, they also gave up more scoring chances to the Swedes.

With an average age of 18 years, 11 months, it was Canada's fifth-youngest team at the tournament. Their composure rattled, they faced the task of having to win a quarter-final en route to gold.

In the six years the tournament format awarded each pool winner a bye to the semifinal, only Russia in 1999 had won gold via a win in the quarters.

The loss to Sweden marked a sea change in Canada's attitude. It started to sink in that gold was not assured.

"We thought we were a little bit invincible before then," said Alzner. "We turned into a team that knew we had to be desperate every single game."

There was the danger, however, that the young team would not recover its confidence in time for the games to follow.

When they weren't at the rink, the Canadian players spent most of their time back at the hotel scanning the internet and reading email. After the loss to Sweden, the players read comments from some people at home doubting their ability to win another gold. That galvanized the team and drew them closer together in an us-against-the-world mentality.

"That struck a chord with everybody and kind of fired us up," Alzner recalled. "We were all more focused after that. We turned it up and were snapping the puck a little bit more."

Canada scored a 4–1 win over minnow Denmark in their next game. Even though their subsequent 4–2 quarter-final win over Finland booked Canada into the semis, there was a sense they were playing with white knuckles. The chemistry and confidence still wasn't quite there.

Swedish goaltender Jhonas Enroth stones Steven Stamkos in the gold-medal game. Canada struggled to get the puck to the Swedish net, managing only 20 shots in regulation time.

There wasn't any non-hockey talk in the dressing room now.

A subplot to the tournament was Hartsburg's decision to go with Steve Mason in goal for the medal round, even though some hockey pundits felt he should put Bernier in net.

Canada rarely had goaltending controversies extending into the tournament, as one of the two goalies usually established himself as the starter either during camp or in pre-tournament games.

The day of Canada's semifinal against the United States was tumultuous for Mason, who found out before the game that the London Knights had traded him to Kitchener. The timing couldn't have been worse, and Mason's focus was going to be even further tested.

Mason persevered. So did the team in front of him. Cockiness was a character flaw of this team, but it was balanced out by emotional resiliency.

Even when it looked doubtful Canada was strong enough to win gold again and the goaltending question loomed over the team, the players seemed unaffected off the ice.

They were still enjoying the experience of playing for their country. When it came to dealing with the media, they were a bunch of chatterboxes and relished the attention.

"We had a colourful group of guys," agreed Alzner. "When you get back to the hotel, you talk about the game for half an hour and then it's about having fun and being buddies. That's something that really helped us. We were tight-knit.

"You look at the guys now, where they are in their career, they're still talking lots and still letting that colourful attitude and personality come through."

Canada was also buoyed by the ever-growing army of fans from home who followed them to Europe. If Canadians didn't make up the majority of people in the stands, their raucous support made them the loudest of any country's contingent.

A 4–1 semifinal win over the United States put the Canadians back on firmer ground emotionally. They regained confidence, but not the arrogance they'd brought with them to the tournament. Mason quieted his critics with a 33-save performance against the Americans.

Craig Hartsburg made the toughest call a coach might face late in an international tournament: switching starting goaltenders. Hartsburg decided to go with Steve Mason (shown here) in place of Jonathan Bernier during the medal round.

Shawn Matthias crashes into goaltender Jhonas Enroth just as Matt Halischuk slides the puck into the net for the golden goal in the fourth minute of overtime.

"All we needed was to realize we could beat the good teams again," Alzner said.

But once again, Canada would face Sweden—now established as the tournament favourite with a fast, dangerous attack. Hartsburg was ill with the flu and had just 24 hours to prepare his team for the gold-medal game the next day.

The Canadians were ready for payback versus the Swedes. They'd matured over the course of the world junior tournament, but they would be pushed to the limit to get the gold.

Canada lost Legein to a shoulder injury in the first period, but led 2–0 after two periods on goals from Marchand and Giroux.

There was a sense of déjà vu in the third, however, as Jonathan Carlsson scored at 5:13 and Thomas Larsson tied it up with 38 seconds remaining in regulation and the Swedish net empty.

The extra game Canada had played in the quarter-final was taking its toll by the end of the championship game, as the Swedes outshot Canada 14–3 in the third period.

"We were literally halfway through the third period and it was like a switch went on for them and turned off for us," recalled Kyle Turris, Canada's scoring leader in the tournament.

Hartsburg had a job to do in the dressing room before overtime to calm down his distraught players.

"The first thing was to get them off thinking 'Well, we just blew the gold medal,'" Hartsburg said. "We had to get them settled down because there were kids who were devastated by it and they were pretty close to tears. We needed one shot and we talked about that immediately."

And as it turned out, it was just one shot. After Mason made three saves on the Swedes, Matt Halischuk swarmed their net and shovelled the puck past Jhonas Enroth at 3:36 of overtime. Canada's post-game celebration was a whirl of joy, gratitude, and relief.

Halischuk's goal will go down in history as one of the many big ones a Canadian has scored in the world junior championship. But as a defining moment, Canada might not have won without the dose of humility served to them in their earlier loss to the Swedes.

"You hate to say when you lose it's good, but it was the best thing that happened to the team," Hartsburg said.

Marchand was named player of the game for Canada in the final. He'd taken only two minor penalties the whole tournament and finished second in team scoring behind Turris with four goals and two assists.

Marchand agreed that both he and his teammates grew up during the 2008 championship.

"I think we thought it was going to come way too easy for us," Marchand said. "After that loss, we realized we had to suck it up and do everything we can to win the tournament."

Alzner often thinks about that roller coaster of a world junior tournament now that he's playing in the NHL.

"I look back on things like that, big games in tournaments like world juniors, for help sometimes when we do get into a sticky situation on the ice and I personally need something to propel me to play a little bit better," he says.

Riley Holzapfel waves the maple leaf after the gold-medal win over Sweden. In the last six minutes of regulation time, a tired Canadian team had given up a two-goal lead.

2009

OTTAWA
THE LAST GASP

GORD MILLER

In his second trip to the world juniors, 18-year-old John Tavares provided offensive skill up the middle for the Canadian team in Ottawa.

Jordan Eberle didn't have time to think about how his life was about to change, or about how close he was to scoring one of the most famous goals in Canadian hockey history. His only concern was how much time was left on the clock in the semifinal game of the 2009 world junior championship against Russia.

To be exact, at the moment the puck went into the net there were 5.4 seconds left.

Eberle had tied the score at five, gathering up a bouncing puck on a centring pass from John Tavares that had caromed off a Russian defender and onto his waiting stick. Seeing that Russian netminder Vadim Zhelobnyuk had gone down, Eberle went to his favourite move: forehand, backhand, up.

The Ottawa crowd exploded, and Eberle was mobbed by jubilant teammates. "I don't remember much," Eberle said, recalling the moments after the goal. "Except that P. K. Subban slammed into me pretty hard. My shoulder was sore for a while."

"I looked around and saw the Russians kneeling on the ice," Tavares said. "They were absolutely crushed."

In the broadcast booth high above the ice, I could feel the building shake from the roar of the crowd. There was no time to react, so I said the first words that came to mind: "CAN ... YOU ... BELIEVE IT!"

It was more of a statement than a question, because the truth was, I couldn't believe it.

———————

In a motel room near Comox, British Columbia, Al Murray, watching the game on television, smiled. The chief scout for Hockey Canada had known Eberle for years, having coached and later scouted him in their native Regina. Murray had seen that move countless times before, most often in the Eberle family driveway.

"My son Jake and Jordan went to school together and were teammates in all kinds of sports," Murray remembered. "We'd swing by Jordan's house and there he'd be in the driveway, with a stick and a tennis ball, going forehand, backhand, roof, over and over again."

Despite having such a close relationship with the chief scout, Eberle's spot on the 2009 national junior team was far from guaranteed. A prolific scorer in minor hockey, Eberle was often overlooked—his hometown Regina Pats didn't take him until the seventh round of the WHL draft.

Even with Murray in charge of player selection, Eberle wasn't invited to try out for the 2008 world junior team, one of the few highly ranked prospects for the NHL draft who wasn't there. The following summer, when Eberle was invited to the August evaluation camp in Ottawa, he struggled.

Eberle had just been drafted in the first round by Edmonton, and seemed anxious to prove that his new-found status was deserved. When the coaching staff finished the evaluations from the camp, Eberle was rated last among the 44 players in attendance. "He was awful," Murray said later, laughing.

———————

Like so many memorable moments for Canada at the world junior championships, Eberle's magical goal was the product of some hard work and more than a little good luck.

The road to a fifth straight gold medal began with a bumpy summer. Two weeks after the evaluation camp, head coach Benoit Groulx unexpectedly stepped down, taking a job with the AHL's Rochester Americans.

Picking one assistant over the other to be the head coach would be awkward, and finding someone on short notice outside the program wouldn't be easy either, since the coach would be asked to leave his junior team for nearly a month.

And so, Hockey Canada president Bob Nicholson picked up the phone and once again called an old friend: Pat Quinn.

Quinn was already one of Canada's most decorated international coaches, having guided the Canadian men's team to gold at the 2002 Olympics in Salt Lake City.

In addition, he had answered the call in the spring of 2008, coaching the Canadian under-18 team to gold in the World Championship in Kazan, Russia.

Picking Quinn to coach the under-18s was a surprising choice to say the least. While Quinn had a wealth of experience, his years in the NHL had been marked by whispers that he didn't get along with young players.

Now, fresh off another gold medal and two years removed from his last NHL job, Quinn once again accepted Nicholson's invitation. "I wanted to put that whole thing about young players behind me," he said. "And besides, I was bouncing off the walls."

Quinn's 2009 Canadian junior team included six players who had been with him the previous spring in Kazan. One of the six was Eberle, who had played well for Quinn on the under-18 team and had overcome his bad August camp with a blistering start to his season in Regina.

This Team Canada was younger than usual, as eight players, including Steven Stamkos and Drew Doughty, had not been released by their NHL teams. On the eve of the tournament, chief scout Al Murray made a bold prediction.

"He's not the biggest guy or the fastest skater," Murray said. "But when it's all said and done, I think Jordan Eberle will score some big goals for this team."

After three games, it didn't seem as if any heroics would be required in Ottawa, because drama was in short supply. Canada opened with an 8–1 win over the Czechs, beat Kazakhstan 15–0, and then won 5–1 against Germany. The aggregate score of 28–2, combined with the fact that Canada had won the previous four world junior tournaments, had critics wondering if the competition had become too one-sided.

But on New Year's Eve Canada faced the United States in the first tough test of the tournament—and almost failed it miserably.

Less than 13 minutes in, the Americans had seized a 3–0 lead, silencing the Ottawa crowd and forcing Quinn to call a time out. "Have you forgotten how to play?" Quinn asked his bewildered players. But he calmed them, and urged them to get back to basics.

"He has this unbelievable presence," Eberle said later. "Everything about him is big: his head, his hands, his voice."

But Quinn was more than just a figurehead; he was also a veteran NHL coach who knew how to run a bench. He immediately began double-shifting his best player, John Tavares of the Oshawa Generals. Tavares was a breakout star in the 2008 tournament in the Czech Republic, and now was one of only four returning players in Ottawa.

Two explosive first-period goals by John Tavares led a rally from an early 3–0 deficit to a key opening-round victory over the United States.

Tavares scored two quick goals, and Eberle scored before the end of the period to tie the score at three. The game was fiercely contested the rest of the way before Canada scored two empty-net goals to win 7–4.

"We hadn't really been challenged to that point," Eberle remembered. "We were way too jacked up at the start of that game. It was a good lesson for us."

It was already being called a classic, the most exciting game Canada had ever played at the WJC. It was inconceivable that just three days later, the team would play in an even better one.

———

"Right from the start, that Russia game was wild," Eberle said. "We'd score, and they'd come right back, and every time we thought we were finally in control, they'd come back again."

A last-minute icing call in the third period against the Russians set in motion events that led to one of the most memorable goals in the history of Canadian hockey: Jordan Eberle's tally with 5.4 seconds left that took the 2009 semifinal into overtime. Here, the puck comes to Eberle at the edge of Vadim Zhelobnyuk's crease.

Canada took a quick 1–0 lead, but the Russians answered, a chain of events that would repeat itself four times, as Canada took leads of 2–1, 3–2 (on a goal by Eberle), and 4–3, only to see the Russians come back every time.

Now, with 2:20 to go, there was a scramble to the right of Canadian goaltender Dustin Tokarski. Russia's Dimitri Klopov poked home the loose puck for his second score of the game and the Russians led for the first time, 5–4. The Ottawa crowd fell silent.

As he did against the United States, Quinn tried to steady his team. When Russia's Dmitri Kugryshev iced the puck with 1:24 left, Quinn called a time out and pulled Tokarski from the Canadian goal.

Quinn normally left tactics to his assistants, but this time he ran the time out himself, at one point telling Eberle, "If the puck is on the right hand side, get to the net." It was a play Quinn had used countless times in the final minutes of games in the NHL. (Later, he was asked how many times it had worked. "Not very often," he said with a chuckle.)

With 41 seconds left, Klopov gained control of the puck in his own zone. Despite having time and space to move the puck ahead, he fired down the ice at the empty Canadian net, perhaps looking for the hat trick. He missed. It was icing, and the faceoff came back to the Russian zone. Far from being distraught, Klopov and his Russian teammates were laughing as they prepared for the faceoff.

"When I saw that, I was really hoping it would come back and bite them," Eberle said.

After Canada had won a third straight faceoff in the Russian zone, Cody Hodgson got a good shot away with 24 seconds left, but Zhelobnyuk kicked it to the corner. The puck went to Nikita Filatov, who tried to clear it on his backhand, but Ryan Ellis read the play and moved to cut it off. Ellis slammed into the boards, actually knocking the puck down with his shoulder to keep it in. Instead of blindly throwing the puck toward the goal, Ellis squeezed it by two Russian defenders along the boards.

In the ensuing scramble, Tavares poked the puck free. Russian defenceman Vyacheslav Voinov went to clear it, but Hodgson deftly lifted his stick. The puck went back to Tavares, who saw three Russian players around him. "I knew there wasn't much time left, and when I saw all those Russians along the wall, I just threw it blindly toward the net, thinking maybe there was an opening," he recalled.

Jordan Eberle was sliding across the goalmouth on his knees when he answered Canadian fans' prayers against the Russians.

Goaltender Dustin Tokarski had won a Memorial Cup with Spokane in the spring of 2008 before landing the starter's job with the Canadian juniors. Coach Pat Quinn gave Tokarski a vote of confidence despite his struggles in games against the United States and Russia.

Remembering Quinn's instructions, Eberle left the battle along the boards and moved to the slot. When Russian defenceman Dmitri Kulikov tried to block the shot, the puck bounced off his shin pad and went right to Eberle, whose momentum was carrying him to the front of the Russian goal. Forehand, backhand, up. Tie game.

Unlike Paul Henderson's goal in the 1972 Summit Series, Mario Lemieux's goal in the 1987 Canada Cup, or Sidney Crosby's gold-medal clincher in Vancouver in 2010, Jordan Eberle's goal didn't win the game for Canada. Pat Quinn thinks that's why it's so widely remembered.

"If Henderson doesn't score, or Lemieux or Crosby don't score, those games continue, and who knows what happens," Quinn said. "If Jordan Eberle doesn't score, the game is over and there's no gold medal."

The rest of the game was something of an anticlimax. Canada dominated the OT but didn't score, sending the game to a shootout. Tavares and Eberle scored on the first two shots for Canada, while Russian coach Sergei Nemchinov mysteriously left his best player, Filatov, to shoot third. He never got the chance. Tokarski stopped the first two Russian shooters and the game was over.

Two days later, Eberle had three points as Canada beat Sweden 5–1 to win a fifth straight goal medal.

Jordan Eberle isn't much for collecting souvenirs. The puck he put in the Russian net went back into play and was never recovered. Eberle kept using the same stick in the OT, the shootout, the gold-medal game, and even two more games in the WHL until the shaft finally snapped. Eberle discarded the stick, but the Pats equipment man, knowing it was the one he had used to score the now famous goal, retrieved it and kept it for him.

Eberle's biggest thrill came two months later, when he met Paul Henderson, who welcomed him into the exclusive club of Canadians who had scored iconic international goals. "Congratulations, Jordan," Henderson said. "You'll be talking about that goal for the rest of your life."

Of all the moments I have called, the one I am asked about most is "the Eberle goal." More than a year after he scored it, I was walking through my neighbourhood and

came across a bunch of kids playing road hockey. Sure enough, one of them went forehand, backhand, roof and looked over at me, smiling.

"C'mon," he said. "Say it."

"CAN ... YOU ... BELIEVE IT!" I boomed, my voice echoing down the street. The kids raised their sticks, roaring their approval.

Even now, it gives me chills.

Eberle's goal against Russia wasn't a game-winner, but it was a game-saver and kept Canada's hopes alive for a fifth straight gold medal.

2010

SASKATOON
THE END OF THE GOLDEN RUN

ROY MacGREGOR

Brayden Schenn goes airborne to deck U.S. forward Derek Stepan in the neutral zone. Two tight games between Canada and the United States kept fans in Saskatchewan on the edge of their seats.

Crunch!

Crunch!

Crunch!

These are not the sounds of the game being played—though there was much physical contact, as usual, at the 2010 world junior hockey championship—but the sound of people walking to and from the rink, the sound of heavy boots on hard, frozen snow, the sounds that carry at –30°C and below.

Welcome to the true home of the winter game. It is not an actual place—not Windsor, Nova Scotia; not Kingston, Ontario; not Montreal, all of which claim to have been the true birthplace of hockey—but a climate, the game Canadian weather created born of necessity where one must find a way to keep warm as well as keep moving over ice as slippery as a soaped glass.

"In a land so inescapably and inhospitably cold," Bruce Kidd and John Macfarlane wrote many years ago, "hockey is the dance of life, an affirmation that despite the deathly chill of winter we are alive."

And nowhere is the game more alive than on the Canadian prairies. Here is where the hockey rink became the natural community gathering place for towns otherwise fragmented by immigrants arriving from Europe with different languages

Jake Allen won the starting job, but he was pulled from the Canadian goal in the third period of the gold-medal game.

and different churches. Here—just on the outside of Saskatoon—is where little Floral once stood, the small community where a neighbour returned Katherine Howe's kindness during the Great Depression by dropping off a gunny sack containing a pair of old skates. Katherine's awkward son, Gordie, tried them out on the pond back of the house, "fell in love with hockey that day"—and the rest is history.

Those who love hockey could not help but love a WJC held in Regina and Saskatoon in the dead of Canadian winter. Crunching snow, early dark, battery jumps in the parking lots, 50/50 draws worth as much as a new home, volunteers happily paying $50 apiece for the "privilege" of giving up their holiday time in exchange for long days at the rink helping stage this remarkable event.

Team Canada even arrived with its own compelling storyline from the Prairies: Travis Hamonic, a 19-year-old defenceman with the Moose Jaw Warriors who had grown up in little St. Malo, Manitoba, and who used to drive to the rink on his Ski-Doo, hockey bag thrown over the back and sticks held across the handlebars. Hamonic was the youngest of four children and hoped, one day, to be like older brother Jesse, who played. Their father, Gerald, had been head of the local minor hockey system until he died suddenly of heart failure. Travis had been only 10 at the time and had dedicated his junior career to his father's memory. Deeply religious, he wore No. 3 to honour the Holy Trinity—Father, Son, and Holy Spirit—and before each game would write a private message to his father on the blade of his stick, quickly taping over the secret words before anyone else could see.

The City of Saskatoon itself even offered a charming connection between the national game and local politics, with Mayor Don Atchison having once been the goaltender for the local junior team, the Saskatoon Blades, and later enjoying a brief minor-league professional career in which he tended net for the Johnston Jets, the wonky team that inspired *Slap Shot*, the 1977 cult movie about hockey. Atchison's locker was next to Ned Dowd's, a player who took notes for his sister Nancy, who wrote the Hollywood screenplay. Dowd took Atchison's crazy sense of humour and the personality of the team's other goalie, Louis Levasseur, and out of that created Denis Lemieux ("You feel shame"), a character as beloved as Paul Newman's Reggie

Dunlop and the infamous Hanson Brothers. "Everything in that movie is true," claims the mayor of Saskatoon.

A much more evident truth is that the "world juniors" has come to mean something very, very special to all Canadians—especially when played in Canada. It has become as much a part of the annual Christmas break as Boxing Day sales and New Year's hangovers. It is an 11-day festival that begins the day after Christmas and extends into the heart of winter itself, as the game of cold and ice should. It also helps, of course, that Canada wins the tournament often, thereby calming the insecurities that fly up each time the country that gave the world this game has to give the world credit for playing it as well as, even sometimes better than, Canadians themselves.

Team Canada came to Saskatoon with a chance to mark its sixth successive victory in the championship. Victory in Saskatoon on the final day would mean that this string would surpass the record five in a row that Canada set in the 1990s and matched in Ottawa in 2009. Canada's success had already proved to be a remarkable accomplishment—five gold, four silver, and three bronze over the past 12 championships—and stood as a powerful statement that the game at the youth level has never been in as excellent shape as it is today.

The Canadian team rallied around Travis Hamonic, who had to watch the final from the sidelines with a separated shoulder.

The pride Canadian players bring is obvious. "When you pull on a world junior jersey," Team Canada forward and Regina native Jordan Eberle, the hero of the gold-medal victory in Ottawa, said when he came to his home province, "you're expected to win gold. That's just how it is. For me and for every kid on this team, we grew up watching this tournament. It's a special event. Kids grow up dreaming of playing in it."

"These kids are all prospects for the NHL," added Taylor Hall, the Windsor Spitfires star many were predicting (accurately, it turned out) would go first overall in the NHL draft the following June. "I think fans have an interest in watching that. When I was a little kid, there was nothing better than watching the world juniors with my buddies on Boxing Day. It's something special to Canadians. It's a combination of hockey, for sure, and holidays. I find it attracts even non–hockey fans."

Willie Desjardins, the Saskatchewan-born coach of the Canadian team, tried to put it all into perspective when he said one beauty of the tournament is that, each year, it contains "a little bit of the unknown and a little bit of the unexpected." And while the outcome could often be a surprise, the interest in the tournament is no surprise at all. "It's the time of year," Desjardins said. "Everybody's home with their families and it's something they do together.

"It's hockey and it's Canada."

The 2009 WJC had been decided in Ottawa by that 6–5 final, a score held to be almost sacred in Canadian hockey circles when it came to discussing the greatest of games ever played in hockey. Paul Henderson's dramatic last-minute goal in the 1972 Summit Series had given Canada a 6–5 victory over the Soviet Union. Wayne Gretzky's pass to Mario Lemieux and Lemieux's rifle shot had given Canada the 1987 Canada Cup by a 6–5 score. It seemed only fitting that one of the greatest WJC games ever played should also end 6–5.

Even before the medal round, Saskatoon had enjoyed a world junior match between Canada and the United States that set the stage, brilliantly, for the final. Before a record crowd of 15,171 at Credit Union Centre—the stands bleeding red with screaming Canadian fans—Team U.S.A. and Team Canada fought to a 4–4 tie that ultimately went to a shootout. It had been a game for the ages so far as early-round matches go, the lead changing twice, the swift Americans scoring two short-handed goals, the determined Canadians coming back from being down 4–2 and scoring short-handed to tie the game in the dying minutes. Canada's Jordan Eberle, the previous year's hero, had scored twice, Stefan Della Rovere once, and Alex Pietrangelo had delivered the tying goal by intercepting a clearing pass and roofing a shot just under the crossbar. Philip McRae, Jordan Schroeder, Tyler Johnson, and Danny Kristo had all scored for Team U.S.A.

In the wild shootout that was held to settle matters, Canada scored on all three

of its shots (Eberle, Nazem Kadri, and Brandon Kozun), while the Americans matched goal for goal (Kristo and Jeremy Morin) until the final shooter of the night (Schroeder) failed to score when Canadian goaltender Jake Allen scissored his pads closed to deny the shot.

It was clear, by this game, that the Americans had become the new rivals to the Canadians—two teams perfectly matched on the ice and two countries forever rubbing up against each other off the ice. It was fitting that the two North American rivals were meeting in a gold-medal game held in—as hockey promoter Bill Hunter put it years ago when Saskatoon was wooing the St. Louis Blues—the very *heart* of the continent. As Canadian poet Al Purdy had once said, victory in hockey, especially against the United States, serves "as a Canadian specific to salve the anguish of inferiority at being good at something the Americans aren't."

The shootout victory over Team U.S.A. gave Canada a bye into the semifinals. The Americans now had to play Finland in order to survive. And survive the Americans did, defeating Finland to advance against pre-tournament favourite Sweden and then winning that match 5–2 to reach the final. Canada, on the other hand, had a skate in the park by comparison, as they next met unheralded Switzerland, the tournament surprise when they bumped out Russia with a 3–2 overtime victory. Drained and missing their best defenceman to injury, the Swiss had fallen easily to Canada, 6–1.

It set up a rematch that was jokingly referred to as "Groundhog Day in Saskatoon"—the Canadians and Americans meeting again on the same ice to settle

Taylor Hall celebrates Greg Nemisz's goal that tied the score 2–2 in the first period of the gold-medal game.

the score once and for all. "A shootout loss is not really a loss," rationalized Team U.S.A.'s Kristo. "It shows up as a loss, but it's not really a loss."

If the Americans found inspiration in avenging that shootout, then the Canadians had theirs in Travis Hamonic. The young defenceman from little St. Malo, Manitoba, had gone down with a separated shoulder in the final moments of the semifinal. He wouldn't be suiting up in the game he had worked so hard to get to, and he wouldn't be playing for the gold medal he had dreamed since childhood of winning. This time he wouldn't be writing that private message to his late father before the game and then taping over the blade so only he would know what he said. Now, the message was for him, and completely public. "We're going to try and go out there and win it for him," said Canadian forward Brayden Schenn.

The Canadians scored on their first shot, and then their fifth, while the Americans

Jordan Eberle scored eight goals in six games in the 2010 tournament, but there would be no repeat of 2009's magical goal in his second bid for gold.

matched the Canadian goals and then moved ahead to take a 3–2 lead. When Canada tied the game at 3–3 early in the second period, the American side pulled goaltender Mike Lee in favour of Jack Campbell, who had played so well in the New Year's classic that Canada had finally taken 5–4 in the shootout. Campbell was an instant standout, continually stopping what seemed, at times, a Canadian stampede to the American net.

It was not to be the only goaltending change, though, with Canada pulling Jake Allen after the Americans scored twice in the third period and replacing Allen with Martin Jones. The change seemed to fire up the Canadians, with Jordan Eberle once again the Canadian hero as he scored twice on the brilliant Campbell in a span of 2:49 to, once again, force overtime in the gold-medal game. Eberle's two, combined with Canadian goals from Luke Adam, Greg Nemisz, and Taylor Hall, matched the five goals from five different Team U.S.A. players: Chris Kreider, Jordan Schroeder, John Carlson, Jerry D'Amigo, and Derek Stepan.

But there would be no shootout this time. And no sixth straight gold medal for Canada. Instead, the dramatic game was ended at 4:21 of the overtime when Team U.S.A. broke up ice on a three-on-one break and rushing defenceman Carlson, with his second goal of the night, beat Jones fairly with a hard blast from the left circle.

Final score, 6–5. Just like all the great games ever played.

And Travis Hamonic, shoulder in a sling, had a medal for his father—just not the gold one he had prayed for.

American John Carlson's overtime goal silenced the crowd in Saskatoon and denied the Canadians a sixth consecutive gold medal.

2011

BUFFALO
THE BORDER CROSSING

ROY MacGREGOR

Carter Ashton hoists an opponent along the boards in Canada's 10–1 romp over Norway. The Canadians had things their own way throughout the tournament up to the third period of the gold-medal game.

It is shortly after midnight, January 6, 2011. Traffic is still heavy on the Peace Bridge that spans the Niagara River between Fort Erie, Ontario, and Buffalo, New York. Vehicles holding red-jerseyed, face-painted, hoarse Canadians who, earlier in the evening, had packed the HSBC Arena to witness the most astonishing collapse in world junior championship history are slowly making their way home.

In one car sits Dan Visentin, the driver, who refuses to turn on the radio because he knows only too well what they will be saying and he does not wish to hear the one word that is bouncing about the airwaves: "choke," the ultimate curse word in hockey. Besides Dan, the car holds Liz, his wife, like Dan a schoolteacher, and his parents, Italo and Rita, who decades ago immigrated to Canada and found their dream life in Niagara Falls. They were now following the great dream of their grandson, Mark, and had just witnessed its shattering.

The green light signalled them up to the booth. Dan rolled down the window, preparing to hand over the four passports.

"How ya doing tonight?" the Canadian border guard asked.

"Depressed," Dan answered.

The guard flicked through the top passport, paused and looked up, surprised.

"You're a Visentin," he said.

Canadian goaltender Mark Visentin knew all about the loneliest position in the game.

"I'm the father."

The guard handed back the passports. "Don't worry," he said. "You have a great kid there—you got to be proud of him."

"We are."

"He's going to be a great goalie one day."

"We know."

The first time Mark Visentin tried playing goal, he "fell in love with it." His hero was "CuJo"—Curtis Joseph of the Toronto Maple Leafs—and he tried to emulate Joseph's style. He played on backyard rinks and driveways and in the street in little Waterdown, Ontario. He even played with the family dog, Sheeba, the golden retriever who had grown up with him, changing from a puppy who happily chased balls that missed the net Mark was guarding to a faithful old dog, herself a teenager now, who was simply content to get a pat on the head and her ears scratched. There was no one in her life as important as Mark, her lifelong playmate.

Goaltenders, as the entire hockey world has long known, are both different people and special people. The great Russian goaltender Vladislav Tretiak called it the most "noble" position in all of sport. Gump Worsley argued it was "not a job that would interest any normal, straight-thinking human." Hall of Famer Jacques Plante once asked, "How would you like it if you were sitting in your office and you made one little mistake. Suddenly, a big red light went on and 18,000 people jumped up and started screaming at you, calling you a bum and an imbecile and throwing garbage at you."

Mark Visentin's a reflective young man who possesses an understanding of the potential rewards and gut-wrenching risks that his position entails. "The goaltender can be a game-changer," he says, "and that is a great feeling. But if you're going to do that, you have to accept the ups and downs."

Heading into the 2011 world junior championship, it had been all ups. A brilliant minor hockey goaltender, he had made the leap to major junior at 16. At 17, six weeks short of his 18th birthday, he became a first-round draft pick (chosen 27th overall) of the Phoenix Coyotes. He was already a junior star with the Niagara IceDogs and hoped to have a professional career, but as he was also an excellent student he had a backup plan: a degree at nearby Brock University. He had a girlfriend, Harmony, and life could hardly be better for a kid just turned 18.

Team Canada 2011 came to Buffalo with tremendous promise and a few questions. The team had been selected with an eye to assembling a roster of, as head coach Dave Cameron put it, "200-foot players." He did not, fortunately, mean height, but rather style. Cameron and management wanted solid, working-class players who were comfortable at both ends of the ice. With a number of flashier juniors left off the team, there were naturally questions raised concerning who would do the scoring, but there were also questions raised as to who would stop the scoring from the other side. From a list of top junior goaltenders the choice came down to two: Olivier Roy, a 19-year-old native of Causapscal, Quebec, playing for the Acadie-Bathurst Titan, and 18-year-old Mark Visentin.

Roy, the more experienced of the two, had been chosen to start Canada's first three games, but when Canada lost a 6–5 shootout to another pre-tournament favourite, Sweden, the decision was made to give Visentin a chance the next game—which would be Switzerland and a game that, of course, Canada could be expected to win handily.

It was not an auspicious debut. The Canada-Switzerland game was barely a minute old when, back of the Canadian net, two Swiss forwards came up with a puck that should already have been cleared safely away by the Canadian defence. Inti Pestoni came around the net and flipped a soft shot that somehow slipped in between Visentin's right pad and the post.

Oooooooooooooops.

It was, however, the only goal the pesky Swiss could manage. Canada went on to a 4–1 victory and the chance to meet nemesis Team U.S.A.—the gold-medal winner in Saskatoon only the year before—in the 2011 semifinal. Visentin, who had stopped the 21 other shots directed his way, was philosophical about the first. "I didn't want that to happen," he said. "But it's over and you can't change that."

He talked about how he had been working on his "mental focus" as much as his angles. He had been learning not to get down on himself, not to doubt—the debilitating bug that all goaltenders must fight off from time to time. "There were 59 minutes left," he told himself. More than enough time to repair matters.

He talked about the possibility of him now facing the Americans. A year earlier he had watched the championship being played out in Saskatoon and the final had been "a heartbreaker." He wanted to be a part of the avenging of Saskatoon.

He got his wish. Visentin started against the arch-rival Americans and played well, with Canada winning 4–1 to advance once again to the key gold-medal match. What was surprising was the opponent: Russia. The Russians had barely been on the radar heading into the tournament, losing their first two matches to Canada (6–3) and Sweden (2–0), but they had since fashioned the two most remarkable comebacks of 2011. Down 3–1 against the Finns, they had won 4–3 in overtime, then had tied the Swedes in the dying seconds of Sunday's semifinal game to force overtime and get to a shootout, which they won.

Instead of the anticipated United States–Canada match, the gold medal had come down to Canada vs. Russia.

———————

These Russians could not be taken lightly—not after such dramatic comebacks against Finland and Sweden—and the Canadians did not take them lightly. Team Canada captain Ryan Ellis opened the scoring with a blast from the point on an early Canadian power play. Before the first period was over, Canada was up 2–0 on big Carter Ashton's goal. When Brayden Schenn made it 3–0—a seemingly insurmountable lead—it marked Schenn's 18th point of the tournament, tying him for the all-time Team Canada single tournament scoring lead with Dale McCourt, who had set the mark in 1977—back before Hockey Canada had established the Program of Excellence.

To gain some sense of the shock to come, it is worth noting that those who were voting on the tournament's top players handed in their ballots at the end of the second period. Schenn, to no surprise, was named tournament MVP as well as best forward. Ellis was named the top defenceman. And top goaltender title went to Team U.S.A.'s Jack Campbell.

And then it happened. In less than five minutes of play, the Russians managed six shots on young Visentin and scored three times—and the period was not even half over. You could almost see the blood drain from the red-painted faces of the Canadian fans who had packed the HSBC Arena to cheer on what had appeared a certain Canadian victory.

The Russians moved ahead 4–3 when Artemi Panarin managed to elude three Canadian checkers to slip the puck past Visentin and scored again in the dying moments to make it 5–3, all five Russian goals coming in a third period that was

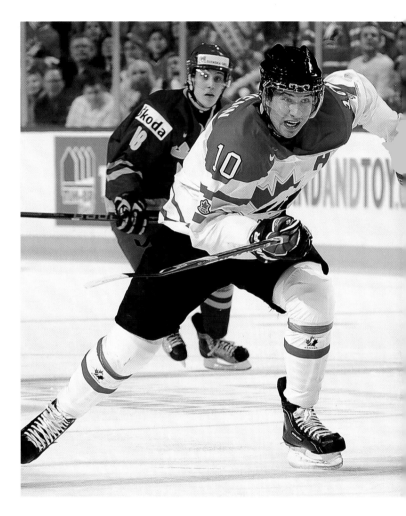

already being tagged "a monumental collapse." Many were even saying the word that losing players and coaches most dread: "choke."

Who, people wanted to know, was to blame for this humiliation? Cameron for failing to pull his goalie as the Russians had done? Team Canada scouts and officials for failing to add snipers? Or Mark Visentin, the goaltender who couldn't stop the Russian flood? As Jacques Plante so eloquently put it more than half a century earlier, the goalie gets the blame, no matter what.

The Russian national anthem was played, and the Canadians, silver medals hanging like albatrosses around their necks, left the ice and hurried through the media availability without even looking up. Mark Visentin had sobbed openly on the ice and cried some more in the dressing room. He heard Hockey Canada's André Brin asking some of the other players if anyone was ready to speak to the waiting media.

"I'll come out," he volunteered, surprising Brin.

In his second trip to the tournament, Brayden Schenn racked up 18 points, more than any other player in the history of the Program of Excellence.

The gathered media were even more surprised. Here was this 18-year-old kid who had just been at the centre of a crushing turn of events and he was ready to talk. A few in the media noted how clear his eyes were: shouldn't he be off somewhere crying?

And yet he stood there, towering over the microphones and notepads, head held high, and he spoke for as long as there were questions—even though no language could possibly provide equal answers.

———

Mark Visentin dressed slowly, still processing what had happened. The teammates said their goodbyes—painful and poignant—and Mark found Harmony waiting outside, as arranged, and the two began the long drive back in the dark. He knew his parents and grandparents would have already crossed over and he made it through without comment, without a border guard recognizing his name. He drove slowly

Left: Canadian captain Ryan Ellis brought savvy puck-handling skills to the blue line in his third WJC.

Above: Defenceman Maxim Berezin lines up Carter Ashton in the final. With the gold medal on the line, the older, bigger Russians physically wore down the Canadians.

Mark Visentin is beaten for a goal in the third period against the Russians. He showed dignity beyond his years in the wake of a wrenching defeat in the gold-medal game.

back to his parents' home in Waterdown. No radio for them, either. He didn't need to hear his own words played back to him.

"I like to get stuff done and not leave it," he told me a couple of days later.

He put no blame on the defence that, at times, let him down, no blame on the forwards who had their own breakdowns. He took full responsibility.

"I'm not the guy who blames his team," he said. "You really wish you could have provided a couple of saves when they were needed."

He had felt the tide turning. He watched the spark go into the Russians and knew that it had gone out of his own team. "We pushed the panic button a bit," he said. "We tried to get back but….

"No one to blame but me. I try to make myself accountable for what happens."

He was, however, being held accountable by others, perhaps too shocked or too angry to allow for perspective. Hockey means so much to Canadians, and success has been so regular, that only success seems acceptable. People who might not expect their own teen to clean up his room or take out the garbage were not only expecting, but demanding, that these teenagers take on the best hockey teams in the world and remain, always, the best hockey team in the world.

Yet even those who knew this made no sense were concerned. What, they wondered, would be the long-term effect of such an experience? They needed to be reminded that in Game 5 of the 1972 Summit Series, the original Team Canada had been up 4–1 in the third period in Moscow only to have the Soviets score four unanswered goals and win. The goaltender in net for that "monumental collapse" was Tony Esposito, who was in the prime of his Hall of Fame career.

"People lose perspective," Dan Visentin said of his son a few days after the game. "Mark will be fine. He's got his whole future in front of him."

Mark, however, had driven home that night in silence, thinking more on his past. "It was weird," he remembered. "There was just so much to take in." He thought about former coaches, teammates. He was grateful for his relationship with his family, with Ben Vanderklok, a coach with the Niagara IceDogs who had been working so hard with Mark on the importance of personal mental toughness.

"It was a tough pill to swallow," he said of what had happened. "But I think I'm a better person for it."

If he could handle this, he knew, he could handle anything. He knew now that he was strong enough to leave it behind him, to move on. There would be more "ups" coming.

No one was up when Mark came through the front door that evening. But then, almost immediately, came the sound of an old dog's nails moving along the floor. Sheeba, still going strong at 14, came hurrying toward him, wiggling and tail wagging.

"She was just happy to see me," he said.

And he her, considering the day he had just put in at the most noble position in the game.

EPILOGUE

BOB NICHOLSON,
PRESIDENT AND CEO,
HOCKEY CANADA

The Program of Excellence has grown by our willingness to learn. When we've made mistakes, we've learned from them. When we've had successful approaches, we've tried to repeat them. That said, we had to make sure that we didn't settle for the same old thing. We haven't stayed in one place with our program. We couldn't. We've had to keep evolving, after our victories and our defeats. It's not change for change's sake. We've been forced to adjust because other programs have learned from us and they improve every year. The world junior championship was always a tough tournament to win, but it's tougher now than ever before. The last two tournaments prove the point.

Sweden won its lone WJC title back in 1981, the season before the launch of our Program of Excellence. The Swedes have won world championships and Olympic gold and sent scores of stars to the NHL. They often failed to live up to expectations at the WJC. That, however, has not been the case in recent years. The Swedish Ice Hockey Association has placed a greater emphasis on its junior program and the teams wearing the Tre Kronor are at or near the front of the pack in virtually every season. The Swedes beat our team in the qualifying rounds in Pardubice in the 2008 WJC and, in the rematch with the gold medal on the line, a hard-fought contest went to overtime before Matt Halischuk scored the golden goal.

Through the WJC's first 20 years, U.S. teams were only occasionally a factor. Over the last decade, however, the United States has come away with two golds,

the most recent when they beat our team in overtime of the 2010 gold-medal game in Saskatoon. We know from experience that a gold is hard to win on the road and hardest in the other team's building. You have to give Team U.S.A. full credit for what they were able to do. We go into every tournament now knowing that the United States is going to have a strong team.

Russian teams were the dominant force in the tournament back before the Program of Excellence and almost always a gold-medal threat. Some people have thought that Russia's junior program has been in a downturn because there haven't been breakthrough Russian stars in the NHL since Alexander Ovechkin and Evgeni Malkin. Maybe people have forgotten that it took a last-second goal by Jordan Eberle just to send the semifinal into overtime in 2009. It hardly looked like the Russian program was on hard times when its team stormed back on us in the third period of the gold-medal game in Buffalo.

Those were narrow wins and tough losses, but the greater lesson to learn goes deeper than the gold-medal games: nothing can be taken for granted. No tournament. No game. We saw it in the game the Americans lost to Slovakia in the quarters in Ottawa, and in the Russians' loss to Switzerland in Saskatoon. Any gaps between the teams in this tournament have closed dramatically. Other countries are dedicating more resources and more money to the development of young players. They've moved aggressively and I think that makes what we've accomplished in the last 10 years with the Program of Excellence look all the more impressive. I know that it is going to make our next 10 years an even greater challenge.

I don't think it's a coincidence that our program produced some of Team Canada's greatest moments after our biggest disappointments.

When we were disqualified from the 1987 WJC in Piestany because of the bench-clearing brawl, we came back the next year with a highly disciplined squad and beat a great Soviet team in Moscow. We instilled in our players a better sense of what it was going to take to win, not just technically but also emotionally. Over the years it's been a message we deliver to all the players who come through the program. That said, we don't avoid players who might seem like risks because of their histories in major junior. When Steve Downie came to us for the first time back in December 2005, we told him that he would have to check a lot of his emotions or impulses at the door. The same applied with Steve Ott a few years earlier. Both players and others like them appreciated our position of having open minds about them and they played very well for us.

When we lost in Füssen in 1992, we tried to do something different in the run-up to the tournament. We added players to the lineup on the eve of the round robin, ignoring what we had learned about assembling a team and establishing good chemistry. Our poor result in that tournament forced us to take a long, hard look—not at the players, but at ourselves. We had forgotten how valuable our team building had been to our success. We tried to take a shortcut and the loss fell on us. What might have worked out with a team over the course of a hockey season is tougher to pull off in a short tournament. There's no time for a learning curve. The team has to be ready to play immediately, from the first shift of the first period of the first game. In Füssen, we thought the players would come together—but they simply did not have enough time.

Our greatest assets going forward aren't anything money can buy. They are our people. When I say this, I'm not talking about our players being superior. No, I'm talking about the Canadian Hockey League executives we've developed excellent working relationships with and the coaches who've learned and grown in Hockey Canada's programs over the years. I'm talking about physicians, sports psychologists, trainers, and technical staff who volunteer their time for us. And I'm talking about grass-roots supporters who have contributed in hundreds of different ways to the development of the players who represent this nation at the WJC.

There isn't a particular profile that we seek out for the Program of Excellence. There isn't a "company man." We've had a wide range of characters and they've displayed their mettle at the tournament. They've faced a variety of challenges and been forced to respond to them in ways they could not have anticipated.

Perry Pearn has always been thought of as a tactician and technical coach rather than a fiery, emotional presence. He had to break that mould in Sweden in 1993. Perry's players seemingly had no gas left in the tank when they made it to the gold-medal game. He came up with an emotional speech that many would have thought was out of character. Later, he placed his championship ring on a table and walked out of the dressing room. Those are inspired coaching moments, spontaneous decisions made in the heat of battle.

Brent Sutter faced an entirely different set of challenges with the teams he coached in 2005 and 2006. In his first go-round at the WJC, Brent had a power-house team. His challenge was to keep his players focused and any egos in check. The next year, however, was a very different set of circumstances: a team that went into the gold-medal game as an underdog in the minds of many. Instead of worrying about egos, Brent had to be concerned about nerves and self-doubts. The result was the same—in fact, our team's performance in the 2006 gold-medal game might have been more impressive than the final the year before. The work of Brent and his staff in Vancouver certainly was.

In the wake of victories it's easy to forget just how difficult many big decisions were along the way. Our two most recent WJC gold medals came after our coaches made incredibly tough decisions about their goaltenders. In '08, Craig Hartsburg went with a hunch late in the tournament, going with Steve Mason in the medal round. In '09, Pat Quinn stayed with Dustin Tokarski despite three first-period goals scored by Team U.S.A. late in the round robin—on that occasion his own assistant coaches were sure he'd make the switch. Both Mason and Tokarski were key to their teams' victories.

Everyone who has been involved in the Program of Excellence doesn't just give it his all for a few weeks, or even a season. There's a sense of loyalty and kinship there and an incredible willingness to share and give back. Those who have coached or played another role always come back to help out and work with those who are coming up through the ranks. That includes coaches who went on to helm Stanley Cup winners: Mike Babcock, Ken Hitchcock, and Claude Julien. That includes hockey people like Pat Quinn, who has worked in the game for more than four decades, and others like Guy Boucher, who is barely four decades old.

When Murray Costello and Dennis McDonald founded the Program of Excellence, I don't know if they fully intended its name to work on so many levels. Our WJC program draws on gifted, industrious, tireless people who would never settle for less than excellence and puts them in situations that demand excellence. Good isn't good enough. Excellence is what we aspire to but will never settle for because we believe we can be even better next year. And we know that we have to be better every year.

TEAM ROSTERS

1982

#	NAME	P	S	HT	WT	BORN	HOMETOWN	CLUB	DRAFT STATUS
14	Scott Arniel	F	L	6'1"	170	09/17/62	Kingston, Ont.	Cornell (ECAC)	WPG '81 (2, 22)
5	Paul Boutilier	D	R	5'11"	189	05/03/63	Halifax, N.S.	Sherbrooke (QMJHL)	NYI '81 (1, 21)
10	Garth Butcher	D	R	5'11.5"	181	08/03/63	Regina, Sask.	Regina (WHL)	VAN '81 (1, 10)
1	Frank Caprice	G	L	5'9"	150	05/12/62	Hamilton, Ont.	London (OHL)	VAN '81 (9, 178)
19	Paul Cyr	F	L	5'11"	185	10/31/63	Victoria, B.C.	Victoriaville (QMJHL)	1982 Draft
24	Bruce Eakin	F	L	5'11"	185	09/28/62	Winnipeg, Man.	Lethbridge (WHL)	CGY '81 (10, 204)
16	Marc Habscheid	F	R	5'11"	172	03/01/63	Wymark, Sask.	Victoriaville (QMJHL)	EDM '81 (6, 113)
4	Gord Kluzak	D	L	6'4"	216	03/04/64	Climax, Sask.	Billings (WHL)	1982 Draft
12	Moe Lemay	F	L	5'11"	185	02/18/62	Ottawa, Ont.	Ottawa (OHL)	VAN '81 (5, 105)
30	Mike Moffat	G	L	5'11"	170	02/04/62	Mississauga, Ont.	Kingston (OHL)	BOS '80 (8, 165)
26	Mike Moller	F	R	6'1"	189	06/16/62	Red Deer, Alta.	Lethbridge (WHL)	BUF '80 (2, 41)
2	Randy Moller	D	R	6'2"	205	08/23/63	Red Deer, Alta.	Lethbridge (WHL)	QUE '81 (1, 11)
23	Dave Morrison	F	R	6'1"	189	06/12/62	Kingston, Ont.	Peterborough (OHL)	LA '80 (2, 34)
17	Mark Morrison	F	R	5'8"	150	03/11/63	Tsawwassen, B.C.	Victoriaville (QMJHL)	NYR '81 (3, 51)
21	Troy Murray *C*	F	R	5'11"	189	07/31/62	St. Albert, Alta.	North Dakota (WCHA)	CHI '80 (3, 57)
3	Gary Nylund	D	L	6'4"	207	10/28/63	North Delta, B.C.	Portland (WHL)	1982 Draft
9	James Patrick	D	R	5'9"	165	06/14/63	Winnipeg, Man.	North Dakota (WCHA)	NYR '81 (1, 9)
7	Pierre Rioux	F	R	5'9"	165	02/01/62	Quebec City, Que.	Shawinigan (QMJHL)	Undrafted
11	Todd Strueby	F	L	6'1"	192	06/15/63	Humboldt, Sask.	Saskatoon (WHL)	EDM '81 (2, 29)
20	Carey Wilson	F	R	6'1"	192	05/11/62	Winnipeg, Man.	IFK Helsinki (FIN)	CHI '80 (4, 67)

Head coach: Dave King

Assistant coach: Georges Larivière

Assistant coach: Sherry Bassin

1983

#	NAME	P	S	HT	WT	BORN	HOMETOWN	CLUB	DRAFT STATUS
15	Dave Andreychuk	F	R	6'2"	159	09/29/63	Hamilton, Ont.	Oshawa (OHL)	BUF '82 (1, 16)
5	Paul Boutilier	D	R	5'10.5"	189	05/03/63	Halifax, N.S.	St-Jean (QMJHL)	NYI '81 (1, 21)
2	Joe Cirella	D	R	6'0.5"	189	05/09/63	Stoney Creek, Ont.	Oshawa (OHL)	COL '81 (1, 5)
19	Paul Cyr	F	L	5'11"	185	10/31/63	Port Alberni, B.C.	Victoriaville (QMJHL)	BUF '82 (1, 9)
12	Dale Derkatch	F	L	5'5"	140	10/17/64	Winnipeg, Man.	Regina (WHL)	1983 Draft
8	Mike Eagles	F	L	5'11"	161	03/07/63	Sussex, N.B.	Kitchener (OHL)	QUE '81 (6,,116)
20	Pat Flatley	F	R	6'0.5"	194	10/03/63	Toronto, Ont.	Wisconsin (WCHA)	NYI '82 (1, 21)
4	Gary Leeman	D	R	5'11"	168	02/19/64	Toronto, Ont.	Regina (WHL)	TOR '82 (2, 24)
24	Mario Lemieux	F	R	6'0.5"	176	10/05/65	Montreal, Que.	Laval (QMJHL)	1983 Draft
17	Mark Morrison	F	R	5'8"	159	03/11/63	Delta, B.C.	Victoriaville (QMJHL)	NYR '81 (3, 51)
9	James Patrick *C*	D	L	6'0.5"	178	06/14/63	Winnipeg, Man.	North Dakota (WCHA)	NYR '81 (1, 9)
1	Mike Sands	G	L	5'7"	154	04/06/63	Mississauga, Ont.	Sudbury (OHL)	MIN '81 (2, 31)
7	Brad Shaw	D	R	5'11"	159	04/28/64	Cambridge, Ont.	Ottawa (OHL)	DET '82 (5, 86)
21	Gord Sherven	F	R	5'10.5"	183	08/21/63	Mankota, Sask.	North Dakota (WCHA)	MIN '81 (10, 197)
11	Tony Tanti	F	L	5'9"	189	09/07/63	Mississauga, Ont.	Oshawa (OHL)	CHI '81 (1, 12)
3	Larry Trader	D	L	6'0.5"	194	07/07/63	Barry's Bay, Ont.	London (OHL)	DET '81 (5, 86)
10	Sylvain Turgeon	F	L	5'10.5"	161	01/17/65	Rouyn-Noranda, Que.	Hull (QMJHL)	1983 Draft
18	Pat Verbeek	F	R	5'7"	174	05/24/64	Sarnia, Ont.	Sudbury (OHL)	NJ '82 (3, 43)
30	Mike Vernon	G	L	5'8"	150	02/24/63	Calgary, Alta.	Calgary (WHL)	CGY '81 (3, 56)
14	Steve Yzerman	F	R	5'9"	172	09/05/65	Nepean, Ont.	Peterborough (OHL)	1983 Draft

Head coach: Dave King

Assistant coach: Michel Morin

Assistant coach: Doug Sauter

1984

#	NAME	P	S	HT	WT	BORN	HOMETOWN	CLUB	DRAFT STATUS
30	Allan Bester	G	L	5'7"	150	03/26/64	Hamilton, Ont.	Brantford (OHL)	TOR '83 (3, 48)
20	Lyndon Byers	F	R	6'1"	185	02/29/64	Nipawin, Sask.	Regina (WHL)	BOS '82 (2, 39)
6	Bruce Cassidy	D	L	6'1"	180	05/20/65	Ottawa, Ont.	Ottawa (OHL)	CHI '83 (1, 18)
22	Sylvain Côté	D	R	6'0"	175	01/19/66	Quebec City, Que.	Quebec (QMJHL)	1984 Draft
21	Yves Courteau	F	L	6'1"	185	02/29/64	Pointe-aux-Trembles, Que.	Laval (QMJHL)	DET '82 (2, 23)
9	Russ Courtnall C	F	R	5'10"	175	06/03/65	Victoria, B.C.	Victoriaville (QMJHL)	TOR '83 (1, 7)
3	J.J. Daigneault	D	L	5'11"	181	10/12/65	Montreal, Que.	Canadian National Team	1984 Draft
26	Dale Derkatch	F	L	5'5"	140	10/17/64	Winnipeg, Man.	Regina (WHL)	EDM '83 (7, 140)
23	Gerald Diduck	D	R	6'2"	202	04/05/65	Sherwood Park, Alta.	Lethbridge (WHL)	NYI '83 (1, 16)
11	Dean Evason	F	R	5'10"	175	08/22/64	Brandon, Man.	Kamloops (WHL)	WSH '82 (5, 89)
17	Dave Gagner	F	L	5'10"	185	12/11/64	Chatham, Ont.	Brantford (OHL)	NYR '83 (1, 12)
12	Randy Heath	F	L	5'8"	165	11/11/64	Vancouver, B.C.	Portland (WHL)	NYR '83 (2, 33)
16	Dan Hodgson	F	R	5'11"	170	08/29/65	Fort McMurray, Alta.	Prince Albert (WHL)	TOR '83 (5, 83)
27	Garry Lacey	F	L	5'11"	178	05/24/64	Falconbridge, Ont.	Toronto (OHL)	NYI '82 (3, 63)
19	Gary Leeman	D	R	5'11"	170	02/19/64	Toronto, Ont.	Regina (WHL)	TOR '82 (2, 24)
8	John MacLean	F	R	6'0"	194	11/20/64	Oshawa, Ont.	New Jersey (NHL)	NJ '83 (1, 6)
10	Kirk Muller	F	L	6'0"	189	02/08/66	Kingston, Ont.	Guelph (OHL)	1984 Draft
5	Mark Paterson	D	L	6'0"	195	02/22/64	Nepean , Ont.	Ottawa (OHL)	HFD '82 (2, 35)
4	Brad Shaw A	D	R	5'10"	170	04/28/64	Cambridge, Ont.	Ottawa (OHL)	DET '82 (5, 86)
1	Ken Wregget	G	L	6'1"	182	03/25/64	Brandon, Man.	Lethbridge (WHL)	TOR '82 (3, 45)

Head coach: Brian Kilrea

Assistant coach: Terry Simpson

Assistant coach: Georges Larivière

1985

#	NAME	P	S	HT	WT	BORN	HOMETOWN	CLUB	DRAFT STATUS
14	Bob Bassen	F	L	5'10"	181	05/06/65	Calgary, Alta.	Medicine Hat (WHL)	Undrafted
19	Yves Beaudoin	D	R	5'9"	180	01/07/65	Pointe-aux-Trembles, Que.	Shawinigan (QMJHL)	WSH '83 (10, 195)
2	Brad Berry	D	L	6'2"	190	04/01/65	Bashaw, Alta.	North Dakota (WCHA)	WPG '83 (2, 29)
25	Jeff Beukeboom	D	R	6'4"	210	03/28/65	Lindsay, Ont.	Sault Ste. Marie (OHL)	EDM '83 (1, 18)
1	Craig Billington	G	L	5'10"	155	09/11/66	London, Ont.	Belleville (OHL)	NJ '84 (2, 23)
8	Brian Bradley	F	R	5'9"	183	01/21/65	Kitchener, Ont.	London (OHL)	CGY '83 (3, 51)
6	Wendel Clark	F	L	5'11"	187	10/25/66	Kelvington, Sask.	Saskatoon (WHL)	1985 Draft/Rep.
9	Shayne Corson	F	L	6'2"	185	08/13/66	Barrie, Ont.	Hamilton (OHL)	MTL '84 (1, 8)
11	Adam Creighton A	F	L	6'5"	205	06/06/65	Welland, Ont.	Buffalo (NHL)	BUF '83 (1, 11)
5	Bobby Dollas	D	L	6'3"	210	01/31/65	Montreal, Que.	Winnipeg (NHL)	WPG '83 (1, 14)
30	Norm Foster	G	L	5'7"	175	02/10/65	Vancouver, B.C.	Michigan State (CCHA)	BOS '83 (11, 222)
24	Dan Gratton	F	L	6'0"	182	12/07/66	Brantford, Ont.	Oshawa (OHL)	1985 Draft/Rep.
16	Dan Hodgson C	F	R	5'11"	175	08/29/65	Fort McMurray, Alta.	Prince Albert (WHL)	TOR '83 (5, 83)
12	Jeff Jackson	F	L	6'1"	190	04/24/65	Dresden, Ont.	Hamilton (OHL)	TOR '83 (2, 28)
10	Greg Johnston	F	R	6'1"	205	01/14/65	Barrie, Ont.	Toronto (OHL)	BOS '83 (2, 42)
21	Claude Lemieux	F	R	6'1"	208	07/16/65	Montreal, Que.	Verdun (QMJHL)	MTL '83 (2, 26)
3	John Miner	D	R	5'11"	187	08/28/65	Regina, Sask.	Regina (WHL)	EDM '83 (11, 220)
7	Selmar Odelein	D	R	6'1"	201	04/11/66	Quill Lake, Sask.	Regina (WHL)	EDM '84 (1, 21)
23	Stéphane Richer	F	R	6'2"	185	07/07/66	Ripon, Que.	Granby (QMJHL)	MTL '84 (2, 29)
26	Jim Sandlak	F	R	6'3"	202	12/12/66	Kitchener, Ont.	London (OHL)	1985 Draft/Rep.

Head coach: Terry Simpson

Assistant coach: Ron Lapointe

1986

#	NAME	P	S	HT	WT	BORN	HOMETOWN	CLUB	DRAFT STATUS
1	Craig Billington	G	L	5'10"	160	09/11/66	London, Ont.	Belleville (OHL)	NJ '84 (2, 23)
30	Sean Burke	G	L	6'3"	195	01/29/67	Windsor, Ont.	Toronto (OHL)	NJ '85 (2, 24)
2	Terry Carkner	D	L	6'4"	202	03/07/66	Winchester, Ont.	Peterborough (OHL)	NYR '84 (1, 14)
27	Al Conroy	F	R	5'7"	165	01/17/66	Calgary, Alta.	Medicine Hat (WHL)	Undrafted
9	Shayne Corson	F	L	6'1"	187	08/13/66	Barrie, Ont.	Hamilton (OHL)	MTL '84 (1, 8)
24	Alain Côté	D	R	6'0"	201	04/14/67	Matane, Que.	Boston (NHL)	BOS '85 (2, 31)
22	Sylvain Côté	D	R	6'0"	177	01/19/66	Quebec City, Que.	Hartford (NHL)	HFD '84 (1, 11)
10	Peter Douris	F	R	6'0"	195	02/19/66	Toronto, Ont.	New Hampshire (ECAC)	WPG '84 (2, 30)
22	Jeff Greenlaw	F	L	6'2"	195	02/28/68	Aylmer, Ont.	Canadian National Team	1986 Draft
8	Derek Laxdal	F	R	6'2"	189	02/21/66	Stonewall, Man.	Brandon (WHL)	TOR '84 (8, 151)
20	Scott Mellanby	F	R	6'1"	200	06/11/66	Islington, Ont.	Wisconsin (WCHA)	PHI '84 (2, 27)
5	Dave Moylan	D	L	6'2"	201	08/13/67	Tillsonburg, Ont.	Sudbury (OHL)	BUF '85 (4, 77)
14	Joe Murphy	F	L	5'10"	170	10/16/67	London, Ont.	Penticton (BCHL)	1986 Draft
19	Joe Nieuwendyk	F	L	6'2"	187	09/10/66	Oshawa, Ont.	London (OHL)	CGY '85 (2, 27)
7	Selmar Odelein	D	R	6'1"	190	04/11/66	Quill Lake, Sask.	Regina (WHL)	EDM '84 (1, 21)
12	Gary Roberts	F	L	6'1"	187	05/23/66	Whitby, Ont.	Ottawa (OHL)	CGY '84 (1, 12)
15	Luc Robitaille	F	L	6'1"	185	02/17/66	Montreal, Que.	Hull (QMJHL)	LA '84 (9, 171)
26	Jim Sandlak *C*	F	R	6'3"	207	12/12/66	Kitchener, Ont.	London (OHL)	VAN ' 85 (1, 4)
25	Mike Stapleton	F	R	5'10"	175	05/05/66	Strathroy, Ont.	Cornell (ECAC)	CHI '84 (7, 132)
3	Emmanuel Viveiros	D	L	5'11"	171	01/08/66	St. Albert, Alta.	Prince Albert (WHL)	EDM '84 (6, 106)

Head coach: Terry Simpson

Assistant coach: Michel Parizeau

1987

#	NAME	P	S	HT	WT	BORN	HOMETOWN	CLUB	DRAFT STATUS
4	Steve Chiasson *C*	D	L	6'0"	205	04/14/67	Peterborough, Ont.	Detroit (NHL)	DET '85 (3, 50)
9	Yvon Corriveau	F	L	6'1"	200	02/08/67	Welland, Ont.	Washington (NHL)	WSH '85 (1, 19)
15	Pat Elynuik	F	R	6'0"	181	10/30/67	Foam Lake, Alta.	Prince Albert (WHL)	WPG '86 (1, 8)
10	Theoren Fleury	F	R	5'10"	160	06/29/68	Russell, Man.	Moose Jaw (WHL)	1987 Draft
2	Greg Hawgood	D	L	5'9"	185	08/10/68	St. Albert, Alta.	Kamloops (WHL)	BOS '86 (10,202)
6	Kerry Huffman	D	L	6'2"	185	01/03/68	Peterborough, Ont.	Guelph (OHL)	PHI '86 (2, 22)
5	Chris Joseph	D	R	6'2"	194	09/10/69	Burnaby, B.C.	Seattle (WHL)	1987 Draft
11	Mike Keane	F	R	5'10"	179	09/25/67	Winnipeg, Man.	Moose Jaw (WHL)	Undrafted
22	David Latta	F	L	6'0"	187	01/03/67	Thunder Bay, Ont.	Kitchener (OHL)	QUE '85 (1, 15)
14	Dave McLlwain	F	L	6'0"	176	06/09/67	Seaforth, Ont.	North Bay (OHL)	PIT '86 (9,172)
16	Scott Metcalfe *A*	F	L	6'0"	192	01/06/67	Mississauga, Ont.	Kingston (OHL)	EDM '85 (1, 20)
19	Steve Nemeth *A*	F	L	5'9"	176	02/11/67	Calgary, Alta.	Canadian National Team	NYR '85 (10, 196)
8	Luke Richardson	D	L	6'3"	197	03/26/69	Ottawa, Ont.	Peterborough (OHL)	1987 Draft
21	Stéphane Roy	F	L	6'0"	182	06/29/69	Quebec City, Que.	Granby (QMJHL)	MIN '85 (3, 51)
12	Everett Sanipass	F	L	6'2"	198	02/13/68	Moncton, N.B.	Verdun (QMJHL)	CHI '86 (1, 14)
18	Brendan Shanahan	F	R	6'3"	206	01/23/69	Mimico, Ont.	London (OHL)	1987 Draft
1	Shawn Simpson	G	L	5'11"	157	08/10/68	Ottawa, Ont.	St-Hyacinthe (QMJHL)	WSH '86 (3, 60)
20	Pierre Turgeon	F	L	6'1"	204	08/02/69	Rouyn-Noranda, Que.	Granby (QMJHL)	1987 Draft
30	Jimmy Waite	G	L	5'11"	162	04/15/69	Sherbrooke, Que.	Chicoutimi (QMJHL)	1987 Draft
3	Glen Wesley	D	L	6'1"	192	10/02/68	Red Deer, Alta.	Portland (WHL)	1987 Draft

Head coach: Bert Templeton

Assistant coach: Pat Burns

1988

#	NAME	P	S	HT	WT	BORN	HOMETOWN	CLUB	DRAFT STATUS
17	Warren Babe	F	L	6'3"	192	09/07/68	Bow Island, Alta./	Minnesota (NHL)	MIN '86 (1, 12)
16	Rob Brown	F	L	5'11"	188	04/10/68	St. Albert, Alta.	Pittsburgh (NHL)	PIT '86 (4, 67)
26	Dan Currie	F	L	6'0"	178	03/15/68	Burlington, Ont.	Sault Ste. Marie (OHL)	EDM '86 (4, 84)
21	Eric Desjardins	D	R	6'0"	182	06/14/69	Rouyn-Noranda, Que.	Granby (QMJHL)	MTL '87 (2, 38)
18	Rob DiMaio	F	R	5'10"	187	02/19/68	Calgary, Alta.	Medicine Hat (WHL)	NYI '87 (6, 118)
10	Theoren Fleury *C*	F	R	5'10"	160	06/29/68	Russell, Man.	Moose Jaw (WHL)	CGY '87 (8, 166)
15	Adam Graves	F	L	6'1"	191	01/14/68	Toronto, Ont.	Windsor (OHL)	DET '86 (1, 22)
	Jeff Hackett	G	L	6'0"	183	06/01/68	London, Ont.	Oshawa (OHL)	NYI '87 (2, 34)
2	Greg Hawgood	D	L	5'9"	190	08/10/68	St. Albert, Alta.	Kamloops (WHL)	BOS '86 (10,202)
12	Jody Hull	F	R	6'2"	200	02/02/69	Cambridge, Ont.	Peterborough (OHL)	HFD '87 (1, 18)
5	Chris Joseph	D	R	6'0"	195	09/10/69	Burnaby, B.C.	Canadian National Team	PIT '87 (1, 5)
20	Sheldon Kennedy	F	R	5'10"	170	06/15/69	Elkhorn, Man.	Swift Current (WHL)	1988 Draft
3	Marc Laniel	D	L	6'1"	190	01/16/68	Scarborough, Ont.	Oshawa (OHL)	NJ '86 (3, 62)
10	Trevor Linden	F	R	6'2"	177	04/11/70	Medicine Hat, Alta.	Medicine Hat (WHL)	1988 Draft
7	Wayne McBean	D	L	6'2"	200	02/21/69	Calgary, Alta.	Los Angeles (NHL)	LA '87 (1, 4)
6	Scott McCrady	D	R	6'2"	190	10/30/68	Calgary, Alta.	Medicine Hat (WHL)	NYI '87 (2, 35)
14	Mark Pederson	F	L	6'1"	192	01/14/68	Medicine Hat, Alta.	Medicine Hat (WHL)	MTL '86 (1, 15)
8	Mark Recchi	F	L	5'10"	188	02/02/69	Kamloops, B.C.	Kamloops (WHL)	Undrafted
19	Joe Sakic	F	L	5'11"	185	07/07/69	Burnaby, B.C.	Swift Current (WHL)	QUE '87 (1, 15)
30	Jimmy Waite	G	L	6'0"	163	04/15/69	Sherbrooke, Que.	Chicoutimi (QMJHL)	CHI '87 (1, 8)

Head coach: Dave Chambers

Assistant coach: Jean Bégin

Assistant coach: Ken Hitchcock

1989

#	NAME	P	S	HT	WT	BORN	HOMETOWN	CLUB	DRAFT STATUS
20	Rod Brind'Amour	F	L	6'0"	190	08/09/70	Campbell River, B.C.	Michigan State (CCHA)	STL '88 (1, 9)
25	Andrew Cassels	F	L	5'11"	187	07/23/69	Bramalea, Ont.	Ottawa (OHL)	MTL '87 (1, 17)
27	Rob Cimetta	F	L	6'1"	191	02/15/70	Toronto, Ont.	Toronto (OHL)	BOS '88 (1, 18)
6	Eric Desjardins *C*	D	R	6'1"	190	06/14/69	Rouyn-Noranda, Que.	Montreal (NHL)	MTL '87 (2, 38)
29	Stéphane Fiset	G	L	6'0"	174	06/17/70	Montreal, Que.	Victoriaville (QMJHL)	QUE '88 (2, 24)
4	Corey Foster	D	L	6'3"	203	10/27/69	Ottawa, Ont.	Peterborough (OHL)	NJ '88 (1, 12)
7	Martin Gélinas	F	L	5'11"	195	06/05/70	Shawinigan. Que.	Hull (QMJHL)	LA '88 (1, 7)
21	Sheldon Kennedy *A*	F	R	5'10"	170	06/15/69	Elkhorn, Man.	Swift Current (WHL)	DET '88 (4, 80)
24	Dan Lambert	D	L	5'7"	173	01/12/70	St. Malo, Man.	Swift Current (WHL)	Undrafted
28	Jamie Leach	F	R	6'1"	185	08/25/69	Winnipeg, Man.	Niagara Falls (OHL)	PIT '87 (3, 47)
10	Darcy Loewen	F	L	5'10"	185	02/26/69	Calgary, Alta.	Spokane (WHL)	BUF '88 (3, 55)
8	John McIntyre	F	L	6'1"	182	04/29/69	London, Ont.	Guelph (OHL)	TOR '87 (3, 49)
1	Gus Morschauser	G	L	5'9"	163	03/26/69	Kitchener, Ont.	Kitchener (OHL)	Undrafted
14	Rob Murphy	F	L	6'3"	203	04/07/69	Hull, Que.	Vancouver (NHL)	VAN '87 (2, 2)
16	Yves Racine	D	L	6'0"	194	02/07/69	Matane, Que.	Victoriaville (QMJHL)	DET '87 (1, 11)
26	Mike Ricci	F	L	6'1"	191	10/27/71	Scarborough, Ont.	Peterborough (OHL)	1990 Draft
18	Reginald Savage	F	L	5'10"	185	05/01/70	Montreal, Que.	Victoriaville (QMJHL)	WSH '88 (1, 15)
22	Darrin Shannon	F	L	6'2"	190	12/08/69	Barrie, Ont.	Windsor (OHL)	PIT '88 (1, 4)
5	Geoff Smith	D	L	6'3"	191	03/07/69	Edmonton, Alta.	North Dakota (WCHA)	EDM '87 (3, 63)
2	Steve Veilleux	D	R	6'0"	200	03/09/69	Lachenaie, Que.	Trois-Rivieres, Que./QC	VAN '87 (3, 45)

Head coach: Tom Webster

Assistant coach: Alain Vigneault

1990

#	NAME	P	S	HT	WT	BORN	HOMETOWN	CLUB	DRAFT STATUS
28	Stu Barnes	F	R	5'11"	175	12/25/70	Spruce Grove, Alta.	Tri-City (WHL)	WPG '89 (1, 4)
24	Patrice Brisebois	D	R	6'2"	172	01/27/71	Montreal, Que.	Laval (QMJHL)	MTL '89 (2, 30)
16	Dave Chyzowski *C*	F	L	6'1"	192	07/11/71	Edmonton, Alta.	NY Islanders (NHL)	NYI '89 (1, 2)
15	Mike Craig	F	R	6'1"	167	06/06/71	London, Ont.	Oshawa (OHL)	MIN '89 (2, 28)
19	Kris Draper	F	L	5'10"	189	06/24/71	West Hill, Ont.	Canadian National Team	WPG '89 (3, 62)
29	Stéphane Fiset	G	L	6'0"	178	06/17/70	Montreal, Que.	Victoriaville (QMJHL)	QUE '88 (2, 24)
6	Kevin Haller	D	L	6'2"	180	12/05/70	Trochu, Alta.	Regina (WHL)	BUF '89 (1, 14)
5	Jason Herter	D	R	6'1"	196	10/02/70	Hafford, Sask.	North Dakota (WCHA)	VAN '89 (1, 8)
1	Trevor Kidd	G	L	6'1"	168	03/26/72	Dugald, Man.	Brandon (WHL)	1990 Draft
88	Eric Lindros	F	R	6'4"	218	02/28/73	Toronto, Ont.	Oshawa (OHL)	1991 Draft
4	Stewart Malgunas	D	L	5'11"	184	04/21/70	Prince George, B.C.	Seattle (WHL)	Undrafted
21	Kent Manderville	F	L	6'3"	193	04/12/71	Victoria, B.C.	Cornell (ECAC)	CGY '89 (2, 24)
14	Mike Needham	F	R	5'10"	196	03/25/70	Fort Saskatchewan, Alta.	Kamloops (WHL)	PIT '89 (6, 126)
10	Dwayne Norris	F	R	5'10"	178	01/08/70	St. John's, N.L.	Michigan State (CCHA)	Undrafted
18	Scott Pellerin	F	L	5'11"	195	01/09/70	Shediac, N.B.	Maine (Hky East)	NJ '89 (3, 47)
7	Adrien Plavsic	D	L	6'1"	195	01/13/70	Dollard, Que.	Peoria (IHL)	STL '88 (2, 30)
2	Dan Ratushny *A*	D	R	6'1"	202	10/29/70	Nepean , Ont.	Cornell (ECAC)WPG	'89 (2, 25)
9	Mike Ricci *A*	F	L	6'1"	190	10/27/71	Scarborough, Ont.	Peterborough (OHL)	1990 Draft
12	Steven Rice	F	R	6'1"	209	05/26/71	Waterloo, Ont.	Kitchener (OHL)	NYR '89 (1, 20)
13	Wes Walz	F	R	5'11"	181	05/15/70	Calgary, Alta.	Lethbridge (WHL)	BOS '89 (3, 57)

Head coach: Guy Charron

Assistant coach: Dick Todd

Assistant coach: Perry Pearn

1991

#	NAME	P	S	HT	WT	BORN	HOMETOWN	CLUB	DRAFT STATUS
24	Patrice Brisebois	D	R	6'2"	181	01/27/71	Montreal, Que.	Drummondville (QMJHL)	MTL '89 (2, 30)
15	Mike Craig	F	R	6'0.5"	181	06/06/71	London, Ont.	Minnesota (NHL)	MIN '89 (2, 28)
18	Dale Craigwell	F	L	5'11"	181	04/24/71	Oshawa, Ont.	Oshawa (OHL)	Undrafted
19	Kris Draper	F	L	5'11"	189	05/24/71	West Hill, Ont.	Ottawa (OHL)	WPG '89 (3, 62)
4	Karl Dykhuis	D	R	6'3"	201	07/08/72	Sept-Îles, Que.	Canadian National Team	CHI '90 (1, 16)
9	Pat Falloon	F	R	5'11"	189	09/22/72	Foxwarren, Man.	Spokane (WHL)	1991 Draft
7	David Harlock	D	L	6'2"	205	03/16/71	Toronto, Ont.	Michigan (CCHA)	NJ '90 (2, 24)
8	Greg Johnson	F	L	5'11"	183	03/16/71	Thunder Bay, Ont.	North Dakota (WCHA)	PHI '89 (2, 33)
1	Trevor Kidd	G	L	6'2"	185	03/26/72	Dugald, Man.	Brandon (WHL)	CGY '90 (1, 11)
26	Martin Lapointe	F	L	5'11"	201	09/12/73	Ville St-Pierre, Que.	Laval (QMJHL)	1991 Draft
88	Eric Lindros	F	R	6'5"	223	02/28/73	Toronto, Ont.	Oshawa (OHL)	1991 Draft
21	Kent Manderville	F	L	6'3"	205	04/12/71	Victoria, B.C.	Cornell (ECAC)	CGY '89 (2, 24)
2	Jason Marshall	D	R	6'2"	196	02/22/71	Cranbrook, B.C.	Tri-City (WHL)	STL '89 (1, 9)
10	Brad May	F	L	6'0.5"	207	11/29/71	Markham, Ont.	Niagara Falls (OHL)	BUF '90 (1, 14)
28	Scott Niedermayer	D	L	6'0"	196	08/31/73	Cranbrook, B.C.	Kamloops (WHL)	1991 Draft
29	Félix Potvin	G	L	6'0.5"	174	06/23/71	Anjou, Que.	Chicoutimi (QMJHL)	TOR '90 (2, 31)
12	Steven Rice *C*	F	R	6'0.5"	214	05/26/71	Waterloo, Ont.	Kitchener (OHL)	NYR '89 (1, 20)
22	Pierre Sévigny	F	L	6'0"	185	09/08/71	Trois-Rivières, Que.	St-Hyacinthe (QMJHL)	MTL '89 (3, 51)
16	Mike Sillinger	F	R	5'11"	189	06/29/71	Regina, Sask.	Regina (WHL)	DET '89 (1, 11)
27	John Slaney	D	L	5'11"	189	02/07/72	St. John's, N.L.	Cornell (ECAC)	WSH '90 (1, 9)
6	Chris Snell	D	L	5'11"	201	07/12/71	Oshawa, Ont.	Ottawa (OHL)	Undrafted
11	Scott Thornton	F	L	6'3"	205	01/09/71	London, Ont.	Toronto (NHL)	TOR '89 (1, 3)

Head coach: Dick Todd

Assistant coach: Perry Pearn

Assistant coach: Alain Vigneault

1992

#	NAME	P	S	HT	WT	BORN	HOMETOWN	CLUB	DRAFT STATUS
55	Brad Bombardir	D	L	6'0.5"	196	05/05/72	Powell River, B.C.	North Dakota (WCHA)	NJ '90 (3, 56)
2	Jassen Cullimore	D	L	6'5"	220	12/04/72	Simcoe, Ont.	Peterborough (OHL)	VAN '91 (2, 29)
14	Kimbi Daniels	F	R	6'1.5"	174	01/19/72	Brandon, Man.	Philadelphia (NHL)	PHI '90 (3, 44)
24	Karl Dykhuis	D	R	6'3"	201	07/08/72	Sept-Îles, Que.	Canadian National Team	CHI '90 (1, 16)
	Mike Fountain	G	L	6'0"	168	01/26/72	Gravenhurst, Ont.	Oshawa (OHL)	Undrafted
9	Ryan Hughes	F	L	6'2"	189	1/1/7/72	Montreal, Que.	Cornell (ECAC)	QUE '90 (2, 22)
11	Steve Junker	F	L	6'0"	189	06/25/72	Castlegar, B.C.	Spokane (WHL)	NYI '91 (5, 92)
18	Paul Kariya	F	L	5'10.5"	150	10/16/74	North Vancouver, B.C.	Penticton (BCHL)	1993 Draft
1	Trevor Kidd	G	L	6'2"	185	03/26/72	Dugald, Man.	Canadian National Team	CGY '90 (1, 11)
22	Martin Lapointe A	F	R	5'11"	201	09/12/73	Ville St-Pierre, Que.	Laval (QMJHL)	DET '91 (1, 10)
88	Eric Lindros C	F	R	6'5"	225	02/28/73	Toronto, Ont.	Oshawa (OHL)	QUE '91 (1, 1)
13	Richard Matvichuk	D	L	6'2.5"	187	02/05/73	Edmonton, Alta.	Saskatoon (WHL)	MIN '91 (1, 8)
7	Jeff Nelson	F	L	5'10.5"	189	12/18/72	Prince Albert, Sask.	Prince Albert (WHL)	WSH '91 (2, 36)
44	Scott Niedermayer	D	L	6'0"	203	08/31/73	Cranbrook, B.C.	Kamloops (WHL)	NJ '91 (1, 3)
8	Chad Penney	F	R	6'0.5"	196	09/18/73	St. John's, N.L.	North Bay (OHL)	1992 Draft
19	Patrick Poulin	F	R	6'0.5"	212	04/23/73	Vanier, Que.	St-Hyacinthe (QMJHL)	HFD '91 (1, 9)
17	Andy Schneider	F	L	5'9"	150	03/29/72	Edmonton, Alta.	Swift Current (WHL)	Undrafted
77	John Slaney	D	L	5'10.5"	192	02/07/72	St. John's, N.L.	Cornell (ECAC)	WSH '90 (1, 9)
23	Turner Stevenson	F	R	6'2.5"	209	05/18/72	Port Alberni, B.C.	Seattle (WHL)	MTL '90 (1, 12)
16	David St-Pierre	F	R	6'0"	181	03/26/72	Montreal, Que.	Verdun (QMJHL)	CGY '91 (8, 173)
5	Darryl Sydor A	D	L	6'0"	198	05/13/72	Edmonton, Alta.	Los Angeles (NHL)	LA '90 (1, 7)
12	Tyler Wright	F	R	5'10.5"	176	04/06/73	Kamsack, Sask.	Swift Current (WHL)	EDM '91 (1, 12)

Head scout: Sheldon Ferguson

Head coach: Rick Cornacchia

Assistant coach: Tom Renney

Assistant coach: Gary Agnew

1993

#	NAME	P	S	HT	WT	BORN	HOMETOWN	CLUB	DRAFT STATUS
3	Adrian Aucoin A	D	R	6'1"	194	07/03/73	Gloucester, Ont.	Canadian National Team	VAN '92 (5, 117)
11	Jeff Bes	F	L	6'0"	187	07/31/73	Tillsonburg, Ont.	Guelph (OHL)	MIN '92 (3, 58)
14	Joël Bouchard	D	L	6'0"	185	01/23/74	Montreal, Que.	Verdun (QMJHL)	CGY '92 (6, 129)
19	Alexandre Daigle	F	L	6'0"	170	02/07/75	Laval, Que.	Victoriaville (QMJHL)	1993 Draft
10	Jason Dawe	F	L	5'10.5"	192	05/29/73	Scarborough, Ont.	Peterborough (OHL)	BUF '91 (2, 35)
31	Philippe DeRouville	G	L	6'1"	189	08/07/74	Victoriaville, Que.	Verdun (QMJHL)	PIT '92 (5, 115)
32	Martin Gendron	F	R	5'9"	192	02/15/74	Valleyfield, Que.	St-Hyacinthe (QMJHL)	WSH '92 (3, 71)
7	Chris Gratton	F	L	6'3.5"	203	07/05/75	Brantford, Ont.	Kingston (OHL)	1993 Draft
9	Ralph Intranuovo	F	L	5'9"	170	12/11/73	Scarborough, Ont.	Sault Ste. Marie (OHL)	EDM '92 (4, 96)
18	Paul Kariya	F	L	5'10.5"	150	10/16/74	North Vancouver, B.C.	Maine (Hky East)	1993 Draft
21	Nathan Lafayette	F	R	6'1"	189	02/17/73	Mississauga, Ont.	Newmarket (OHL)	STL '91 (3, 65)
22	Martin Lapointe C	F	R	5'11"	201	09/12/73	Ville St-Pierre, Que.	Laval (QMJHL)	DET '91 (1, 10)
30	Manny Legace	G	L	5'9"	181	02/04/73	Alliston, Ont.	Niagara Falls (OHL)	Undrafted
16	Dean McAmmond	F	L	6'0"	187	06/15/73	Grande Cache, Alta.	Prince Albert (WHL)	CHI '91 (1, 22)
23	Rob Niedermayer	F	L	6'2"	201	12/28/74	Cranbrook, B.C.	Medicine Hat (WHL)	1993 Draft
6	Chris Pronger	D	L	6'6"	190	10/10/74	Dryden, Ont.	Peterborough (OHL)	1993 Draft
33	Mike Rathje	D	L	6'5"	203	05/11/74	Medicine Hat, Alta.	Medicine Hat (WHL)	SJ '92 (1, 3)
29	Jeff Shantz	F	R	6'1"	194	10/10/73	Duchess, Alta.	Regina (WHL)	CHI '92 (2, 36)
15	Jason Smith	D	R	6'3.5"	201	11/02/73	Calgary, Alta.	Regina (WHL)	NJ '92 (1, 18)
2	Brent Tully	D	R	6'3.5"	189	03/26/74	Peterborough, Ont.	Peterborough (OHL)	VAN '92 (4, 93)
4	Darcy Werenka	D	R	6'0.5"	209	05/13/73	Beaumont, Alta.	Brandon (WHL)	NYR '91 (2, 37)
12	Tyler Wright A	F	R	5'11"	170	04/06/73	Kamsack, Sask.	Swift Current (WHL)	EDM '91 (1, 12)

Head scout: Sheldon Ferguson

Head coach: Perry Pearn

Assistant coach: Joe Canale

Assistant coach: Dave Siciliano

1994

#	NAME	P	S	HT	WT	BORN	HOMETOWN	CLUB	DRAFT STATUS
8	Jason Allison	F	R	6'3"	201	05/29/75	North York, Ont.	London (OHL)	WSH '93 (1, 17)
34	Chris Armstrong	D	L	6'0"	194	06/26/75	Whitewood, Sask.	Moose Jaw (WHL)	FLA '93 (3, 57)
5	Drew Bannister	D	R	6'0.5"	205	04/09/74	Sudbury, Ont.	Sault Ste. Marie (OHL)	TB '92 (2, 26)
23	Jason Botterill	F	L	6'3"	205	05/19/76	Winnipeg, Man.	Michigan (CCHA)	1994 Draft
24	Joël Bouchard	D	L	6'0"	192	01/23/73	Montreal, Que.	Verdun (QMJHL)	CGY '92 (6, 129)
20	Curtis Bowen	F	L	6'0.5"	201	03/24/74	Kenora, Ont.	Ottawa (OHL)	DET '92 (1, 22)
19	Anson Carter	F	R	6'0.5"	181	06/06/74	Scarborough, Ont.	Michigan State (CCHA)	WSH '92 (10, 220)
12	Brandon Convery	F	R	6'0"	187	02/04/74	Kingston, Ont.	Niagara Falls (OHL)	TOR '92 (1, 8)
9	Yanick Dubé	F	R	5'9"	170	06/14/74	Gaspé, Que.	Laval (QMJHL)	Undrafted
30	Manny Fernandez	G	L	5'10.5"	163	08/27/74	Sherbrooke, Que.	Laval (QMJHL)	QUE '92 (3, 52)
25	Jeff Friesen	F	L	6'0"	185	08/05/76	Meadow Lake, Sask.	Regina (WHL)	1994 Draft
22	Aaron Gavey	F	L	6'0.5"	181	02/22/74	Sudbury, Ont.	Sault Ste. Marie (OHL)	TB '92 (4, 74)
32	Martin Gendron	F	R	5'9"	198	02/15/74	Valleyfield, Que.	Hull (QMJHL)	WSH '92 (3, 71)
18	Rick Girard	F	L	5'10.5"	176	05/01/74	Edmonton, Alta.	Swift Current (WHL)	VAN '93 (2, 46)
10	Todd Harvey *A*	F	R	5'10.5"	203	02/17/75	Sheffield, Ont.	Detroit (OHL)	DAL '93 (1, 9)
4	Bryan McCabe	D	L	6'2"	201	06/08/75	Calgary, Alta.	Spokane (WHL)	NYI '93 (2, 40)
28	Marty Murray	F	L	5'9"	165	02/16/75	Lyleton, Man.	Brandon (WHL)	CGY '93 (4, 96)
27	Mike Peca	F	R	5'10.5"	174	03/26/74	Toronto, Ont.	Ottawa (OHL)	VAN '92 (2, 40)
14	Nick Stajduhar	D	L	6'2"	205	12/06/74	Kitchener, Ont.	London (OHL)	EDM '93 (1, 16)
1	Jamie Storr	G	L	6'0.5"	161	12/25/75	Brampton, Ont.	Owen Sound (OHL)	1994 Draft
2	Brent Tully *C*	D	R	6'3.5"	201	03/26/74	Peterborough, Ont.	Peterborough (OHL)	VAN '92 (4, 93)
6	Brendan Witt *A*	D	L	6'0"	212	02/20/75	Humboldt, Sask.	Seattle (WHL)	WSH '93 (1, 11)

Head coach: Joe Canale

Assistant coach: Dan Flynn

Assistant coach: Mike Johnston

1995

#	NAME	P	S	HT	WT	BORN	HOMETOWN	CLUB	DRAFT STATUS
3	Chad Allan	D	L	6'1"	190	07/12/76	Davidson, Sask.	Saskatoon (WHL)	VAN '94 (3, 65)
9	Jason Allison *A*	F	R	6'3"	192	05/29/75	North York, Ont.	London (OHL)	WSH '93 (1, 17)
5	Nolan Baumgartner	D	R	6'1"	187	03/23/76	Calgary, Alta.	Kamloops (WHL)	WSH '94 (1, 10)
21	Jason Botterill	F	L	6'4"	209	05/19/76	Winnipeg, Man.	Michigan (CCHA)	DAL '94 (1, 20)
30	Dan Cloutier	G	L	6'1"	182	04/22/76	Sault Ste. Marie, Ont.	Sault Ste. Marie (OHL)	NYR '94 (2, 26)
8	Larry Courville	F	L	6'2"	184	04/02/75	Timmins, Ont.	Oshawa (OHL)	WPG '93 (5, 119)
19	Alexandre Daigle	F	L	6'0"	185	02/07/75	Laval, Que.	Victoriaville (QMJHL)	OTT '93 (1, 1)
24	Eric Daze	F	L	6'5"	204	07/02/75	Montreal, Que.	Beauport (QMJHL)	CHI '93 (4, 90)
22	Shean Donovan	F	R	6'1"	170	01/22/75	Timmins, Ont.	Ottawa (OHL)	SJ '93 (2, 28)
25	Jeff Friesen	F	L	6'0"	183	08/05/76	Meadow Lake, Sask.	Regina (WHL)	SJ '94 (1, 11)
10	Todd Harvey *C*	F	R	6'0"	200	02/17/75	Sheffield, Ont.	Detroit (OHL)	DAL '93 (1, 9)
14	Ed Jovanovski	D	L	6'2"	210	06/26/76	Windsor, Ont.	Windsor (OHL)	FLA '94 (1, 1)
4	Bryan McCabe *A*	D	L	6'1"	200	06/08/75	Calgary, Alta.	Spokane (WHL)	NYI '93 (2, 40)
28	Marty Murray	F	L	5'9"	168	02/16/75	Lyleton, Man.	Brandon (WHL)	CGY '93 (4, 96)
17	Jeff O'Neill	F	R	6'0"	186	02/23/76	King City, Ont.	Guelph (OHL)	HFD '94 (1, 5)
23	Denis Pederson	F	L	6'2"	194	09/10/75	Prince Albert, Sask.	Prince Albert (WHL)	NJ '93 (1, 13)
6	Wade Redden	D	L	6'1"	193	06/12/77	Lloydminster, Sask.	Brandon (WHL)	1995 Draft
12	Jamie Rivers	D	L	6'1"	185	03/16/75	Ottawa, Ont.	Sudbury (OHL)	STL '93 (3, 63)
20	Ryan Smyth	F	L	6'2"	183	02/21/76	Banff, Alta.	Moose Jaw (WHL)	EDM '94 (1, 6)
7	Lee Sorochan	D	L	6'2"	205	09/09/75	Gibbons, Alta.	Lethbridge (WHL)	NYR '93 (2, 34)
1	Jamie Storr	G	L	6'1"	174	12/28/75	Brampton, Ont.	Owen Sound (OHL)	LA '94 (1, 7)
16	Darcy Tucker	F	L	5'10"	163	03/15/75	Endiang, Alta.	Kamloops (WHL)	MTL '93 (6, 151)

Head coach: Don Hay

Assistant coach: Mike Johnston

Assistant coach: Alain Rajotte

1996

#	NAME	P	S	HT	WT	BORN	HOMETOWN	CLUB	DRAFT STATUS
7	Chad Allan *A*	D	L	6'1"	196	07/12/76	Davidson, Sask.	Saskatoon (WHL)	VAN '94 (3, 65)
5	Nolan Baumgartner *C*	D	R	6'1"	200	03/23/76	Calgary, Alta.	Kamloops (WHL)	WSH '94 (1, 10)
19	Jason Botterill *A*	F	L	6'3"	205	05/19/76	Winnipeg, Man.	Michigan (CCHA)	DAL '94 (1, 20)
11	Curtis Brown	F	L	6'0"	182	02/12/76	Seniac, Sask.	Moose Jaw (WHL)	BUF '94 (2, 43)
31	Marc Denis	G	L	6'0"	187	08/01/77	Montreal, Que.	Chicoutimi (QMJHL)	COL '95 (2, 25)
17	Hnat Domenichelli	F	L	5'11"	179	02/17/76	Edmonton, Alta.	Kamloops (WHL)	HFD '94 (5, 83)
9	Christian Dubé	F	R	5'11"	180	04/25/77	Quebec City, Que.	Sherbrooke (QMJHL)	NYR '95 (2, 39)
21	Denis Gauthier	D	L	6'2"	210	10/01/76	Montreal, Que.	Drummondville (QMJHL)	CGY '95 (1, 20)
16	Robb Gordon	F	R	6'0"	195	01/13/76	Surrey, B.C.	Kelowna (WHL)	VAN '94 (2, 39)
3	Jason Holland	D	R	6'2"	200	04/30/76	Morinville, Alta.	Kamloops (WHL)	NYI '94 (2, 38)
12	Jarome Iginla	F	R	6'1"	193	07/01/77	St. Albert, Alta.	Kamloops (WHL)	DAL '95 (1, 11)
14	Daymond Langkow	F	L	5'10"	170	09/27/76	Edmonton, Alta.	Tri-City (WHL)	TB '95 (1, 5)
23	Brad Larsen	F	L	6'0"	200	06/28/77	Vernon, B.C.	Swift Current (WHL)	OTT '95 (3, 53)
8	Alyn McCauley	F	L	5'11"	185	05/29/77	Gananoque, Ont.	Ottawa (OHL)	NJ '95 (4, 79)
24	Craig Mills	F	R	5'11"	190	08/27/76	Toronto, Ont.	Belleville (OHL)	WPG '94 (5, 108)
4	Chris Phillips	D	L	6'2"	200	03/09/78	Fort McMurray, Alta.	Prince Albert (WHL)	1996 Draft
22	Jason Podollan	F	R	6'1"	181	02/18/76	Vernon, B.C.	Spokane (WHL)	FLA '94 (2, 31)
6	Wade Redden	D	L	6'2"	196	06/12/77	Lloydminster, Sask.	Brandon (WHL)	NYI '95 (1, 2)
1	José Théodore	G	L	5'10.5"	174	09/13/76	Laval, Que.	Hull (QMJHL)	MTL '94 (2, 44)
30	Rhett Warrener	D	L	6'1"	209	01/27/76	Saskatoon, Sask.	Florida (NHL)	FLA '94 (2, 27)
18	Mike Watt	F	L	6'1"	214	03/31/76	Egmondville, Ont.	Michigan (CCHA)	EDM '94 (2, 32)
10	Jamie Wright	F	L	5'11"	172	05/13/76	Elmira, Ont.	Guelph (OHL)	DAL '94 (4, 98)

Head coach: Marcel Comeau

Assistant coach: Terry Bangen

Assistant coach: Blair MacKasey

1997

#	NAME	P	S	HT	WT	BORN	HOMETOWN	CLUB	DRAFT STATUS
1	Martin Biron	G	L	6'2"	165	08/15/77	Lac St-Charles, Que.	Beauport (QMJHL)	BUF '95 (1, 16)
14	Daniel Brière	F	R	5'9"	160	10/06/77	Gatineau, Que.	Drummondville (QMJHL)	PHX '96 (1, 24)
31	Marc Denis	G	L	6'1"	193	08/01/77	Montreal, Que.	Chicoutimi (QMJHL)	COL '95 (2, 25)
19	Boyd Devereaux	F	L	6'2"	190	04/16/78	Seaforth, Ont.	Kitchener (OHL)	EDM '96 (1, 6)
4	Jason Doig	D	R	6'3"	216	01/29/77	Montreal, Que.	Granby (QMJHL)	WPG '95 (2, 34)
9	Christian Dubé *A*	F	R	5'11"	186	04/25/77	Sherbrooke, Que.	NY Rangers (NHL)	NYR '95 (2, 39)
3	Hugh Hamilton	D	L	6'1"	175	02/11/77	Leask, Sask.	Spokane (WHL)	HFD '95 (5, 113)
28	Dwayne Hay	F	L	6'1"	192	02/11/77	London, Ont.	Guelph (OHL)	WSH '95 (2, 43)
12	Brad Isbister	F	R	6'3"	225	05/07/77	Calgary, Alta.	Portland (WHL)	WPG '95 (3, 67)
24	Richard Jackman	D	L	6'2"	176	06/28/78	Brampton, Ont.	Sault Ste. Marie (OHL)	DAL '96 (1, 5)
23	Brad Larsen *C*	F	L	6'0"	200	06/28/77	Vernon, B.C.	Swift Current (WHL)	OTT '95 (3, 53)
17	Trevor Letowski	F	R	5'10"	175	04/05/77	Thunder Bay, Ont.	Sarnia (OHL)	PHX '96 (7, 174)
10	Cameron Mann	F	R	6'0"	190	04/20/77	Balmertown, Ont.	Peterborough (OHL)	BOS '95 (4, 99)
18	Alyn McCauley *A*	F	L	5'11"	185	05/29/77	Gananoque, Ont.	Ottawa (OHL)	NJ '95 (4, 79)
7	Chris Phillips *A*	D	L	6'2"	200	03/09/78	Fort McMurray, Alta.	Prince Albert (WHL)	OTT '96 (1, 1)
22	Cory Sarich	D	R	6'3"	175	08/16/78	Bladworth, Sask.	Saskatoon (WHL)	BUF '96 (2, 27)
27	Peter Schaefer	F	L	6'0"	187	07/12/77	Yellow Grass, Sask.	Brandon (WHL)	VAN '95 (3, 66)
25	Joe Thornton	F	L	6'4"	186	07/02/79	St. Thomas, Ont.	Sault Ste. Marie (OHL)	1997 Draft
34	Jesse Wallin	D	L	6'2"	186	03/10/78	North Battleford, Sask.	Red Deer (WHL)	DET '96 (1, 26)
33	Jeff Ware	D	L	6'4"	225	05/29/77	Toronto, Ont.	Toronto (NHL)	TOR '95 (1, 15)
35	Trent Whitfield	F	L	5'11"	180	06/17/77	Alameda, Sask.	Spokane (WHL)	BOS '96 (4, 100)
20	Shane Willis	F	R	6'1"	185	06/13/77	Sylvan Lake, Alta.	Prince Albert (WHL)	TB '95 (3, 56)

Head coach: Mike Babcock

Assistant coach: Mike Pelino

Assistant coach: Réal Paiement

1998

#	NAME	P	S	HT	WT	BORN	HOMETOWN	CLUB	DRAFT STATUS
11	Steve Bégin A	F	L	6'0"	188	06/04/78	Trois-Rivières, Que.	Val-d'Or (QMJHL)	CGY '96 (2, 40)
7	Sean Blanchard	D	L	6'0"	201	03/29/78	Garson, Ont.	Ottawa (OHL)	LA '97 (4, 99)
28	Matt Bradley	F	R	6'1"	188	06/13/78	Stittsville, Ont.	Kingston (OHL)	SJ '96 (4, 102)
3	Eric Brewer	D	L	6'3"	196	04/17/79	Kamloops, B.C.	Prince George (WHL)	1998 Draft
12	Matt Cooke	F	L	6'1"	195	09/07/78	Belleville, Ont.	Windsor (OHL)	VAN '97 (6, 144)
15	Daniel Corso	F	L	5'10"	161	04/03/78	St-Hubert, Que.	Victoriaville (QMJHL)	STL '96 (7, 169)
18	Jean-Pierre Dumont	F	L	6'0"	195	04/01/78	Montreal, Que.	Val-d'Or (QMJHL)	NYI '96 (1, 3)
2	Brad Ference	D	R	6'3"	190	04/02/79	Calgary, Alta.	Spokane (WHL)	VAN '97 (1, 10)
32	Mathieu Garon	G	R	6'0.5"	192	01/09/78	Chandler, Que.	Victoriaville (QMJHL)	MTL '96 (2, 44)
21	Josh Holden	F	L	6'0"	170	01/18/78	Calgary, Alta.	Regina (WHL)	VAN '96 (1, 12)
5	Zenith Komarniski	D	L	6'2"	190	08/13/78	Edmonton, Alta.	Spokane (WHL)	VAN '96 (3, 75)
14	Vincent Lecavalier	F	L	6'4"	180	04/21/80	Île-Bizard, Que.	Rimouski (QMJHL)	1998 Draft
1	Roberto Luongo	G	L	6'2"	185	04/04/79	Montreal, Que.	Val-d'Or (QMJHL)	NYI '97 (1, 4)
6	Manny Malhotra	F	L	6'1"	210	05/18/80	Mississauga, Ont.	Guelph (OHL)	1998 Draft
16	Brett McLean	F	L	5'10"	187	08/14/78	Comox, B.C.	Kelowna (WHL)	DAL '97 (9, 242)
22	Cory Sarich C A	D	R	6'3"	190	08/16/78	Bladworth, Sask.	Saskatoon (WHL)	BUF '96 (2, 27)
19	Alex Tanguay	F	L	6'0"	180	11/21/79	Ste-Justine, Que.	Halifax (QMJHL)	1998 Draft
10	Daniel Tkaczuk	F	L	6'0"	195	06/10/79	Mississauga, Ont.	Barrie (OHL)	CGY '97 (1, 6)
26	Mike Van Ryn	D	R	6'2"	186	05/14/79	London, Ont.	Michigan (CCHA)	1998 Draft
4	Jesse Wallin C A	D	L	6'2"	190	03/10/78	North Battleford, Sask.	Red Deer (WHL)	DET '96 (1, 26)
20	Jason Ward	F	R	6'2"	193	01/16/79	Oshawa, Ont.	Erie (OHL)	MTL '97 (1, 11)
24	Brian Willsie	F	R	6'0"	179	03/16/78	London, Ont.	Guelph (OHL)	COL '96 (6, 146)

Head coach: Réal Paiement

Assistant coach: Peter DeBoer

Assistant coach: Terry Bangen

1999

#	NAME	P	S	HT	WT	BORN	HOMETOWN	CLUB	DRAFT STATUS
28	Bryan Allen	D	L	6'4"	206	08/21/80	Kingston, Ont.	Oshawa (OHL)	VAN '98 (1, 4)
20	Blair Betts	F	L	6'2"	200	02/16/80	Sherwood Park, Alta.	Prince George (WHL)	CGY '98 (2, 33)
31	Tyler Bouck	F	L	6'0"	185	01/13/80	Camrose, Alta.	Prince George (WHL)	DAL '98 (2, 57)
5	Kyle Calder	F	L	6'0"	180	01/05/79	Mannville, Alta.	Regina (WHL)	CHI '97 (5, 130)
14	Brian Campbell	D	L	5'11"	190	05/23/79	Strathroy, Ont.	Ottawa (OHL)	BUF '97 (6, 156)
23	Jason Chimera	F	L	6'2"	190	05/02/79	Edmonton, Alta.	Medicine Hat (WHL)	EDM '97 (5, 121)
19	Harold Druken	F	L	6'0"	205	01/26/79	St. John's, N.L.	Plymouth (OHL)	VAN '97 (2, 36)
9	Rico Fata	F	L	6'0"	205	02/12/80	Sault Ste. Marie, Ont.	Calgary (WHL)	CGY '98 (1, 6)
27	Andrew Ference	D	L	5'11"	190	03/27/79	Sherwood Park, Alta.	Portland (WHL)	PIT '97 (8, 208)
2	Brad Ference	D	R	6'3"	195	04/02/79	Calgary, Alta.	Spokane (WHL)	VAN '97 (1, 10)
32	Brian Finley	G	L	6'3"	185	03/07/81	Sault Ste. Marie, Ont.	Barrie (OHL)	1999 Draft
12	Simon Gagné	F	L	6'0"	180	02/29/80	Ste-Foy, Que.	Quebec (QMJHL)	PHI '98 (1, 22)
35	Brad Leeb	F	R	5'11"	180	08/27/79	Red Deer, Alta.	Red Deer (WHL)	Undrafted
1	Roberto Luongo	G	L	6'2"	193	04/04/79	Montreal, Que.	Acadie-Bathurst (QMJHL)	NYI '97 (1, 4)
17	Adam Mair A	F	R	6'1"	190	02/15/79	Hamilton, Ont.	Owen Sound (OHL)	TOR '97 (4, 84)
36	Kent McDonnell	F	R	6'1"	195	03/01/79	Cornwall, Ont.	Guelph (OHL)	CAR '97 (9, 225)
33	Brenden Morrow	F	L	6'0"	205	01/16/79	Carlyle, Sask.	Portland (WHL)	DAL '97 (1, 25)
24	Robyn Regehr	D	L	6'3"	220	04/19/80	Rosthern, Sask.	Kamloops (WHL)	COL '98 (1, 19)
7	Brad Stuart	D	L	6'2"	217	06/11/79	Rocky Mountain House, Alta.	Regina (WHL)	SJ '98 (1, 3)
10	Daniel Tkaczuk A	F	L	6'1"	190	06/10/79	Mississauga, Ont.	Barrie (OHL)	CGY '97 (1, 6)
26	Mike Van Ryn C	D	R	6'1"	195	05/14/79	London, Ont.	Michigan (CCHA)	NJ '98 (1, 26)
20	Jason Ward	F	R	6'3"	190	01/16/79	Oshawa, Ont.	Windsor (OHL)	MTL '97 (1, 11)

Head coach: Tom Renney

Head scout: Barry Trapp

Assistant coach: Stan Butler

Assistant coach: Claude Julien

2000

#	NAME	P	S	HT	WT	BORN	HOMETOWN	CLUB	DRAFT STATUS
16	Mark Bell	F	L	6'3"	198	08/05/80	St. Paul's, Ont.	Ottawa (OHL)	CHI '98 (1, 8)
33	Mathieu Biron A	D	R	6'6"	220	04/29/80	Lac St-Charles, Que.	NY Islanders (NHL)	NYI '98 (1, 21)
12	Tyler Bouck A	F	L	6'0"	200	01/13/80	Camrose, Alta.	Prince George (WHL)	DAL '98 (2, 57)
3	Jay Bouwmeester	D	L	6'4"	195	09/27/83	Edmonton, Alta.	Medicine Hat (WHL)	2002 Draft
7	Éric Chouinard	F	L	6'3"	200	07/08/80	Cap Rouge, Que.	Quebec (QMJHL)	MTL '98 (1, 16)
1	Brian Finley	G	L	6'3"	180	07/03/81	Sault Ste. Marie, Ont.	Barrie (OHL)	NSH '99 (1, 6)
11	Dany Heatley	F	L	6'3"	195	01/21/81	Calgary, Alta.	Wisconsin (WCHA)	2000 Draft
20	Barret Jackman	D	L	6'1"	203	03/05/81	Fruitvale, B.C.	Regina (WHL)	STL '99 (1, 17)
2	Matt Kinch	D	L	5'11"	185	02/17/80	Red Deer, Alta.	Calgary (WHL)	BUF '99 (5, 146)
31	Jamie Lundmark	F	R	6'0"	185	01/16/81	Edmonton, Alta.	Moose Jaw (WHL)	NYR '99 (1, 9)
6	Manny Malhotra C	F	L	6'2"	210	05/18/80	Mississauga, Ont.	NY Rangers (NHL)	NYR '98 (1, 7)
18	Steve McCarthy	D	L	6'0"	205	02/03/81	Trail, B.C.	Kootenay (WHL)	CHI '99 (1, 23)
10	Chris Nielsen	F	R	6'2"	193	02/16/80	Goodlands, Man.	Calgary (WHL)	NYI '98 (2, 36)
30	Maxime Ouellet	G	L	6'1"	195	06/17/81	Beauport, Que.	Quebec (QMJHL)	PHI '99 (1, 22)
26	Matt Pettinger	F	L	6'1"	205	10/22/80	Victoria, B.C.	Denver (WCHA)	2000 Draft
25	Brandon Reid	F	R	5'8"	165	03/09/81	Kirland, Que.	Halifax (QMJHL)	Undrafted
35	Mike Ribeiro	F	L	5'11"	164	02/10/80	Montreal, Que.	Montreal (NHL)	MTL '98 (2, 45)
9	Brad Richards	F	L	6'0"	180	05/02/80	Murray Harbour, N.L.	Rimouski (QMJHL)	TB '98 (3, 64)
24	Kyle Rossiter	D	L	6'2"	220	06/09/80	Edmonton, Alta.	Spokane (WHL)	FLA '98 (2, 30)
21	Joé Rullier	D	R	6'4"	203	01/28/80	Montreal, Que.	Rimouski (QMJHL)	LA '98 (5, 133)
27	Michael Ryder	F	R	6'0"	190	03/31/80	Bonavista, N.L.	Hull (QMJHL)	MTL '98 (8, 216)
19	Jason Spezza	F	R	6'3"	195	06/13/83	Mississauga, Ont.	Mississauga (OHL)	2001 Draft

Head coach: Claude Julien

Assistant coach: Todd McLellan

Assistant coach: Dean Clark

2001

#	NAME	P	S	HT	WT	BORN	HOMETOWN	CLUB	DRAFT STATUS
33	Alex Auld	G	L	6'3.5"	198	01/07/81	Thunder Bay, Ont.	North Bay (OHL)	FLA '99 (2, 40)
4	Jay Bouwmeester	D	L	6'4"	207	09/27/83	Edmonton, Alta.	Medicine Hat (WHL)	2002 Draft
34	Brad Boyes	F	R	6'0"	181	04/17/82	Mississauga, Ont.	Erie (OHL)	TOR '00 (1, 24)
29	Mike Cammalleri	F	L	5'8.5"	174	06/08/82	Richmond Hill, Ont.	Michigan (CCHA)	2001 Draft
5	Dan Hamhuis	D	L	6'0.5"	194	12/13/82	Smithers, B.C.	Prince George (WHL)	2001 Draft
23	Jay Harrison	D	L	6'3"	205	11/03/82	Whitby, Ont.	Brampton (OHL)	2001 Draft
15	Dany Heatley	F	L	6'2"	205	01/21/81	Calgary, Alta.	Wisconsin (WCHA)	ATL '00 (1, 2)
2	Barret Jackman A	D	L	6'0.5"	201	03/05/81	Fruitvale, B.C.	Regina (WHL)	STL '99 (1, 17)
22	Jason Jaspers	F	L	5'10.5"	183	04/08/81	Thunder Bay, Ont.	Sudbury (OHL)	PHX '99 (4, 71)
17	Jamie Lundmark	F	R	6'0"	185	01/16/81	Edmonton, Alta.	Seattle (WHL)	NYR '99 (1, 9)
16	Derek MacKenzie	F	L	5'11"	178	06/11/81	Sudbury, Ont.	Sudbury (OHL)	ATL '99 (5, 128)
7	Steve McCarthy C	D	L	6'0"	196	02/03/81	Trail, B.C.	Chicago (NHL)	CHI '99 (1, 23)
12	David Morisset	F	R	6'1.5"	203	04/06/81	Langley, B.C.	Seattle (WHL)	STL ' 00 (2, 65)
21	Steve Ott	F	L	6'0"	181	08/19/82	Stoney Point, Ont.	Windsor (OHL)	DAL '00 (1, 25)
30	Maxime Ouellet	G	L	6'1.5"	198	06/17/81	Beauport, Que.	Rouyn-Noranda (QMJHL)	PHI '99 (1, 22)
27	Mark Popovic	D	L	6'1.5"	189	10/11/82	Stoney Creek, Ont.	Toronto St. Michael's (OHL)	2001 Draft
25	Brandon Reid A	F	R	5'9"	170	03/09/81	Kirkland, Que.	Val-d'Or (QMJHL)	VAN '00 (7, 208)
3	Nick Schultz	D	L	6'0.5"	194	08/25/82	Strasbourg, Sask.	Prince Albert (WHL)	MIN '00 (2, 33)
9	Jason Spezza	F	R	6'0.5"	209	06/13/83	Mississauga, Ont.	Windsor (OHL)	2001 Draft
19	Jarret Stoll	F	R	6'0.5"	198	06/24/82	Neudorf, Sask.	Kootenay (WHL)	CGY '00 (2, 46)
28	Raffi Torres	F	L	5'11.5"	209	10/08/81	Markham, Ont.	Brampton (OHL)	NYI '00 (1, 5)
10	Mike Zigomanis	F	R	6'0.5"	194	01/17/81	North York, Ont.	Kingston (OHL)	BUF '99 (2, 64)

Head scout: Barry Trapp

Head coach: Stan Butler

Assistant coach: Kevin Dickie

Assistant coach: Mike Kelly

2002

#	NAME	P	S	HT	WT	BORN	HOMETOWN	CLUB	DRAFT STATUS
34	Jared Aulin	F	R	6'0"	187	03/15/82	Calgary, Alta.	Kamloops (WHL)	COL '00 (2, 47)
4	Jay Bouwmeester	D	L	6'4"	207	09/27/83	Edmonton, Alta.	Medicine Hat (WHL)	2002 Draft.
17	Brad Boyes	F	R	6'0"	187	04/17/82	Mississauga, Ont.	Erie (OHL)	TOR '00 (1, 24)
13	Mike Cammalleri A	F	L	5'9"	181	06/08/82	Richmond Hill, Ont.	Michigan (CCHA)	LA '00 (2, 49)
8	Carlo Colaiacovo	D	L	6'0.5"	183	01/27/83	Toronto, Ont.	Erie (OHL)	TOR '01 (1, 17)
5	Dan Hamhuis	D	L	6'0.5"	198	12/13/82	Smithers, B.C.	Prince George (WHL)	NSH '01 (1, 12)
23	Jay Harrison	D	L	6'3.5"	209	11/03/82	Whitby, Ont.	Brampton (OHL)	TOR '01 (3, 82)
21	Chuck Kobasew	F	R	5'11.5"	194	04/17/82	Osoyoos, B.C.	Kelowna (WHL)	CGY '01 (1, 14)
31	Pascal Leclaire	G	L	6'1.5"	183	11/07/92	St-Gabriel-de-Brandon, Que.	Montreal (QMJHL)	CBJ '01 (1, 8)
18	Jay McClement	F	L	6'0.5"	198	03/02/83	Kingston, Ont.	Brampton (OHL)	STL '01 (2, 57)
30	Olivier Michaud	G	L	5'10.5"	163	09/14/83	Beloeil, Que.	Shawinigan (QMJHL)	Undrafted
10	Garth Murray	F	L	6'0.5"	207	09/17/82	Regina, Sask.	Regina (WHL)	NYR '01 (3, 79)
38	Rick Nash	F	L	6'1.5"	170	06/12/84	Brampton, Ont.	London (OHL)	2002 Draft
14	Steve Ott	F	L	6'0"	178	08/19/82	Stoney Point, Ont.	Windsor (OHL)	DAL '00 (1, 25)
37	Nathan Paetsch	D	L	6'0"	201	03/30/83	Leroy, Sask.	Moose Jaw (WHL)	WSH '01 (2, 58)
27	Mark Popovic	D	L	6'1.5"	189	10/11/82	Stoney Creek, Ont.	Toronto St. Michael's (OHL)	ANA '01 (2, 35)
7	Nick Schultz A	D	L	6'1.5"	203	08/25/82	Strasbourg, Sask.	Minnesota (NHL)	MIN '00 (2, 33)
9	Jason Spezza	F	R	6'2"	209	06/13/83	Mississauga, Ont.	Windsor (OHL)	OTT '01 (1, 2)
16	Jarret Stoll C	F	R	6'0.5"	198	06/24/82	Neudorf, Sask.	Kootenay (WHL)	CGY '01 (2, 46)
20	Brian Sutherby	F	L	6'3"	196	03/01/82	Edmonton, Alta.	Moose Jaw (WHL)	WSH '00 (1, 26)
19	Scottie Upshall	F	L	5'10.5"	178	10/07/83	Fort McMurray, Alta.	Kamloops (WHL)	2002 Draft
22	Stephen Weiss	F	L	6'0"	185	04/03/83	Markham, Ont.	Plymouth (OHL)	FLA '01 (1, 4)

Head coach: Stan Butler

Assistant coach: Marc Habscheid

Assistant coach: Mike Kelly

Goaltending consultant: Andy Moog

2003

#	NAME	P	S	HT	WT	BORN	HOMETOWN	CLUB	DRAFT STATUS
7	Brendan Bell	D	L	6'0.5"	207	03/31/83	Ottawa, Ont.	Ottawa (OHL)	TOR '01 (3, 65)
16	Pierre-Marc Bouchard A	F	L	5'11"	165	04/27/84	Boucherville, Que.	Minnesota (NHL)	MIN '02 (1, 8)
11	Gregory Campbell	F	L	5'10.5"	187	12/17/83	Tillsonburg, Ont.	Kitchener (OHL)	FLA '02 (3, 67)
8	Carlo Colaiacovo	D	L	6'0.5"	187	01/27/83	Toronto, Ont.	Erie (OHL)	TOR '01 (1, 17)
2	Steve Eminger A	D	R	6'1.5"	187	10/31/83	Woodbridge, Ont.	Washington (NHL)	WSH '02 (1, 12)
1	Marc-André Fleury	D	L	6'1.5"	170	11/28/84	Sorel, Que.	Cape Breton (QMJHL)	2003 Draft
27	Boyd Gordon	F	R	6'0"	185	10/18/83	Regina, Sask.	Red Deer (WHL)	STL '02 (1, 17)
29	Brooks Laich	F	L	6'0"	183	06/23/83	Wawota, Sask.	Seattle (WHL)	OTT '01 (6, 193)
31	David LeNeveu	D	L	6'0.5"	170	05/23/83	Fernie, B.C.	Cornell (ECAC)	PHX '02 (2, 46)
15	Joffrey Lupul	F	R	6'1.5"	194	09/23/83	Fort Saskatchewan, Alta.	Medicine Hat (WHL)	ANA '02 (1, 7)
18	Jay McClement	F	L	6'1.5"	194	03/02/83	Kingston, Ont.	Brampton (OHL)	STL '01 (2, 57)
6	Nathan Paetsch	D	L	6'0.5"	194	03/30/83	Leroy, Sask.	Moose Jaw (WHL)	WSH '01 (2, 58)
10	Daniel Paille	F	L	6'0"	201	04/15/84	Welland, Ont.	Guelph (OHL)	BUF '02 (1, 20)
25	Pierre-Alexandre Parenteau	F	R	5'11.5"	178	03/24/83	Boucherville, Que.	Chicoutimi (QMJHL)	ANA '01 (9, 264)
3	Alexandre Rouleau	D	L	6'0.5"	189	07/29/83	Mont-Laurier, Que.	Val-d'Or (QMJHL)	PIT '01 (3, 96)
21	Derek Roy	F	L	5'8.5"	187	05/04/83	Rockland, Ont.	Kitchener (OHL)	BUF '01 (2, 32)
14	Matt Stajan	F	L	6'1.5"	187	12/19/83	Mississauga, Ont.	Belleville (OHL)	TOR '02 (2, 57)
22	Jordin Tootoo	F	R	5'8.5"	185	02/02/83	Rankin Inlet, Nun.	Brandon (WHL)	NSH '01 (4, 98)
19	Scottie Upshall C	F	L	5'11.5"	178	10/07/83	Fort McMurray, Alta.	Kamloops (WHL)	NSH '02 (1, 6)
28	Kyle Wellwood	F	R	5'9.5"	189	05/16/83	Oldcastle, Ont.	Windsor (OHL)	TOR '01 (5, 134)
17	Ian White	D	R	5'9.5"	183	06/04/84	Steinbach, Man.	Swift Current (WHL)	TOR '02 (6, 191)
4	Jeff Woywitka	D	L	6'3"	216	09/01/83	Vermilion, Alta.	Red Deer (WHL)	PHI '01 (1, 27)

Head scout: Blair MacKasey

Head coach: Marc Habscheid

Assistant coach: Mario Durocher

Assistant coach: Mike Kelly

2004

#	NAME	P	S	HT	WT	BORN	HOMETOWN	CLUB	DRAFT STATUS
37	Shawn Belle	D	L	6'1"	184	01/03/85	Edmonton, Alta.	Tri-City (WHL)	STL '03 (1, 30)
8	Tim Brent *A*	F	R	6'0"	186	03/10/84	Cambridge, Ont.	Toronto St. Michael's (OHL)	ANA '02 (2, 37)
22	Brent Burns	F	R	6'4"	200	09/03/85	Barrie, Ont.	Minnesota (NHL)	MIN '03 (1, 20)
9	Jeff Carter	F	R	6'3"	202	01/01/85	London, Ont.	Sault Ste. Marie (OHL)	PHI '03 (1, 11)
29	Braydon Coburn	D	L	6'5"	217	02/27/85	Shaunavon, Sask.	Portland (WHL)	ATL '03 (1, 8)
21	Jeremy Colliton	F	R	6'1"	194	01/13/85	Blackie, Alta.	Prince Albert (WHL)	NYI '03 (2, 58)
28	Sidney Crosby	F	L	5'10"	185	08/07/87	Cole Harbour, N.S.	Rimouski (QMJHL)	2005 Draft
27	Nigel Dawes	F	L	5'8"	176	02/09/85	Winnipeg, Man.	Kootenay (WHL)	NYR '03 (5, 149)
24	Stephen Dixon	F	L	5'11"	188	09/07/85	Halifax, N.S.	Cape Breton (QMJHL)	PIT '03 (7, 229)
1	Marc-André Fleury	G	L	6'1.5"	173	11/28/84	Sorel, Que.	Pittsburgh (NHL)	PIT '03 (1, 1)
15	Ryan Getzlaf	F	R	6'3"	206	05/10/85	Regina, Sask.	Calgary (WHL)	ANA '03 (1, 19)
5	Josh Gorges	D	L	6'0"	188	08/14/84	Kelowna, B.C.	Kelowna (WHL)	Undrafted
35	Josh Harding	G	R	6'1"	183	06/18/84	Regina, Sask.	Regina (WHL)	MIN '02 (2, 38)
6	Kevin Klein	D	R	6'0.5"	197	12/13/84	Kitchener, Ont.	Guelph (OHL)	NSH '03 (2, 37)
2	Derek Meech	D	L	5'11"	194	10/21/84	Winnipeg, Man.	Red Deer (WHL)	DET '02 (7, 229)
20	Daniel Paille *C*	F	L	6'0"	203	04/04/84	Welland, Ont.	Guelph (OHL)	BUF '02 (1, 20)
3	Dion Phaneuf	D	L	6'2"	205	04/10/85	Edmonton, Alta.	Red Deer (WHL)	CGY '03 (1, 9)
18	Michael Richards	F	L	5'11"	195	02/11/85	Kenora, Ont.	Kitchener (OHL)	PHI '03 (1, 24)
32	Brent Seabrook	D	R	6'2"	225	04/20/85	Tsawwassen, B.C.	Lethbridge (WHL)	CHI '03 (1, 14)
12	Anthony Stewart	F	R	6'1"	230	01/05/85	Scarborough, Ont.	Kingston (OHL)	FLA '03 (1, 25)
25	Maxime Talbot *A*	F	L	5'10"	181	02/11/84	St-Bruno, Que.	Gatineau (QMJHL)	PIT '02 (8, 234)
19	Jeff Tambellini	F	L	5'10"	190	04/13/84	Port Moody, B.C.	Michigan (CCHA)	LA '03 (1, 27)

Head scout: Blair MacKasey
Head coach: Mario Durocher
Assistant coach: Dean Chynoweth
Assistant coach: Jim Hulton
Goaltending coach: Ian Clark

2005

#	NAME	P	S	HT	WT	BORN	HOMETOWN	CLUB	DRAFT STATUS
25	Cam Barker	D	L	6'3"	220	04/04/86	Winnipeg, Man.	Medicine Hat (WHL)	CHI '04 (1, 3)
35	Réjean Beauchemin	G	L	6'2"	198	05/03/85	Winnipeg, Man.	Prince Albert (WHL)	PHI '03 (6, 191)
4	Shawn Belle	D	L	6'1"	229	01/03/85	Edmonton, Alta.	Tri-City (WHL)	STL '03 (1, 30)
37	Patrice Bergeron *A*	F	R	6'1"	186	07/24/85	Quebec City, Que.	Providence (AHL)	BOS '03 (2, 45)
7	Jeff Carter *A*	F	R	6'4"	207	01/01/85	London, Ont.	Sault Ste. Marie (OHL)	PHI '03 (1, 11)
29	Braydon Coburn	D	L	6'5"	220	02/27/85	Shaunavon, Sask.	Portland (WHL)	ATL '03 (1, 8)
21	Jeremy Colliton	F	R	6'1"	202	01/13/85	Blackie, Alta.	Prince Albert (WHL)	NYI '03 (2, 58)
9	Sidney Crosby	F	L	5'10"	193	08/07/87	Cole Harbour, N.S.	Rimouski (QMJHL)	2005 Draft
17	Nigel Dawes	F	L	5'8"	187	02/09/85	Winnipeg, Man.	Kootenay (WHL)	NYR '03 (5, 149)
14	Stephen Dixon	F	L	5'10"	198	09/07/85	Halifax, N.S.	Cape Breton (QMJHL)	PIT '03 (7, 229)
11	Colin Fraser	F	L	6'1"	187	01/28/85	Surrey, B.C.	Red Deer (WHL)	PHI '03 (3, 69)
15	Ryan Getzlaf	F	R	6'3"	209	05/10/85	Regina, Sask.	Calgary (WHL)	ANA '03 (1, 19)
33	Jeff Glass	G	L	6'1"	180	11/19/85	Cochrane, Alta.	Kootenay (WHL)	OTT '04 (3, 89)
19	Andrew Ladd	F	L	6'1"	202	12/12/85	Maple Ridge, B.C.	Calgary (WHL)	CAR '04 (1, 4)
17	Clarke MacArthur	F	L	6'0"	187	04/06/85	Lloydminster, Alta.	Medicine Hat (WHL)	BUF '03 (3, 74)
24	Corey Perry	F	R	6'2"	198	05/16/85	Peterborough, Ont.	London (OHL)	ANA '03 (1, 28)
3	Dion Phaneuf *A*	D	L	6'2"	216	04/10/85	Edmonton, Alta.	Red Deer (WHL)	CGY '03 (1, 9)
18	Michael Richards *C*	F	L	5'10"	198	02/11/85	Kenora, Ont.	Kitchener (OHL)	PHI '03 (1, 24)
2	Brent Seabrook	D	R	6'1"	224	04/20/85	Tsawwassen, B.C.	Lethbridge (WHL)	CHI '03 (1, 14)
12	Anthony Stewart	F	R	6'1"	233	01/05/85	Scarborough, Ont.	Kingston (OHL)	FLA '03 (1, 25)
20	Danny Syvret	D	L	5'10"	200	06/13/85	Millgrove, Ont.	London (OHL)	Undrafted
6	Shea Weber	D	R	6'3"	220	08/14/85	Sicamous, B.C.	Kelowna (WHL)	NSH '03 (2, 49)

Head scout: Blair MacKasey
Head coach: Brent Sutter
Assistant coach: Peter DeBoer
Assistant coach: Jim Hulton
Assistant coach: Rob Cookson
Goaltending coach: Ian Clark

2006

#	NAME	P	S	HT	WT	BORN	HOMETOWN	CLUB	DRAFT STATUS
25	Cam Barker *A*	D	L	6'3"	220	04/04/86	Winnipeg, Man.	Medicine Hat (WHL)	CHI '04 (1, 3)
22	Daniel Bertram	F	R	5'11"	175	01/14/87	Calgary, Alta.	Boston College (Hky East)	CHI '05 (2, 54)
21	Michael Blunden	F	R	6'3"	213	12/15/86	Gloucester, Ont.	Erie (OHL)	CHI '05 (2, 43)
19	David Bolland *A*	F	R	5'11"	176	06/05/86	Mimico, Ont.	London (OHL)	CHI '04 (2, 32)
6	Luc Bourdon *A*	D	L	6'2"	199	02/16/87	Shippagan, N.B.	Val-d'Or (QMJHL)	VAN '05 (1, 10)
16	Dustin Boyd	F	L	6'0"	185	07/16/86	Winnipeg, Man.	Moose Jaw (WHL)	CGY '04 (3, 98)
17	Kyle Chipchura *C*	F	L	6'1"	209	02/19/86	Vimy, Alta.	Prince Albert (WHL)	MTL '04 (1, 18)
9	Andrew Cogliano	F	L	5'9"	178	06/14/87	Woodbridge, Ont.	Michigan (CCHA)	EDM '05 (1, 25)
14	Blake Comeau *A*	F	R	6'1"	207	02/18/86	Meadow Lake, Sask.	Kelowna (WHL)	NYI '04 (2, 47)
7	Steve Downie	F	R	5'10"	189	04/03/87	Queensville, Ont.	Peterborough (OHL)	PHI '05 (1, 29)
30	Devan Dubnyk	G	L	6'5"	200	05/04/86	Calgary, Alta.	Kamloops (WHL)	EDM '04 (1, 14)
20	Guillaume Latendresse	F	L	6'2"	222	05/24/87	Ste-Catherine, Que.	Drummondville (QMJHL)	MTL '05 (2, 45)
12	Kristopher Letang	D	R	5'11"	190	04/24/87	Laval, Que.	Val-d'Or (QMJHL)	PIT '05 (3, 62)
23	Ryan O'Marra	F	R	6'1"	194	06/09/87	Mississauga, Ont.	Erie (OHL)	NYI '05 (1, 15)
4	Ryan Parent	D	L	6'2"	183	03/17/87	Sioux Lookout, Ont.	Guelph (OHL)	NSH '05 (1, 18)
33	Justin Pogge	G	L	6'3"	205	04/22/86	Penticton, B.C.	Calgary (WHL)	TOR '04 (3, 90)
36	Sasha Pokulok	D	L	6'5"	230	05/25/86	Vaudreuil-Dorion, Que.	Cornell (ECAC)	WSH '05 (1, 14)
37	Benoit Pouliot	F	L	6'3"	179	09/29/86	Ottawa, Ont.	Sudbury (OHL)	MIN '05 (1, 4)
27	Tom Pyatt	F	L	5'11"	180	02/14/87	Thunder Bay, Ont.	Saginaw (OHL)	NYR '05 (4, 107)
10	Kris Russell	D	L	5'10"	166	05/02/87	Caroline, Alta.	Medicine Hat (WHL)	CBJ '05 (3, 67)
3	Marc Staal	D	L	6'3"	196	01/13/87	Thunder Bay, Ont.	Sudbury (OHL)	NYR '05 (1, 12)
29	Jonathan Toews	F	L	6'2"	185	04/29/88	Winnipeg, Man.	North Dakota (WCHA)	2006 Draft

Head coach: Brent Sutter

Assistant coach: Craig Hartsburg

Assistant coach: Clément Jodoin

Goaltending coach: Ian Clark

2007

#	NAME	P	S	HT	WT	BORN	HOMETOWN	CLUB	DRAFT STATUS
3	Karl Alzner	D	L	6'2"	209	09/24/88	Burnaby, B.C.	Calgary (WHL)	2007 Draft
22	Dan Bertram	F	R	5'10"	183	01/14/87	Calgary, Alta.	Boston College (Hky East)	CHI '05 (2, 54)
6	Luc Bourdon	D	L	5'5"	211	02/16/87	Shippagan, N.B.	Moncton (QMJHL)	VAN '05 (1, 10)
11	Marc-André Cliche	F	R	6'0.5"	187	03/23/87	Rouyn-Noranda, Que.	Lewiston (QMJHL)	NYR '05 (2, 56)
9	Andrew Cogliano	F	L	5'9"	186	06/14/87	Woodbridge, Ont.	Michigan (CCHA)	EDM '05 (1, 25)
7	Steve Downie *A*	F	L	5'10.5"	203	04/03/87	Queensville, Ont.	Peterborough (OHL)	PHI '05 (1, 29)
26	Cody Franson	D	R	6'3"	204	08/08/87	Sicamous, B.C.	Vancouver (WHL)	NSH '05 (3, 79)
38	Sam Gagner	F	R	5'10.5"	190	08/10/89	Oakville, Ont.	London (OHL)	2007 Draft
15	Darren Helm	F	L	6'0"	183	01/21/87	St. Andrews, Man.	Medicine Hat (WHL)	DET '05 (5, 132)
31	Leland Irving	G	L	6'0"	177	04/11/88	Swan Hills, Man.	Everett (WHL)	CGY '06 (1,26)
5	Kristopher Letang *C*	D	L	5'11.5"	207	04/24/87	Ste-Julie, Que.	Val-d'Or (QMJHL)	PIT '05 (3, 62)
20	Bryan Little	F	R	5'10.5"	201	11/23/87	Cambridge, Ont.	Barrie (OHL)	ATL '06 (1, 12)
17	Brad Marchand	F	L	5'9"	183	05/11/88	Hammonds Plains, N.S.	Val-d'Or (QMJHL)	BOS '06 (3, 71)
12	Kenndal McArdle	F	L	5'11.5"	205	01/04/87	Burnaby, B.C.	Vancouver (WHL)	FLA '05 (1, 20)
19	James Neal	F	L	6'2.5"	203	09/03/87	Whitby, Ont.	Plymouth (OHL)	DAL '05 (2, 33)
23	Ryan O'Marra	F	R	6'2"	207	06/09/87	Mississauga, Ont.	Saginaw (OHL)	NYI '05 (1, 15)
4	Ryan Parent	D	L	6'2"	194	03/17/87	Sioux Lookout, Ont.	Guelph (OHL)	NSH '05 (1, 18)
1	Carey Price	G	L	6'2"	217	08/16/87	Anahim Lake, B.C.	Tri-City (WHL)	MTL '05 (1, 5)
27	Tom Pyatt *A*	F	L	5'11"	186	02/14/87	Thunder Bay, Ont.	Saginaw (OHL)	NYR '05 (4, 107)
10	Kris Russell	D	L	5'10"	162	05/02/87	Caroline, Alta.	Medicine Hat (WHL)	CBJ '05 (3, 67)
14	Marc Staal *A*	D	L	6'4"	207	01/13/87	Thunder Bay, Ont.	Sudbury (OHL)	NYR '05 (1, 12)
29	Jonathan Toews *A*	F	L	6'1.5"	203	04/29/88	Winnipeg, Man.	North Dakota (WCHA)	CHI '06 (1, 3)

Head scout: Jim Hammett

Head coach: Craig Hartsburg

Assistant coach: Curtis Hunt

Assistant coach: Clément Jodoin

Goaltending coach: Corey Hirsch

2008

#	NAME	P	S	HT	WT	BORN	HOMETOWN	CLUB	DRAFT STATUS
27	Karl Alzner *C*	D	L	6'2"	209	09/24/88	Burnaby, B.C.	Calgary (WHL)	WSH '07 (1, 5)
1	Jonathan Bernier	G	L	6'0"	185	08/07/88	Laval, Que.	Lewiston (QMJHL)	LA '06 (1, 11)
11	Zach Boychuk	F	L	5'9"	176	10/04/89	Airdrie, Alta.	Lethbridge (WHL)	2008 Draft
8	Drew Doughty	D	R	6'0"	190	12/08/89	London, Ont.	Guelph (OHL)	2008 Draft
18	Colton Gillies	F	L	6'4"	189	02/12/89	Surrey, B.C.	Saskatoon (WHL)	MIN '07 (1, 16)
28	Claude Giroux	F	R	5'11"	172	01/12/88	Ottawa, Ont.	Gatineau (QMJHL)	PHI '06 (1, 22)
2	Josh Godfrey	D	R	6'0"	187	01/15/88	Kingston, Ont.	Sault Ste. Marie (OHL)	WSH '07 (2, 34)
32	Matt Halischuk	F	R	5'11"	173	06/01/88	Mississauga, Ont.	Kitchener (OHL)	NJ '07 (4, 117)
4	Thomas Hickey	D	L	5'11"	182	02/08/89	Calgary, Alta.	Seattle (WHL)	LA '07 (1, 4)
21	Riley Holzapfel	F	L	5'11"	185	08/18/88	Regina, Sask.	Moose Jaw (WHL)	ATL '06 (2, 43)
21	Stefan Legein *A*	F	R	5'9"	170	11/24/88	Oakville, Ont.	Niagara (OHL)	CBJ '07 (2,37)
17	Brad Marchand *A*	F	L	5'9"	183	05/11/88	Hammonds Plains, N.S.	Val-d'Or (QMJHL)	BOS '06 (3, 71)
30	Steve Mason	G	R	6'3"	186	05/29/88	Oakville, Ont.	London (OHL)	CBJ '06 (3, 69)
22	Shawn Matthias	F	L	6'4"	213	02/19/88	Mississauga, Ont.	Belleville (OHL)	DET '07 (2, 47)
3	Logan Pyett *A*	D	R	5'10"	199	05/26/88	Milestone, Sask.	Regina (WHL)	DET '06 (7, 212)
15	Luke Schenn	D	R	6'2"	210	11/02/89	Saskatoon, Sask.	Kelowna (WHL)	2008 Draft
34	Wayne Simmonds	F	R	6'2"	175	08/26/88	Pickering, Ont.	Owen Sound (OHL)	LA '07 (2, 61)
10	Steven Stamkos	F	R	6'0"	183	02/07/90	Unionville, Ont.	Saginaw (OHL)	2008 Draft
23	P.K. Subban	D	R	5'11"	204	05/13/89	Toronto, Ont.	Belleville (OHL)	MTL '07 (2, 43)
12	Brandon Sutter *A*	F	R	6'3"	170	02/14/89	Red Deer, Alta.	Red Deer (WHL)	CAR '07 (1, 11)
20	John Tavares	F	L	6'0"	196	09/20/90	Oakville, Ont.	Oshawa (OHL)	2009 Draft
19	Kyle Turris	F	R	6'2"	170	08/14/89	New Westminster, B.C.	Wisconsin (WCHA)	PHX '07 (1, 3)

Head scout: Al Murray

Head coach: Craig Hartsburg

Assistant coach: Curtis Hunt

Assistant coach: Clément Jodoin

Goaltending coach: Corey Hirsch

2009

#	NAME	P	S	HT	WT	BORN	HOMETOWN	CLUB	DRAFT STATUS
32	Keith Aulie	D	L	6'6"	215	06/11/89	Rouleau, Sask.	Brandon (WHL)	CGY '07 (4, 116)
24	Jamie Benn	F	L	6'1.5"	202	07/18/89	Victoria, B.C.	Kelowna (WHL)	DAL '07 (5, 129)
11	Zach Boychuk *A*	F	L	5'10"	175	10/04/89	Airdrie, Alta.	Lethbridge (WHL)	CAR '08 (1, 14)
28	Patrice Cormier	F	L	6'1.5"	201	06/14/89	Cap-Pele, N.B.	Rimouski (QMJHL)	NJ '08 (2, 54)
15	Stefan Della Rovere	F	L	5'11"	200	02/25/90	Maple, Ont.	Barrie (OHL)	WSH '08 (7, 204)
25	Chris DiDomenico	F	R	5'11"	170	02/20/89	Woodbridge, Ont.	Saint John (QMJHL)	TOR '07 (6, 164)
14	Jordan Eberle	F	R	5'10"	181	05/15/90	Regina, Sask.	Regina (WHL)	EDM '08 (1, 22)
8	Ryan Ellis	D	R	5'9.5"	176	01/03/91	Freelton, Ont.	Windsor (OHL)	2009 Draft
22	Tyler Ennis	F	L	5'8"	165	10/06/89	Edmonton, Alta.	Medicine Hat (WHL)	BUF '08 (1, 26)
7	Angelo Esposito	F	R	6'1"	180	02/20/89	Montreal, Que.	Montreal (QMJHL)	PIT '07 (1, 20)
17	Cody Goloubef	D	R	6'1"	194	11/30/89	Oakville, Ont.	Wisconsin (WCHA)	CBJ '08 (2, 37)
4	Thomas Hickey *C*	D	L	5'11"	194	02/08/89	Calgary, Alta.	Seattle (WHL)	LA '07 (1, 4)
18	Cody Hodgson *A*	F	R	5'11"	189	02/18/90	Markham, Ont.	Brampton (OHL)	VAN '08 (1, 10)
29	Evander Kane	F	L	6'1"	180	08/02/90	Vancouver, B.C.	Vancouver (WHL)	2009 Draft
3	Tyler Myers	D	R	6'7.5"	213	02/01/90	Calgary, Alta.	Kelowna (WHL)	BUF '08 (1, 12)
31	Chet Pickard	G	L	6'1"	216	11/29/89	Winnipeg, Man.	Tri-City (WHL)	NSH '08 (1, 18)
10	Alex Pietrangelo	D	R	6'2.5"	204	01/18/90	King City, Ont.	Niagara (OHL)	STL '08 (1, 4)
12	Brett Sonne	F	L	6'0"	187	05/16/89	Maple Ridge, B.C.	Calgary (WHL)	STL '07 (3, 85)
5	P.K. Subban *A*	D	R	5'11"	206	05/13/89	Toronto, Ont.	Belleville (OHL)	MTL '07 (2, 43)
20	John Tavares *A*	F	L	6'0"	203	09/20/90	Oakville, Ont.	Oshawa (OHL)	2009 Draft
2	Colten Teubert	D	R	6'3"	189	03/08/90	White Rock, B.C.	Regina (WHL)	LA '08 (1, 13)
30	Dustin Tokarski	G	L	5'11"	189	09/16/89	Watson, Sask.	Spokane (WHL)	TB '08 (5, 122)
16	Dana Tyrell	F	L	5'9.5"	182	04/23/89	Airdrie, Alta.	Prince George (WHL)	TB '07 (2, 47)

Head scout: Al Murray

Head coach: Pat Quinn

Assistant coach: Dave Cameron

Assistant coach: Willie Desjardins

Assistant coach: Guy Boucher

Goaltending coach: Frédéric Chabot

2010

#	NAME	P	S	HT	WT	BORN	HOMETOWN	CLUB	DRAFT STATUS
20	Luke Adam	F	L	6'2"	201	06/18/90	St. John's, N.L.	Cape Breton (QMJHL)	BUF '08 (2, 44)
1	Jake Allen	G	L	6'1"	191	08/07/90	Fredericton, N.B.	Montreal (QMJHL)	STL '08 (2, 34)
7	Gabriel Bourque	F	L	5'9"	183	01/25/91	Squatec, Que.	Baie-Comeau (QMJHL)	NSH '09 (5, 132)
26	Jordan Caron	F	L	6'2"	200	11/02/90	Sayabec, Que.	Rimouski (QMJHL)	BOS '09 (1, 25)
28	Patrice Cormier C	F	L	6'1.5"	201	06/14/90	Cap-Pelé, N.B.	Rimouski (QMJHL)	NJ '08 (2, 54)
22	Jared Cowen	D	L	6'5"	226	01/25/91	Allan, Sask.	Spokane (WHL)	OTT '09 (1, 9)
24	Calvin de Haan	D	L	6'0"	182	05/09/91	Carp, Ont.	Oshawa (OHL)	NYI '09 (1, 12)
19	Stefan Della Rovere A	F	L	5'10.5"	200	02/25/90	Maple, Ont.	Barrie (OHL)	WSH '08 (7, 204)
14	Jordan Eberle A	F	R	5'10"	181	05/15/90	Regina, Sask.	Regina (WHL)	EDM '08 (1, 22)
6	Ryan Ellis A	D	R	5'9.5"	184	01/03/91	Freelton, Ont.	Windsor (OHL)	NSH '09 (1, 11)
4	Taylor Hall	F	L	6'0"	181	11/14/91	Kingston, Ont.	Windsor (OHL)	2010 Draft
3	Travis Hamonic	D	R	6'0"	219	08/16/90	St. Malo, Man.	Moose Jaw (WHL)	NYI '08 (2, 53)
12	Adam Henrique	F	L	5'11"	188	02/06/90	Burford, Ont.	Windsor (OHL)	NJ '08 (3, 82)
31	Martin Jones	G	R	6'3.5"	187	01/10/90	North Vancouver, B.C.	Calgary (WHL)	Undrafted
9	Nazem Kadri A	F	L	6'0"	174	10/06/90	London, Ont.	London (OHL)	TOR '09 (1, 7)
17	Brandon Kozun	F	R	5'7"	156	03/08/90	Calgary, Alta.	Calgary (WHL)	LA '09 (6, 179)
15	Brandon McMillan	F	L	5'11"	185	03/22/90	Delta, B.C.	Kelowna (WHL)	ANA '08 (3, 95)
16	Greg Nemisz	F	R	6'3"	199	06/05/90	Courtice, Ont.	Windsor (OHL)	CGY '08 (1, 25)
27	Alex Pietrangelo A	D	R	6'3"	207	01/18/90	King City, Ont.	St. Louis (NHL)	STL '08 (1, 4)
5	Marco Scandella	D	L	6'2.5"	217	02/23/90	Montreal, Que.	Val-d'Or (QMJHL)	MIN '08 (2, 55)
10	Brayden Schenn	F	L	6'0"	194	08/22/91	Saskatoon, Sask.	Brandon (WHL)	LA '09 (1, 5)
2	Colten Teubert A	D	R	6'3"	195	03/08/90	White Rock, B.C.	Regina (WHL)	LA '08 (1, 13)

Head scout: Al Murray

Head coach: Willie Desjardins

Associate coach: Dave Cameron

Assistant coach: Steve Spott

Assistant coach: André Tourigny

Goaltending coach: Ron Tugnutt

2011

#	NAME	P	S	HT	WT	BORN	HOMETOWN	CLUB	DRAFT STATUS
25	Carter Ashton	F	L	6'3"	219	04/01/91	Saskatoon, Sask.	Tri-City (WHL)	TB '09 (1, 29)
22	Tyson Barrie	D	R	5'10"	190	07/26/91	Victoria, B.C.	Kelowna (WHL)	COL '09 (3, 64)
11	Casey Cizikas	F	L	5'11"	191	02/27/91	Mississauga, Ont.	Mississauga St. Michael's (OHL)	NYI '09 (4, 92)
28	Brett Connolly	F	R	6'2"	181	05/02/92	Prince George, B.C.	Prince George (WHL)	TB '10 (1, 6)
7	Sean Couturier	F	L	6'3"	192	12/07/92	Bathurst, N.B.	Drummondville (QMJHL)	2011 Draft
2	Jared Cowen A	D	L	6'5"	227	01/25/91	Allan, Sask.	Spokane (WHL)	OTT '09 (1, 9)
24	Calvin de Haan A	D	L	6'0"	189	05/09/91	Carp, Ont.	Oshawa (OHL)	NYI '09 (1, 12)
3	Simon Després	D	L	6'4"	222	07/27/91	Laval, Que.	Saint John (QMJHL)	PIT '09 (1, 30)
21	Cody Eakin	F	L	6'0"	187	05/24/91	Winnipeg, Man.	Swift Current (WHL)	WSH '09 (3, 85)
6	Ryan Ellis C	D	R	5'10"	184	01/03/91	Freelton, Ont.	Windsor (OHL)	NSH '09 (1, 11)
17	Marcus Foligno	F	L	6'1"	200	08/10/91	Sudbury, Ont.	Sudbury (OHL)	BUF '09 (4, 104)
5	Erik Gudbranson	D	R	6'4"	211	01/07/92	Orleans, Ont.	Kingston (OHL)	FLA '10 (1, 3)
16	Curtis Hamilton	F	L	6'3"	202	12/04/91	Kelowna, B.C.	Saskatoon (WHL)	EDM '10 (2, 48)
12	Quinton Howden	F	L	6'2"	192	01/21/92	Oak Bank, Man.	Moose Jaw (WHL)	FLA '10 (1, 25)
19	Ryan Johansen	F	R	6'2"	193	07/31/92	Port Moody, B.C.	Portland (WHL)	CBJ '10 (1, 4)
9	Zack Kassian	F	R	6'3"	226	01/24/91	LaSalle, Ont.	Windsor (OHL)	BUF '09 (1, 13)
20	Louis Leblanc	F	R	5'11"	181	01/26/91	Kirkland, Ont.	Montreal (QMJHL)	MTL '09 (1, 18)
4	Dylan Olsen	D	L	6'2"	223	01/03/91	Calgary, Alta.	Minnesota-Duluth (WCHA)	CHI '09 (1, 28)
31	Olivier Roy	G	L	5'11"	186	07/12/91	Causapscal, Que.	Acadie-Bathurst (QMJHL)	EDM '09 (5, 133)
10	Brayden Schenn A	F	L	6'0"	199	08/22/91	Saskatoon, Sask.	Brandon (WHL)	LA '09 (1, 5)
8	Jaden Schwartz	F	L	5'10"	184	06/25/92	Wilcox, Sask.	Colorado College (WCHA)	STL '10 (1, 14)
30	Mark Visentin	G	L	6'1"	198	08/07/92	Waterdown, Ont.	Niagara (OHL)	PHX '10 (1, 27)

Head scout: Kevin Prendergast

Head coach: Dave Cameron

Assistant coach: Ryan Huska

Assistant coach: André Tourigny

Assistant coach: George Burnett

Goaltending coach: Ron Tugnutt

CONTRIBUTORS

MIKE BABCOCK coached the Detroit Red Wings to the Stanley Cup in 2008 and the Canadian men's hockey team to an Olympic gold medal in 2010.

BRENDAN BELL has played for the Toronto Maple Leafs, the Phoenix Coyotes, and the Ottawa Senators. He was a first-team all-star in the Ontario Hockey League with the Ottawa 67's.

MURRAY COSTELLO was president of Hockey Canada and president of the Canadian Amateur Hockey Association. He played for the Chicago Blackhawks, Boston Bruins, and Detroit Red Wings, in a 163-game NHL career. He was inducted into the Hockey Hall of Fame in 2005 as a builder.

DAMIEN COX is the *Toronto Star*'s hockey columnist and a regular on Sportsnet's radio and television broadcasts. He has written and co-written several books about hockey.

DEAN EVASON is an assistant coach with the Washington Capitals. He played over 800 games in the NHL and also coached in the Western Hockey League.

SHELDON FERGUSON is director of amateur scouting for the Carolina Hurricanes.

TERRY KOSHAN writes about the NHL and major junior hockey for the *Toronto Sun*. He has covered many Memorial Cup tournaments and world junior championships since joining the paper in 1996.

STÉPHANE LEROUX covers junior hockey at RDS.

ROY MacGREGOR has been a columnist at *The Globe and Mail* for the last decade. His book *Home Team: Fathers, Sons and Hockey* was shortlisted for a Governor General's Award.

BOB McKENZIE has been a hockey commentator on TSN since the late 1980s. He first covered the world juniors on air in 1990.

GORD MILLER joined TSN in 1990 and has been the network's lead NHL play-by-play announcer since 2002. His work at the 2008 world junior championship earned him a Gemini nomination.

STEVE MILTON is a long-time columnist with *The Hamilton Spectator*. He covered the 1985 WJC.

DAVE MORRISON is head of the amateur scouting department for the Toronto Maple Leafs. He played professional hockey for 18 seasons before retiring in 1999.

BOB NICHOLSON has been the president and CEO of the Canadian Hockey Association since 1998 and serves as Canada's representative to the International Ice Hockey Federation. In the years since he was named senior vice-president of the association in 1992, the Program of Excellence has won ten gold medals, six silver, and two bronze at the IIHF world under-20 tournament.

FRANK ORR is a member of the media wing of the Hockey Hall of Fame. He has covered many Stanley Cups and international tournaments for the *Toronto Star*.

MIKE SANDS is a retired professional hockey player who played six games in the NHL with the Minnesota North Stars and has worked for the NHL Central Scouting Bureau. He currently serves as the director of amateur scouting for the Calgary Flames.

DONNA SPENCER has covered the world junior championships and other major international tournaments for the Canadian Press for over a decade. She is based in Calgary.

JESSE WALLIN is the coach of the Red Deer Rebels. He is a former first-round draft pick of the Detroit Red Wings.

TOM WEBSTER is a retired professional hockey player and head coach. He currently serves as an amateur scout for the Calgary Flames.

TIM WHARNSBY writes about hockey for CBC.ca. He previously worked for the *Toronto Sun* and *The Globe and Mail*.

ED WILLES joined *The Province* (Vancouver) as its general sports columnist in 1982, and has worked for newspapers in western Canada for three decades. He has also written two hockey books.

INDEX

PHOTO CREDITS